THE PSYCHIC FACTORS OF CIVILIZATION

BY

LESTER F. WARD

AUTHOR OF "DYNAMIC SOCIOLOGY," "OUTLINES OF SOCIOLOGY," "PURE SOCIOLOGY," "APPLIED SOCIOLOGY"

SECOND EDITION

GINN & COMPANY

BOSTON · NEW YORK · CHICAGO · LONDON

76.6

The Athenæum Press
GINN & COMPANY · PROPRIETORS · BOSTON · U.S.A.

The true place which mind fills in the scheme of nature is the most important truth to be learned in the study of philosophy. . . . The true order of development is from the non-psychic to the psychic, and from the less psychic to the more psychic, and not, as is popularly supposed, from the highest toward the lowest manifestations of this property. This great psychic paradox lies at the base of philosophy, and has ever been its fundamental bane. — *Dynamic Sociology*, II, 76.

Le véritable esprit général de la sociologie dynamique consiste à concevoir chacun de ces états sociaux consécutifs comme le résultat nécessaire du précédent et le moteur indispensable du suivant, selon le lumineux axiome du grand Leibnitz : *Le présent est gros de l'avenir.* — AUGUSTE COMTE : *Philosophie Positive*, IV, 263.

PREFACE TO THE SECOND EDITION.

Il est souvent plus difficile de faire reconnaître une vérité que de la découvrir. — JEAN LAMARCK: *Philosophie Zoologique*, Vol. II, p. 411.

Since the appearance of the first edition of this work in 1893, there have emanated from the same pen three others — namely: Outlines of Sociology (1898), Pure Sociology (1903), and Applied Sociology (1906) — belonging to the same general system of ideas. In the preface to the second edition of Dynamic Sociology, which appeared in 1897, after reviewing the phenomenal progress of sociology since the date of the first edition (1883), I said:

"The history of scientific psychology has been somewhat similar to that of sociology, and a lack of adequate preparation in that branch led me to undervalue its importance as the body of truth upon which the latter science directly reposes. This defect I have sought to supply in a volume published in 1893, entitled The Psychic Factors of Civilization. I would therefore beg those who find this work deficient from the psychological side to acquaint themselves with the later one before judging this from that point of view."

The advance in psychology since 1893 has, however, been along lines widely different from those followed in this work, and although there has arisen what is called a science of "social psychology," still this stands quite aloof from the fundamental problem of the rôle of mind in civilization, and nothing has been done to advance this subject beyond the point to which this work carries it. No revision of the work itself, therefore, is called for, but it is important to point out its relations to the later works mentioned, especially as the latter purposely avoid, as far as possible, any restatement of the principles set forth in this one. In so far as these deal with the psychological aspect they either accept these principles and build upon them, or else they lay down new ones. In Outlines of Sociology these principles are used as postulates in Chapters V and VII, while considerable advance is made upon them in Chapter VIII. In Pure Sociology and Applied Sociology they form the solid basis upon which is constructed a complete system of sociology, but naturally in working out that system much has been done in the direction of amplifying and expanding the psychological conceptions that underlie both spontaneous social evolution and conscious social improvement.

This work is therefore to be regarded as one of the steps — the second taken by the writer — in the natural development of a system of social philosophy, and any extended revision or material alteration of it would throw it out of its natural position in that system and deprive it of its historical value as a phase in the normal growth both of the system and of the mind that conceived it.

L. F. W.

WASHINGTON, February 20, 1906.

PREFACE.

> What is writ is writ —
> Would it were worthier!
>
> BYRON.

> J'ay seulement faict icy un amas de fleurs estrangieres, n'y ayant fourny du mien que le filet à les lier. — MONTAIGNE: *De la Physionomie*, p. 47.

I have sought in this book to set forth two aspects of mind — its cause and its use. But these two are really but one, since its use is its cause.

Since I put the finishing strokes, ten years ago, upon a system of social science which I called Dynamic Sociology my mind at least, if not my pen, has been at work along two lines suggested by the recognized imperfection of that scheme. I have been prompted, on the one hand, to build the superstructure higher, and on the other, to lay the foundations deeper. In the first of these directions I have not only been impelled by my own inward sense, but I have been quite strongly urged by others who thought it was my duty to make a direct application of the principles of dynamic sociology to the living issues of the times, and who believed it better that this be done by one who had them in his grasp than left to others who might never fully feel their true significance.

In the opposite direction, that of strengthening the foundations, the pressure has been entirely from within, and yet it is to this that I have yielded, partly because it was much stronger, and partly because I realized that it properly belonged to me to do, while the other more properly belongs to that trained army of social economists, now so rapidly increasing, who are studying and teaching by the inductive method.

The object of the present work is to determine the precise rôle that mind plays in social phenomena. In the preface to the former one I enumerated five of the comprehensive principles embodied in it to which attention had not previously been specially directed. Three of these related to the domain of mind. As I am still, so far as I am aware, alone in insisting upon the reality and importance of these principles, I will repeat them here:—

"2. The theory of the Social Forces, and the fundamental antithesis which they imply between Feeling and Function.

3. The contrast between these true Social Forces and the guiding influence of the Intellect, embodying the application of the Indirect Method of Conation and the essential nature of Invention, of Art, and of Dynamic Action.

4. The superiority of Artificial, or Teleological, Processes over Natural, or Genetic, Processes."

I then recognized, and so stated in the same preface, that there had been "adumbrations" of most or all of these principles, but the reader of the present work will perceive that all I said of them in the earlier one was itself only an adumbration of the full truth as I have here sought to present it. I need not say, however, that I have undertaken considerably more than merely to expand the various conceptions vaguely hinted at or somewhat clearly set forth in 1883; I have joined others with them and constructed out of all the data that lay at my hand what may without exaggeration be regarded as a practically distinct system, albeit closely connected with and directly affiliated upon the other.

Partly to show this affiliation and enable the reader to appreciate, and if desired, to follow out the intimate relations and connections that bind the two systems together, and partly to indicate to what extent the leading tenets of the new were foreshadowed in the old scheme, I have introduced as preludes to all chapters and parts for which they could be found, passages from Dynamic Sociology embodying, if not the central thought, at least some collateral or subordinate idea involved in the discussion to follow. In a few cases I have borrowed such passages from some of the numerous contributions of a more or less popular character which I have made since the appearance of that work. Some chapters, however, there are which have had such a modern origin in my own mind that no such earlier expressions could be found.

In addition to passages of this class, designed to indicate the growth within me of the general scheme, and thus by historical associations to aid the reader in his endeavor to travel with me along the same road, I have hoped not merely to embellish the work but in a certain way to strengthen it by putting at the heads of the chapters in the form of mottos the thoughts of others that seem to embody or foreshadow the principles involved. These utterances of the poets, prophets, and wise men of all ages show that there is scarcely a thought or a truth that has not found expression in some form, and that no scheme can hope to do more than organize ideas already expressed, and focalize the scattered light that pervades the intellectual world. At the same time the rarity of such utterances — the search required to find an expression of truths so vitally important — is more a matter of surprise than their actual discovery, and abundantly proves the need of systematic efforts to collect them together, arrange them in logical order, and bring their combined weight to bear upon the thought and action of the age. I have thus sought to make this work something more than the product of a single brain; I have sought to make it embody the wisdom of the world so far as it relates to this theme. Those who prefer may regard it as a collection of exotic flowers of thought for which I have only furnished the thread of logic that ties them together.

L. F. W.

WASHINGTON, June 18, 1893.

CONTENTS.

INTRODUCTION.

PART I.

SUBJECTIVE FACTORS.

CHAPTER I.

TWO KINDS OF PHILOSOPHY.

CHAPTER II.

THE DUAL NATURE OF MIND.

CHAPTER III.

THE PSYCHOLOGIC PROCESS.

CHAPTER IV.

SUBJECTIVE PSYCHOLOGY.

CHAPTER V.

OBJECTIVE PSYCHOLOGY.

CHAPTER VI.

THE CONATIVE FACULTY.

CHAPTER VII.

ORIGIN AND FUNCTION OF PLEASURE AND PAIN.

CHAPTER XI.

REFUTATION OF PESSIMISM.

CHAPTER XII.

HAPPINESS.

CHAPTER XIII.

FEELING, FUNCTION, AND ACTION.

CHAPTER XIV.

THE TRANSFORMING AGENCY.

CHAPTER XXI.

INTUITION.

CHAPTER XXII.

INTUITIVE PERCEPTION.

CHAPTER XXIII.

INTUITIVE REASON.

CHAPTER XXIV.

PRINCIPLE OF DECEPTION.

CHAPTER XXVIII.

PSYCHOLOGY OF INVENTION.

CHAPTER XXIX.

INVENTIVE GENIUS.

CHAPTER XXX.

CREATIVE GENIUS.

CHAPTER XXXI.

SPECULATIVE GENIUS.

CHAPTER XXXIV.

MELIORISM.

CHAPTER XXXVIII.

SOCIOCRACY.

INTRODUCTION.

In any department of phenomena the laws, whose establishment gives it the character of a true science, depend upon the operation of certain *forces* prevailing within that department which underlie, or rather constitute, the causes of which the phenomena are the effects. — *Dynamic Sociology*, I, 458–459.

Quoique la conception statique de l'organisme social doive, par la nature du sujet, constituer la première base rationelle de toute la sociologie, comme je viens de l'expliquer, il faut néanmoins reconnaître que non-seulement la dynamique sociale en forme la partie la plus directement intéressante, principalement de nos jours, mais surtout, sous le point de vue purement scientifique, qu'elle seule achève de donner, à l'ensemble de cette science nouvelle, son caractère philosophique le plus tranché, en faisant directement prévaloir la notion qui distingue le plus la sociologie proprement dite de la simple biologie, c'est à dire l'idée mère du progrès continu, ou plutôt du développement graduelle l'humanité. — AUGUSTE COMTE: *Philosophie Positive*, IV, 262.

Die Philosophen vor Kant, wenige ausgenommen, haben die Erklärung des Hergangs unseres Erkennens von der verkehrten Seite angegriffen. Sie giengen nämlich dabei aus von einer sogenannten Seele, einem Wesen, dessen innere Natur und eigenthümliche Funktion im Denken bestände, und zwar ganz eigentlich im abstrakten Denken, mit blossen Begriffen, die ihr um so vollkommener angehörten, als sie von aller Anschaulichkeit ferner lagen. — SCHOPENHAUER: *Welt als Wille und Vorstellung*, II, 312–313.

While many of the minor doctrines promulgated in Dynamic Sociology in 1883 have been laid hold of by different classes of writers and made the basis for further sociologic and economic discussion, it is noteworthy that the two most fundamental and important of all, viz., those relating to the nature of the social forces and to the control of those forces, have been, so far as I am aware, completely ignored. This fact alone would seem to justify a renewed attempt to draw attention to these two paramount considerations. If it cannot be shown that society is a domain of true natural forces the claim to the possibility of a social science must be abandoned. Supposing such a claim to be sustained, if it cannot be shown that social phenomena can be controlled as physical phenomena are controlled by a knowledge of the laws according to which they occur, the hope of improving the social condition of man as his physical condition has been improved must be given up. All therefore that is essentially dynamic in sociology, whether in the more literal sense of dealing with a force, or in the freer sense of involving movement or progress, hinges directly upon these two doctrines, and must stand or fall with them.

It is the purpose of the present work to elaborate these two conceptions and to show what scientific foundation they possess. They are sufficiently distinct to be treated separately, and their logical order is that in which they have been mentioned. This renders possible a convenient subdivision of the work into its two parts, the first part dealing exclusively with the forces of society and the second with the mode of directing those forces.

A closer view will show that this subdivision has a wider justification in the essential nature of the problem itself. At the same time it will show that the two questions to be discussed are not so greatly unlike in their internal elements as not to belong to the same general branch of science. Indeed, a little inspection of them will reveal the fact that in dealing with either the one or the other we are necessarily dealing with the phenomena of mind, but at the same time it is clear that the first relates to a very different department of mind from that to which the second relates. In other words, we have before us a twofold psychic problem, and it should surprise no one to learn that sociology as a whole rests primarily upon psychology. This is its natural basis in the hierarchy of the sciences. Even the social activities of animals are due to their psychic faculty, and this is as true of bees and ants as it is of wolves or buffaloes. Human society, therefore, which is the highest product of evolution, naturally depends upon mind which is the highest property of matter.

The chief difficulty in enforcing this truth lies in the vagueness of the popular conception of mind. It will be shown in its proper place how it has come about that most persons are in the habit of including under the term *mind* only so much as is properly embraced by the word *intellect.* The feelings and emotions are excluded, and it becomes necessary to explain that, in its true scientific sense, mind properly includes all phenomena above those which are simply vital, or relate only to life.

The first task is therefore to show that it is this little studied and imperfectly understood side of mind that constitutes the groundwork of the social forces. Reasons will be given for looking upon this affective faculty or department of mind as subjective, in contradistinction to the thinking faculty, which will be looked upon as objective. These two phases or departments of mind constitute a basis for the subdivision of the science of psychology into its two great natural branches, and we have *subjective psychology* on the one hand and *objective psychology* on the other. These branches of the science are capable of being treated separately, though not independently. Though they are but the obverse and reverse of the same coin, still, as much study may be devoted to the separate inscriptions on the two sides as each may require.

So simple and natural is this subdivision of psychology that the wonder is that it has not always been employed. Yet so far is this from being the case that Kant was the first philosopher distinctly to formulate it, and he immediately abandoned it and seemed to regard the objective branch as constituting the whole of philosophy. Most modern writers on mind, as well as all ancient ones, likewise either ignore the subjective branch, or recognize it only in its highest and most derivative aspect, viz., in the will or conative faculty, which they do not analyze or trace to its source in simpler phenomena. Even so logical a writer as Mr. Alexander Bain, as shown by the titles of his two important works on "The Senses and the Intellect," and "The Emotions and the Will," which appeared in this order, does not adopt the simple classification I have indicated, but uses the Senses to introduce the intellect directly, and deals with the Emotions afterward as if they constituted all there is of the feelings.

Finally, no one seems to have seen in the subjective phenomena of mind any great causational factor as the motive power of human activities or as a basis for the scientific treatment of social phenomena ; and this is as true of those who are devoting themselves to social science as to those who confine their labors to any department of mental science.

The second task will be to point out in what manner the social forces can be brought under the control of the intellect. Here it is true, we are fairly back in the well-trodden field of objective psychology. It is in this field that all the great thinkers of past ages have displayed the highest flights of genius. Surely we ought to be able to profit largely by the labors of so many wise men. But the moment we approach the problem in hand we find that it has been practically untouched. Although fairly within the great domain of intellect, reason, and thought, which has so absorbed the energies of the race, we find that this only practical avenue to its exploration has been lost sight of, and that all this wealth of learning and depth of penetration have been expended on problems that are without value to sociology and incapable of being applied to any system looking to the well being of the race. In fact it would seem that every faculty of the mind had been discovered, analyzed, and exhaustively described except the only one that has been employed in the work of human progress, and this has gone unperceived. The so-called faculties of the intellect have been unduly multiplied to furnish material for metaphysical research, but the primary and original faculty, that which distinguishes intellect from everything else and has lifted man above the brute, cannot be found included among these manifold faculties.

The second problem, therefore, viz., that of objective psychology as the directive element in sociology, is as new and unsolved as the first, and we find ourselves confronted not only by a new sociology but by a new psychology.

The following then are the two theorems which require to be established :

1. The phenomena of subjective psychology, viz., the feelings taken collectively, properly called the soul of man, constitute the dynamic element of society, or the social forces.

2. The initial, original, or primary characteristic of objective psychology, viz., the intellect proper, or intuitive faculty, constitutes the directive element of society, and only means by which the social forces can be controlled.

PART I.

SUBJECTIVE FACTORS.

Imagine the world peopled by myriads of living and active beings of all kinds and forms of diversity. They are all in contact with all the other objects existing about them, and a prey to all the vicissitudes which a constantly changing world presents. Without feeling, they must be without sense or intimation of danger, and rapidly, through frequent exposure to those agencies which destroy their organization, they would, one by one, disappear before the adverse elements that everywhere surround them. The utter extinction of every form under these circumstances could be but a question of time, and all actual life would vanish from the globe. But let us suppose some to be slightly endowed with the susceptibility to pain. These would, in proportionate degrees, shun the agencies calculated to destroy their organization, because such would also be, on the hypothesis, the ones which would produce pain. The forms thus endowed would, therefore, survive longer in proportion to the degree of sensitiveness to pain. Thus, under the now clearly understood law of "natural selection," the number of sentient beings would increase, while the insentient ones would become extinct, and we should have the world substantially as we actually see it. — *Dynamic Sociology*, II, 114–115.

If we open almost any modern text-book of psychology, we shall find mind divided into 'Intellect, Feeling, and Will': and we shall be told that these are 'three aspects of mind' — that the 'Feelings' are *qualia* of other mental contents and inseparable from them. We dissent from this view, and hope to substantiate our rejection of it by considering mental phenomena in connection with our biological origin and neurological development. — DR. HERBERT NICHOLS: *Philosophical Review*, July, 1892 (Vol. I, p. 404).

CHAPTER I.

TWO KINDS OF PHILOSOPHY.

L'homme n'est qu'un roseau le plus faible de la nature, mais c'est un roseau pensant. — PASCAL: *Pensées*, II, p. 84.

All that which until recent times was included under the name philosophy, but which, if not abandoned altogether, is now divided up into a great number of special branches, may be comprehended under the two general heads, Cosmology and Psychology. As soon as men began to think on abstract questions they set about trying to find out either *where* they were or *what* they were; i.e., they either studied the world in which they found themselves, or else they studied themselves. In studying the world they did not study this world which immediately surrounded them, but all worlds — the great world or universe. In studying themselves they did not study the physical man, perceptible to the senses, but the immaterial part, or mind. The study of the universe, at first largely theological, and later more and more naturalistic and scientific, may be properly called cosmology. The study of the mind, in which at first the human and the divine were much confounded, but which later was more and more restricted, and at last definitely connected with the brain and nervous system, now goes by the name of psychology.

Passing over the great theological cosmologies as set forth in the sacred books of India, China, Assyria, Persia, Egypt, Phenicia, and Palestine, mention may be made of the more rational cosmologies of Greece, such as those of Thales, Pythagoras, Anaximander, Democritus, the Stoics, and Aristotle, those of the Alexandrian school, and that of Lucretius in Rome, the Christian cosmologies of St. Augustine, and the schoolmen, including that of Cosmas Indicopleustes, and among moderns, the more rational speculations of Bacon, Hobbes, Descartes, and Spinoza, culminating in the substantial discoveries of Copernicus, Kepler, Galileo. Leibnitz, and Newton.

Looking next at the efforts to explore the mind, it may be said to have commenced much later and to have been more exclusively confined to the great intellectual races of Europe. Beginning with Socrates and Plato, the movement was given a definite form by Aristotle, who drew in his physics and metaphysics the same distinction here made between cosmology and psychology. In medieval times metaphysics was a leading branch of learning, and in the hands of Thomas Aquinas, Duns Scotus, and the other dialecticians, was brought to the highest point of scholastic nicety. The more serious study of the mind was inaugurated by Descartes, Spinoza, and Locke, continued by Berkeley, and brought to its greatest perfection by the Scottish and German schools, Reid, Hume, Stewart, Brown, Hamilton, in Scotland, and Kant, Fichte, and Hegel, in Germany.

The above may be taken as a bare outline, without any attempt at completeness, of these two great streams of human thought down to the beginning of the scientific era.

Both of these great branches of philosophy have undergone within the past hundred years an almost complete revolution. This has, of course, been due primarily to the ushering in of the scientific epoch, by which not only have the students of both the macrocosm and the microcosm been put into possession of a vastly increased fund of knowledge about which to philosophize, but an almost entirely new method of reasoning has been made necessary, viz., the inductive or scientific method. In addition to these two causes, however, there is a third, which is perhaps more potent than either of the others. This is a change in the attitude or spirit of inquiry. Whereas before, it was often considered sufficient if the proof of any proposition was brought forward in due logical form, according to Aristotle's *dictum de omni et nullo*, and the truth or falsity of the premises was scarcely ever challenged, under the scientific spirit the objective truth of the proposition was regarded as the real end to be attained, instead of the faultlessness of the reasoning process.

The revolution in cosmologic philosophy brought about by these causes resulted, as already intimated, in replacing the barren speculations and ingenious theories of how the universe might have originated and might be constituted, by that mass of known truth and of legitimate deductions therefrom which constitutes to-day the philosophy of science.

The revolution in psychologic philosophy, also due to the accumulation of facts and the gradual adoption of the scientific method and spirit, has been two-fold. The normal advance, parallel to that made in cosmology, has culminated in the new science of psychology, as taught in the leading institutions of learning, often under the names physiological and experimental psychology and psycho-physics, which studies the phenomena of mind from the standpoint of scientific observation and experimentation. This is undoubtedly the true road to a knowledge of mind in its relations to body, and, though still a young science, it promises the most important results.

But experimental psychology cannot claim to have done away entirely with the necessity for the study of mind from the broader and more strictly philosophical standpoint, and such a study, under the vivifying influence of the scientific spirit, has inaugurated another revolution or change of front in psychology which has already begun to make itself felt, and promises a grander future even than that promised by the experimental study of the organs of the mind. This enthusiastic claim will be better understood when it is shown that there is included in this promise nothing less than the establishment upon a psychological basis of a true science of sociology in all respects parallel and identical with the other less complex sciences of the hierarchy. It is to this branch of psychologic progress that I desire to direct special attention, and it is this revolution in the study of mind that constitutes at once the inspiration of this book and the hope for the future of social science.

CHAPTER II.

THE DUAL NATURE OF MIND.

The fundamental distinction here forshadowed rises immediately out of that which subsists between subject and object. Sense may be defined as the subjective, intellect as the objective, side of mind. — *Dynamic Sociology*, I, 381.

Nur so viel scheint zur Einleitung oder Vorerinnerung nöthig zu sein, dass es zwei Stämme der menschlichen Erkenntniss gebe, die vielleicht aus einer gemeinschaftlichen, aber uns unbekannten Wurzel entspringen, nämlich Sinnlichkeit und Verstand, durch deren ersteren uns Gegenstände *gegeben*, durch den zweiten aber *gedacht* werden. — KANT: *Kritik der reinen Vernunft*, pp. 51–52.

Unsere Erkenntniss entspringt aus zwei Grundquellen des Gemüths, deren die erste ist, die Vorstellungen zu empfangen (die Receptivität der Eindrücke), die zweite das Vermögen, durch jene Vorstellungen einen Gegenstand zu erkennen (Spontaneität der Begriffe); durch die erstere wird uns ein Gegenstand gegeben, durch die zweite wird dieser im Verhältniss auf diese Vorstellung (als blose Bestimmung des Gemüths) gedacht. — KANT: *Ibid.*, p. 81.

We do not infer the existence of objective realities by any act of the Reason; in fact, the strict application of logical processes tends rather to shake than to confirm the belief in the External World; but our Minds being at first subjectively impressed by the qualities of matter, we gradually learn to interpret and combine the impressions they make upon our consciousness, so as to derive from them a more or less definite *notion* of the object. — W. B. CARPENTER: *Mental Physiology*, pp. 177–78.

It has become a trite remark that the most difficult problems presenting themselves to the mind of man for solution have always been the first to be attacked. This is well exemplified by the manner in which the early philosophers began the study of themselves as distinguished from their surroundings. They did not begin with the study of their bodies, much less of the bodies of animals that are constructed upon substantially the same general plan as their own. They began by the study of mind, the most mysterious and intangible subject conceivable. Not only so, but instead of investigating their powers of tasting, smelling, feeling, hearing, and seeing the objects about them, which would have been comparatively simple, they plunged at once into all the intricacies and complexities of the thinking and knowing faculty. Plato devoted his life to the elaboration of his doctrine of the *idea,* Aristotle laid down the laws of syllogistic reasoning, and the later philosophers down to Kant scarcely did more than iterate and imitate the teachings and methods of these ancient masters and draw out their theories of mind into fine-spun subtleties. Mingled with these in a vague way were prolonged discussions upon the nature of the human will and the divine will, which was held to be "free" and was treated as something wholly *sui generis.* Along with all these doctrines there also went profuse dissertations on the "soul," usually conceived as a distinct entity and endowed with immortality. Thus the intellect, the will, and the soul, each ontologically conceived, became, after the universe itself, the chief subjects of philosophy. The critical analysis of modern times has shown each of these fields of investigation to be vast and involved, its facts and phenomena to be compound and complex, and its history and genesis to lead far back through the labyrinth of organic evolution to the dawn of the psychic faculty.

The manifold speculations about the mind, by which was always meant the intellect, for it was not conceived that either the will or the soul really belonged to the mind, were chiefly confined to the department which is now called epistemology, i.e., to the question whether there is any real external world, or whether it may not be all simply a subjective train of mental operations. Descartes thought he was at least sure of his own existence because he was able to think, and Bishop Berkeley, Hume, and many other learned men could get no further than this. Locke did a noble work in showing that ideas come through the senses, and Kant carried this truth further by predicating the dual nature of the mind, i.e., its division into sense (*Sinnlichkeit*) and intellect (*Verstand*). He aptly characterized these, sometimes as the two trunks of human intelligence, sometimes as the two fundamental sources of the mind, but, as will be seen later, he made no further use of the first-named of them than to show that through it alone the intellect receives the materials for thought; or, as he expresses it: it is through sense that the object is given and through intellect that it is thought.

Reid and Stewart of the Scottish school showed still more clearly this dependence of the intellect upon the senses as the primary source of all ideas, and this relation may now be said to be accepted by all philosophers. But beyond this stage at which the intellect is shown to consist of variously compounded and elaborated perceptions derived through the senses, scarcely another step has been taken in the direction of completing the explanation of this relation, or of connecting it with the soul on the one hand or with the will on the other. When the emotions are to be treated they are treated independently of all this previously established psychological truth, and when the conative powers are to be dealt with they are dealt with as a distinct faculty without antecedent or bond of adhesion to any other branch of the system of psychic phenomena.

That a natural connection exists between all these departments of mind it is one of the chief purposes of these pages to show.

CHAPTER III.

THE PSYCHOLOGIC PROCESS.

Mind has two sides, an obverse and a reverse. The one begins with sensation and ends with sentiment; the other begins with perception and ends with reason. The one constitutes the feelings, the other the intellect. The tendency in all ages has been to ignore the former of these great divisions of the mind, which is essentially the primary one; or, if recognizing it at all, to sublimate it into an intangible something called the will, which no two philosophers could agree in defining, and no one succeed in comprehending; while, at the same time, the glories of the intellect have been unduly extolled, and the impression created that mind consists solely of intellect and will. — *Dynamic Sociology*, II, 123.

Hier ist eine Stufenleiter derselben. Die Gattung ist Vorstellung überhaupt (*repraesentatio*). Unter ihr steht die Vorstellung mit Bewusstsein (*perceptio*). Eine Perception, die sich lediglich auf das Subject als die Modification seines Zustandes bezieht, ist Empfindung (*sensatio*); eine objective Perception ist Erkenntniss (*cognitio*). Diese ist entweder Anschauung oder Begriff (*intuitus vel conceptus*). Jene bezieht sich unmittelbar auf den Gegenstand und ist einzeln; dieser mittelbar vermittelst eines Merkmals, was mehreren Dingen gemein sein kann. — KANT: *Kritik der reinen Vernunft*, p. 261.

Taking as the basis of the knowledge possessed by Man of any object external to him (and therefore of the External World generally), *first*, a subjective Sensation called forth by the presence of that object; *secondly*, the recognition of the *externality* of the cause of that sensation; and *thirdly*, the formation of a *notion* respecting the quality of the object which called it forth, — we have next to inquire into the mode in which such elementary Notions or Cognitions (which are afterwards to be combined into the composite Idea of the object) are generated. — W. B. CARPENTER: *Mental Physiology*, p. 184.

Every sensation, to be known as one, must be perceived; and must so be in one respect a perception. Every perception must be made up of combined sensations: and must so be in one respect sensational . . . Sensations are primary undecomposable states of consciousness; while perceptions are secondary decomposable states, consisting of changes from one primary state to another. Hence, as continuance of the primary states is inconsistent with the occurrence of changes, it follows that consciousness of the changes is in antagonism with consciousness of the states between which they occur. So that perception and sensation are, as it were, ever tending to exclude each other, but never succeeding. Indeed, consciousness continues only in virtue of this conflict. — HERBERT SPENCER : *Principles of Psychology*, I, p. 475.

The first of these elements, originally an excitement, becomes a simple sensation ; then a compound sensation ; then a cluster of partially presentative and partially representative sensations, forming an incipient emotion ; then a cluster of exclusively ideal or representative sensations, forming an emotion proper ; then a cluster of such clusters, forming a compound emotion ; and eventually becomes a still more involved emotion composed of the ideal forms of such compound emotions. The other element, beginning with that immediate passage of a single stimulus into a single motion, called reflex action, presently comes to be a set of associated discharges of stimuli producing associated motions, constituting instinct. Step by step arise more entangled combinations of stimuli, somewhat variable in their modes of union, leading to complex motions similarly variable in their adjustments ; whence occasional hesitations in the sensori-motor processes. Presently is reached a stage at which the combined clusters of impressions, not all present together, issue in actions not all simultaneous ; implying representation of results, or thought. — HERBERT SPENCER : *Data of Ethics*, I, p. 105.

When the end of the finger is placed against any material object two results follow. There is produced a ***sensation*** depending upon the nature of the object, and there is conveyed to the mind a ***notion*** of the nature of the object. The sensation and the notion are not one and the same but two distinct things, capable of being contemplated separately. If the object, as is the usual case, be neither hot nor cold relatively to the temperature of the body, and do not penetrate the tissues nor derange the part in contact with it by any caustic property, the sensation will be what may be called *indifferent*, i.e., it will be neither painful nor pleasurable. Nevertheless, if the object be such as to be capable of producing any sensation at all, i.e., be not a mere gas, incapable of affecting the part, it will be distinct, and one can prolong it at will and fix the attention upon it while partially or wholly excluding the notion it conveys to the mind. On the other hand, in such a case one may, and most naturally does, quite ignore the sensation, and may fix the attention more or less exclusively upon the notion produced by the object. If this latter course is pursued it is clear that the notion conveyed is due to the nature of the object, since it will differ with different objects. In other words it is this notion which affords the mind a knowledge of the nature of the object. The process by which this notion or knowledge is produced is called *perception.*

The primary psychologic process, therefore, is the production of a sensation and nearly or quite simultaneously with this the production of a perception.[1] As the sensation resides wholly in the organism or *subject* experimenting, it may appropriately be called *subjective;* and as the perception relates exclusively to the object the nature of which it reveals, it may with equal propriety be called *objective.* This initial step in the psychologic process furnishes, therefore, the basis or primary element of both the subjective and the objective branch of mind. The following out of the subsequent phenomena which succcessively flow from the repetition, multiplication, combination and coördination of sensations constitutes Subjective Psychology ; while the similar following out of the phenomena which flow from the corresponding repetition, multiplication, combination and coördination of perceptions constitutes Objective Psychology.

The finger-tip has been selected for illustration because it is known that this part of the human organism has from prolonged use been differentiated physiologically through the laws of development for affording, more delicately than any other part, a knowledge of the nature of the objects with which it is brought in contact. Its perceptive power has been specialized by an adjustment of the nerve-tips or papillæ to this end. Such specialization is common in the animal kingdom, reaching much

[1] More properly but less commonly the phenomenon is called a *percept* and the act a *perception.*

greater perfection, for example, in the tips of the vibrissæ of the cat and of the antennæ in insects. But the process might be traced by experimenting with any other part of the body not aponeurotic (e.g., hair or nails), only it would be seen that here the subjective part of the process would manifest itself relatively much stronger while the notion gained of the nature of the object would be correspondingly less definite.

The sense of feeling was also chosen for the purpose of illustrating the psychologic process because it displays both parts of the process to better advantage than any of the other four senses. This is because all the other senses are are too much specialized either in one direction or the other for certain economic purposes. The nerve papillæ of the tongue and palate which give the sense of taste are specialized to dissolve nutritious substances and yield pleasure during their passage to the stomach ; also to reject nauseous ones by yielding pain. They furnish no notion of any other qualities, and give no further idea of an insoluble substance than would be obtained by placing it upon the back of the hand. This sense, when only soluble substances are considered, may therefore be regarded as occupying the extreme subjective end of the scale.

The sense of smell also occupies a position near what may be called the subjective pole. The olfactory nerve is specialized to detect odors, chiefly either pleasant or unpleasant, but from its location is withdrawn from contact with ordinary substances. If liquids, or solids in the comminuted form, are introduced into the antra, unless themselves odorous, they usually cause pain more or less distinctly from threatening to injure the delicate tissues of the nerve. Inert gases such as air are imperceptible. What constitutes odorousness has long been a disputed question, and the ingenious theory has lately been proposed that only volatile and chemically unstable substances are odorous,[1] i.e., that only gases are capable of affecting the

[1] Prof. F. W. Clarke advanced this theory in a still unpublished paper read before the Philosophical Society of Washington on Nov. 7, 1885. See Bulletin Phil. Soc., Vol. VIII, p. 27.

olfactory nerve in the manner to produce the sensation of an odor.

The next sense in the order of increasing objectivity with correspondingly decreasing subjectivity is that of hearing, but the step is a long one, and it is obvious that the sensation produced by sound, unless the vibrations are so violent as to produce pain or manifest disturbance of the apparatus, is practically *nil*. On the other hand a very definite idea of the nature of the object emitting the sound is produced; not, indeed, of its form or texture, but of its sound-producing properties. By virtue of this objective capability of the sense of hearing it becomes one of the great avenues of conveying knowledge to the mind.

Finally, at the extreme objective pole we find the sense of sight. Unless the light be so brilliant as mechanically to injure the optic nerve it is impossible to detect any sensation in the act of seeing. But of all the senses this is the one that furnishes the most complete notion of the object.

With regard to the material vehicle of the five senses we may say that the gustatory sense requires a liquid, the olfactory sense (should Prof. Clarke's theory be confirmed) a gaseous, the tactual sense a solid, the auditory sense usually a gaseous (the atmosphere[1]), and the visual sense an ethereal (the universal ether) medium.

The order in passing from the subjective to the objective pole is that just given, viz., 1, taste; 2, smell; 3, touch; 4, hearing; 5, sight.

[1] Solids and liquids are also, of course, conductors of sound in varying degrees, but it is the air that directly affects the organ of hearing.

CHAPTER IV.

SUBJECTIVE PSYCHOLOGY.

The phenomena of feeling constitute the true basis of all that part of philosophy which at all involves the interest of man. They are, in short, the foundation-stones of the social science. What function is to biology, feeling is to sociology. — *Dynamic Sociology*, II, 123.

Sensation is the consciousness of the change which the contact of the object effects in the state of the molecules at the point of contact. This bears no direct proportion to the amount of disturbance produced, but depends far more upon the degree of *sensitiveness* of the part affected. This sensitiveness is due to the specialization of the tissues for this express purpose, which results from the operation of natural selection or adaptation. The physiological meaning of these degrees of sensitiveness in different tissues is, that the nerve-fibers are so arranged at points where it is advantageous to the organism to have them so, that slight disturbances at their termini convey comparatively powerful discharges to the interior centers, and the greater the disproportion between the amount of disturbance and the amount of the discharge the more sensitive the part is said to be. — *Dynamic Sociology*, I, 381–382.

The peculiarity of Feeling, therefore, is that there is nothing but what is subjectively subjective; there is no object different from self, — no objectification of any mode of self. — SIR WILLIAM HAMILTON: ***Metaphysics***, II. p. 432, Lecture 42.

External Objects impressed upon the Senses occasion, first in the Nerves, on which they are impressed, and then in the Brain, Vibrations of the small, and as one may say, infinitesimal, medullary Particles. — DAVID HARTLEY: *Observations on Man, Prop.* IV.

These vibrations are motions backwards and forwards of the small particles; of the same kind with the oscillations of pendulums, and the tremblings of the particles of sounding bodies. They must be conceived to be exceedingly short and small, so as not to have the least efficacy to disturb or move the whole bodies of the nerves or brain. — DAVID HARTLEY: *Ibid.*, (*Discussion of Prop.* IV).

The first tendency in every consciousness is pure pain-pleasure, complete subjectivity which, however, in higher consciousness is so quickly lost through practically consentaneous differentiation that all traces of it seem wholly extinguished. Pure subjectivity must be pronounced the most evanescent of all characters in developed minds and yet the most constant. It is the inevitable precedent in every sensation and in every perception. We always experience pleasure or pain before the pleasurable or painful. — HIRAM M. STANLEY: *Philosophical Review*, July, 1892 (Vol. I, p. 439).

Subjective psychology proper deals exclusively with sensations and their various combinations. It takes no account of intellectual processes. The simplest sensations are those mentioned at the beginning of the last chapter, viz., those which are neither painful nor pleasurable, but indifferent. These are more abundant than might be at first supposed, and their importance will be considered in the next chapter. Subjective psychology has very little to do with them. Its chief object is to explain the nature and importance of the other two classes of sensations — painful and pleasurable — which may be grouped together in contrast with indifferent ones and called *intensive*. Reasons will be given later for regarding intensive sensations as primary and indifferent sensations as secondary.

The only senses that afford intensive sensations directly are taste, smell, and touch. Objects brought into contact with the nerves of any of these senses may produce directly either painful or pleasurable effects. In case of sounds so violent as to injure the ear, or light so brilliant as to affect the eye unfavorably, it is no longer hearing or sight but feeling that is involved. Feeling is preëminently the pain-sense,[1] few objects being capable of producing pleasing effects by direct contact, though some such there are, as when soft fur is touched or

[1] The above was written in January, 1892, and I was first made acquainted with the fact that Goldscheider had "positively demonstrated isolated specific pain nerves" on reading the suggestive articles of Dr. Herbert Nichols in the Philosophical Review for July and September. See that review, Vol. I, pp. 406-407.

warm water is felt under certain conditions of the system. Taste and smell, on the contrary, are more especially pleasure-senses, although there are plenty of bitter, sour, and nauseous objects and offensive odors.

The pains and pleasures yielded by sounds and colors are not direct and original but indirect and derivative. It is true that no sensation is possible that is not conveyed to the brain by the proper nerves, but this is only to say that in order for a sensation to exist the organism must be conscious of it. The pain caused by burning the hand, however, is definitely located in the injured part. The pleasure afforded by savory food or fragrant flowers is felt in the organs of taste and smell themselves. But the pleasing effect of melody is not felt in the ear, it is experienced, as is commonly said, by the mind. Much less is the enjoyment of a landscape a sensation located in the eye. It is a diffused state of the psychic organism, and is wrongly called *intellectual* by some. Both these classes of feelings are properly called *emotional.*

This leads to the most important branch of subjective psychology, viz., the emotions. Emotions may be called secondary sensations, i. e., sensations that are not produced directly by the object through contact of its appropriate medium with the nerve, but are reflected from the brain along special nerve fibers to certain specialized emotional ganglia within the organism. They constitute in fact a distinct sense, the oft-mentioned sixth sense, if any one prefers so to designate it. Not, however, the so-called "moral sense" of certain ethical writers, by which we are said to be able to distinguish instinctively right from wrong (which is not a sense in the physiological acceptation of the word), but a true physiological sense, consisting, like the other five, of nerves specialized to afford a particular class of sensations. If, however, we are to arrange the senses in the ascending order of their objectivity and number them accordingly, the emotional sense would stand first instead of last, since it is as exclusively subjective as the sense of sight is exclusively objective. An emotion yields no perception. It was pointed out that the senses of taste and smell are chiefly subjective, that their principal function is to cause pleasurable (or painful) sensations. But not only do these senses give rise to a great number of such sensations differing as the nature of the object differs, but they really acquaint the mind with as many different qualities residing in the objects. That is to say, they yield perceptions of the gustatory and olfactory qualities of objects capable of affecting them, but of no other qualities. But the emotional sense furnishes the mind with no knowledge whatever of the object producing the emotion. It furnishes sensation only, although the nature of the sensations differ widely according to the objects, and are infinitely multiplied.

It appears then that the nervous apparatus of a developed organism yields two great classes of sensations which may be roughly classed as *external* and *internal.* I say roughly, because this distinction is not absolute. The nerves of taste, smell, hearing, and sight are internal, but not so much so that the medium through which they are reached does not actually penetrate to them from without and act directly upon them as literally as a blow with a whip acts upon the external nerves of the part of the body that it strikes. In emotions, on the contrary, there is no medium except the nerve currents themselves. The specialized emotional ganglia are located in many parts of the body but not in all parts. Large numbers of them are connected with the cerebro-spinal system, but the great emotional centers are located in the sympathetic system. It is unnecessary to enter here into a detailed account of the intricate relations subsisting between the cerebro-spinal and sympathetic systems, relations which are not as yet all fully understood, and about which there is still considerable controversy. The general facts have long been established and these are sufficient for the present purpose. The sympathetic system is essentially internal; its operations are chiefly or wholly unconscious and cannot be controlled at will, although they are profoundly affected by mental states, however these may have been brought about ; it controls the involuntary operations of the internal organs, such as circulation, digestion, assimilation, and glandular secretion ; and, finally, it is the seat of the principal emotions. Here a distinction must be drawn between sensation and emotion. In a popular sense an emotion is a sensation, but not in the same sense in which the term is applied to external impressions. It was remarked above that feeling is primarily a pain-sense. All the nerves of feeling, so far as known, belong to the cerebro-spinal system, and all organs which are exposed to injury receive fibers from that system whether they receive any from the sympathetic system or not. Those organs, such as the liver, kidneys, ovaries, etc., which are supplied with fibers from the sympathetic only are so far internal as not to require the protection of a sensory apparatus.

The emotional centers, therefore, while they are not specialized for experiencing the sensation of pain from the contact of foreign substances, and therefore do not in this meaning belong to the sense of feeling, are nevertheless capable of affording the most intense feelings both of pain and pleasure. We may leave unsettled the question whether the emotions are confined exclusively to the sympathetic system or whether the cerebrospinal system may contribute somewhat to their production, the fact remains that there exists a diffused, but powerful emotional sense distinct from all the other senses, but capable of yielding the deepest and most important of all the feelings.

CHAPTER V.

OBJECTIVE PSYCHOLOGY.

Perception is the quality of that state of consciousness of the tissue affected, which arises from the character of the object; it is the result of differences of sensations produced by differences of objects; or, still more clearly, of different sensations caused by different objects. . . . Perception of the lowest form consists in the impression thus made by the object upon the afferent nerve and the ganglion to which it immediately leads. . . . It is simply the recognition by the sensitive nerve-matter affected that it has been thus affected, the manner in which it is affected denoting the properties of the object. This is the root of the idea of *knowledge*. In thus recognizing the properties of an object, the nervous system, however simple, in so far *knows* the object. The term *cognition* is preferable to recognition, since it does not presuppose an antecedent acquaintance with the same properties. — *Dynamic Sociology*, I, 382–383.

Die Vernunft ist weiblicher Natur: sie kann nur geben, nachdem sie empfangen hat. — SCHOPENHAUER: *Welt als Wille und Vorstellung*, I, 59.

The white medullary Substance of the Brain is also the immediate Instrument, by which Ideas are presented to the Mind: or, in other words, whatever Changes are made in this Substance, corresponding Changes are made in our Ideas; and *vice versâ*. — DAVID HARTLEY: *Observations on Man*, *Prop.* II.

Objective psychology in its properly limited sense deals exclusively with perceptions and their elaboration by the brain. The contact of an object or medium with the nerve of sense is called an impression; the effect produced upon the nerve is referred to the brain and becomes a sensation, which, for reasons that will hereafter be given, appears to reside at the immediate point impressed. If not so strong as to absorb consciousness in the sensation itself a perception results, affording a notion of the nature of the object which caused the sensation. If pain is produced no such notion is gained. If a pleasure-nerve is affected the notion is limited to the few qualities residing in objects capable of appealing to such senses, e. g., sweet, sour, bitter, fragrant, etc. The notions of melody, harmony, and discord, as also of colors, are allied to these last, but differ in not being accompanied by proper sensations. They are perceptions of the lowest class. Uniformly, the less distinct the sensation the more clear the perception. The senses of hearing and sight, therefore, are devoted exclusively to furnishing perceptions.

Perception, like sensation, though residing in the brain appears to be located at the receptive end of the nerves of sense. Perceptions are registered in the brain by a physiological process not wholly understood, but about which much is known. This registration is permanent, i.e., it remains during a longer or shorter period depending upon many conditions. Among these conditions are the importance of the perception, the quality of the brain, the age of the subject, etc.

The structure and mechanism of the brain are such that a plurality of registered perceptions gives rise to a process of combination, comparison, and coördination. Every individual from birth to death is incessantly receiving impressions through the appropriate senses which are duly recorded and constitute his stock of raw material for thought. The process of elaborating this raw material is distinguished from all other psychic operations as *intellectual*. The cerebral apparatus by which it is accomplished is the organ of the intellect.

The first step in the purely intellectual process is the grouping together of the several perceptions furnished by any object and the formation therefrom of a *conception*.[1] of it. This con-

[1] *Concept* would be the proper term and is properly so used, but it has also acquired a much larger meaning, as datum, axiom, or fundamental idea. *Conception* in psychology should be confined to the act of conceiving by the mind. Its use in this sense may have been derived from the physical fact of conception which, before much was known about physiology was supposed by many to be itself a mental process. Weismann (Essays, Vol. II. London, 1892, pp. 106–107) remarks apropos to this belief: "Some writers regard inheritance by means of

ception is then used as a psychological unit of comparison with other conceptions. Where two such conceptions are compared the mind declares whether they are similar or dissimilar, and such declaration is called in logic a *judgment*, while the formula by which it is expressed is called a *proposition*. If such judgment be not erroneous it constitutes a *truth*, which Mr. George Henry Lewes has acutely defined as "the recognition of identity." Judgments thus formed in great numbers in the mind relative to all the multitudinous phenomena of experience become in turn distinct psychological units of a higher order to be themselves compared and co-ordinated.

A still more complex process consists in arranging like with like to form a group and then selecting from that group those properties which all have in common and no others, giving rise to an *idea* in the Platonic sense; and then proceeding with the classification of unlike ideas. But the mind does not stop here. It goes on and makes groups of these groups, ever widening the circle, the larger groups having less and less properties in common, and the smaller groups more and more. This process is termed *generalization* and may be carried up until all things whatsoever shall be embraced in the ultimate generalization. Before the biological sciences were founded philosophers from Plato down labored to find illustrations of this process. Now they are abundant and familiar even to school children, and the study of classification in plants and animals, entirely aside from the knowledge of nature which it affords, is of more value as a lesson in logic than all the rules and formulas of that science if committed to memory. One may struggle for four

fertilization as a purely immaterial occurrence: thus Harvey, in his remarkable and minutely thought-out theory of heredity, imagined conception as a mental process, the folds of the mucous membrane lining the uterus corresponding to the convolutions of the brain, and giving rise to the foetus under the influence of the semen; just as the brain, under the influence of external impressions, gives rise to thoughts. The term 'conception,' when figuratively applied to mental processes, —a term which has been obviously derived from conception on the part of a woman,—is here reversed, and used to explain the very process from which it is itself derived."

years to comprehend the Platonic idea without succeeding, but the moment a distinct conception is gained of what is meant by a genus or an order in natural history the Platonic idea is mastered.

Reason is more especially the faculty by which the mind reaches conclusions. It does this from a use of all the materials in its possession, but chiefly by the aid of conceptions, judgments, and other of the higher psychological units. The two leading methods are deduction and induction, both of which are too familiar to require description. Both are essentially classificatory, the former valuable in verifying hypotheses or suspected relationships among ideas, the latter often leading to the unexpected discovery of new truth.

To all these intellectual operations text-book writers append treatises on memory and imagination. But memory is the general condition to the whole process and consists in the fact that not only perceptions but conceptions, judgments, and ideas are more or less permanently registered and may be called up as occasion requires. The phenomena of the association of ideas also rests upon this fact. Imagination cannot transcend experience. Its materials must all be stored up for use. It can only form new or strange combinations of them, can multiply them into exaggerations or combine them in unnatural ways. The same is true of the creative faculty in art, usually treated as a form of the imagination. But here the process consists essentially in a *selection of the best* from all the materials at hand. Everything in the real world is imperfect but there exist ideals, and the true artist selects from these and realizes to the extent of his power his idea of a perfect combination.

Objective psychology, as already remarked, is about the only department of the mind that the older philosophers deemed worthy of study, and the process above sketched constituted the greater part of the field covered by them. But there is another department, hitherto almost wholly ignored, yet the one which is historically the primary intellectual process, and is at the same time practically the most important of all intellectual processes. To distinguish it from all the other forms of reasoning I propose to call this process *intuition.* The power of carrying on this kind of mental activity may be called the *intuitive faculty.* The probable explanation of the neglect of this faculty by writers on the mind is its identity with what we call *sagacity* or *cunning,* which, whether displayed by animals or men, is considered to be a low element. That the principle of deception lies at the foundation of it I have formerly shown, and shall more fully establish in Chap. XXIV, which makes it of the greatest importance to ethical and social science, while this reputed sin is many times atoned for by its achievements in the domain of non-sentient things in constituting the sole condition to the origin and progress of material civilization. But the proper treatment of this important part of objective psychology cannot be undertaken until the nature of the conative powers, so constantly associated with it, shall have been set forth, and it will be best to postpone the whole subject until the second part of the work is reached, where it will constitute the essential basis of the entire discussion.

CHAPTER VI.

THE CONATIVE FACULTY.

The simpler truths of physics, chemistry, etc., have been found to present difficulties, puzzles, and paradoxes, at every step in their investigation. It is therefore not surprising that the far more subtile phenomena of mind should present enigmas and paradoxes even more remarkable, and thus baffle the common intellect and that of the philosopher as well. That the phantom of the will is such a paradox there is no doubt. Already far more deeply cherished beliefs in various departments have been remanded by science to the limbo of paradoxical myths, and I see no reason for clinging with such pertinacity to the will after it is shown to be only a *will-o'-the wisp.* — *Dynamic Sociology*, I, 398.

Affectus coërceri nec tolli potest, nisi per affectum contrarium et fortiorem affectu coërcendo. — SPINOZA: *Ethica*, Pars IV, *Propositio* VII.

Although the conative faculty properly belongs to subjective psychology it would have been inconvenient to treat it before the general principles of objective psychology were set forth. This is in consequence of the important part which the ideo-motor apparatus performs in producing voluntary action. Of this I shall presently speak.

We have seen that impressions which are not strong enough to produce any but what have been called indifferent sensations are conveyed to the brain in the form of perceptions and constitute the raw material for thought. That is to say, they are reflected to the cortical layers and other specialized fibers and plexuses devoted to the process of ideation as described in the last chapter. But impressions which are strong enough to produce what were called intensive sensations, after being carried to the brain along the *afferent* nerves are reflected back along a different set of nerves, designated as *efferent* nerves, to the muscles connected with the organ impressed. These nerves possess an entirely different function, namely, that of causing the appropriate muscles to contract and the organ to move. Hence they are called motor nerves, and the entire nervous system has this motor apparatus everywhere accompanying the sensor apparatus. The great distinguishing characteristic of an animal organism is its ability to move—to move itself bodily (except in the few cases of the lower forms that are fixed to a support), or at least to move its parts. This movement is accomplished entirely by means of the motor nerves communicating with the appropriate muscles.

It will be observed that the motor apparatus is only stimulated to act by intensive sensations, that is, by such as cause pleasure or pain, be this ever so slight, a fact which is of prime importance in considering the conative powers. But the reason for it is clear. The movements caused by such sensations are not irregular and aimless but have a definite character and purpose. They always take place in the direction *away from* a pain-producing object and *towards* a pleasure-producing object. The simplest animal movement known is that which is called *reflex action*, by which the afferent nerve carries the impression direct to the brain or principal ganglionic center and the motor impulse is directly reflected back to the organ impressed, resulting in its movement. So simple is this that it may be made to take place in a dead frog's leg, provided the nerves are still intact.

From this simple origin the phenomena may be followed through a great variety and complexity of forms until it becomes impossible to analyze them and distinguish their several elements. The sensori-motor apparatus permeates the organism and extends to all the organs that are at all exposed. A few of the internal organs, as previously stated, are destitute of sensori-motor nerves and provided only with sympathetic ones, and one of the most convincing proofs of the purpose of this arrangement is that while the ovaries belong to this latter class the corresponding but exposed testes are provided with sensori-motor nerves from the cerebro-spinal system.

The sympathetic system also has motor attachments, as is evidenced by its control of the peristaltic muscular movements of the intestines, the valves of the arteries, the systole and diastole of the heart and circulatory vessels, the action of secretory glands, etc., but all this is carried on unconsciously, or more properly speaking, is presided over by the great subordinate ganglionic centers and is not referred to the brain or general organ of consciousness. If therefore it appears to form an exception to the general law that movement can only take place in obedience to intensive sensations, this is based on the assumption that those ganglionic centers are incapable of experiencing sensations, an assumption by no means warranted by physiology. The nervous system must be regarded as compound, i. e., as composed of many individuals, the subordinate ganglionic centers, each endowed with a consciousness of its own, and all *integrated* into a general system having the brain as the supreme center of consciousness. This supreme consciousness is the *ego* of the philosophers, and nothing that is not referred to it is perceived by the integrated organism or ego. Physiological economy requires that most of the internal vital processes shall be performed without expense to the general consciousness ; the sensations calling forth these ceaseless actions are extremely slight, and only when derangements occur too great to be repaired by the lower centers are these sensations referred to the higher one and brought within the range of consciousness proper. But the proposition must be rigidly adhered to that there can be no motion without sensation, and these unconscious sensations, if the expression were permissible, must be regarded as the sensations of individual beings distinct from the ego, which is no more aware of them than it is of those of any other organism not itself.

It is to be remarked, however, that there seems to exist a faint but incessant current connecting these lower centers with the supreme center and producing a constant recognition of the activity of all the vital functions; for it can be nothing else than this that constitutes the *enjoyment* of health. It is the pleasure of normal activity throughout all the organs of the body, steadily reported by the subordinate centers to the supreme center. Conversely in low states of health the pain of imperfect performance of function is similarly reported, producing all the grades of pathologic states to complete prostration and death.

Thus far we have considered only those actions which result from the sensori-motor apparatus. But in highly developed organisms there is another apparatus, more complicated in its nature, called the *ideo-motor* apparatus. This exists in all organisms in which there is a true brain having registered upon it any of the impressions described in the last chapter — perceptions, conceptions, judgments, ideas, generalizations, thoughts. The process of ideation is carried on in the cortical layers in communication with each other by means of longitudinal and transverse fibers, with the *fornix* and *corpus callosum*, and with the sensorium at the *thalami optici* and *corpora striata*. These organs are provided with efferent nerves connecting them with the muscular system along which there occurs a motor discharge producing muscular activities which are the legitimate ends for which ideas are formed. The resultant actions are those which are commonly understood as *rational* actions. All others are the simple animal impulses with which the reason has nothing to do. Such actions come as clearly within the generic definition of being the result of intensive senations and tending away from pain-producing and towards pleasure-producing causes, as do the sensori-motor actions or movements. They differ only in their intellectual origin and consequent higher character. Naturally they are less vivid and less strong, but they are also more persistent and enduring. They result from what is called *conviction*, and where judgments and conclusions are objectively true they are successful in their results. But if such judgments and conclusions involve error they must in so far fail, and history and experience have proved that so complicated is the process of ideation that error is nearly or quite as common as truth, so that ideo-motor actions of the more important kinds are often even less reliable than mere animal impulses. This is chiefly due to insufficient data supplied to the mind, and constitutes the great argument for the inculcation of the maximum amount of the most important knowledge which alone can render ideas trustworthy and ideo-motor actions safe.

It will be observed that in treating the conative faculty I have not made use of the term *will*. This is because this term, like many others in our language, has only a popular and not a technical or scientific meaning. Psychology is the physics of the mind, and its phenomena are as uniform and its laws as exact as are those of the physics of the inorganic world. If this were not so it would not be a science, and there would be no use in attempting to treat it at all. The physical law of mind is that motor impulses follow sense impressions as effect follows cause. As in mechanical physics, so in mental physics, the effect is proportioned to the cause and acts in the direction of the cause. In the microcosm as in the macrocosm there are multiplied causes always operating, and these, in the nature of things, are constantly influencing one another in every conceivable way, sometimes working together to strengthen the effects, more commonly conflicting either directly or obliquely and variously modifying them. In mind as in matter the actual effect is always the exact resultant of these causes, and if equal and opposite, equilibrium is the consequence, while if oblique, or varied in quantity and direction, some form of constrained motion results. The actual movement observed is merely an index to the causes producing it, and notifies the observer as to what were the prevailing impulses.

What is popularly termed the will is merely the expression of the psychological fact that this, that, or the other impulse actually did prevail because stronger than all others. If we seek for any other rational basis for the will we never find it. To suppose with some that the rational motives constitute the will and may be made to dominate the physical impulses is unsound, since not only do they often fail to do so in the best minds, but, as above remarked, if they did, the result would often be less safe than it is in the actual case. To the claim that the will consists in causing good motives to prevail over bad ones the answer is that from the nature of the mental mechanism this must always be the case, since the only movements possible are those which seek the good or shun the bad. This of course is from the standpoint of the organism, i.e., egoistic ; but if it be maintained that by the good is only meant the altruistic, then this altruistic motive must also be the prevailing egoistic one, otherwise we have an effect without a cause, and psychology ceases to be a science.

CHAPTER VII.

ORIGIN AND FUNCTION OF PLEASURE AND PAIN.

The normal operations of the organism must be maintained; life must be preserved; the species must be perpetuated. Natural selection has therefore made those acts which secure these ends pleasurable, and those that threaten to defeat them painful. Any species in which these sensations are not sufficiently lively to secure the performance of the acts necessary to maintain and perpetuate its life, and to defend it from external dangers, must rapidly become extinct, and only those species have survived in which the sensations were sufficiently developed for these purposes. — *Dynamic Sociology*, I, 388–389.

The objects which nature must be regarded as aiming to accomplish by the introduction of pleasure and pain are the preservation, perpetuation, and improvement of sentient organisms. Pleasure and pain are merely the means to these several ends, all of which are more or less remote in appearance from the means employed. . . . There is no necessary connection between a given pleasurable or painful sensation, and the result it accomplishes in preserving, perpetuating, or perfecting the organism experiencing it. This result is brought about through a kind of pre-established harmony, not indeed of a supernatural kind, but consisting, on the contrary, of a purely mechanical adaptation of the means to the end, which are connected by the highest causal necessity, yet in such a manner that the creature obeying the mandate of the former does so without the least necessary conception or even knowledge of the latter. — *Dynamic Sociology*, II, 120–121.

Pains are the correlatives of actions injurious to the organism, while pleasures are the correlatives of actions conducive to its welfare. . . . It is an inevitable deduction from the hypothesis of Evolution, that races of sentient creatures could have come into existence under no other conditions. — HERBERT SPENCER: *Principles of Psychology*, I, p. 279. Those races of beings only can have survived in which, on the average, agreeable or desired feelings went along with activities conducive to the maintenance of life, while disagreeable and habitually-avoided feelings went along with activities directly or indirectly destructive of life; and there must ever have been, other things equal, the most numerous and long-continued survivals among races in which these adjustments of feelings to actions were the best, tending ever to bring about perfect adjustment. — HERBERT SPENCER: *Ibid.*, I, p. 280.

Je dois cependant signaler ici une heureuse remarque de M. de Blainville sur le siége de l'impression: outre l'affection directe de l'organe principal de la satisfaction du besoin considéré, il y a toujours une affection sympathique à l'orifice du canal qui doit introduire l'agent destiné à cette satisfaction, soit qu'il s'agisse de l'incrétion d'aliments solides, liquides, ou gazeux: il en est de même, en sens inverse, pour les divers besoins d'excrétion, toujours ressentis sympathiquement à l'extrémité du canal excréteur. — AUGUSTE COMTE: *Philosophie Positive*, III, 517.

Mind, like all other vital function, must originate in some very simple and elementary form as demanded at some critical moment for the preservation of the organism. It is tolerably obvious that this could not be any objective consciousness, any cognitive act, like pure sensation, for this has no immediate value for life. It was not as awareness of object or in any discriminating activity that mind originated, for mere apprehension would not serve the being more than the property of reflection the mirror. The demand of the organism is for that which will accomplish immediate movement to the place of safety. — HIRAM M. STANLEY: *Philosophical Review*, July, 1892 (vol. I, p. 433).

Wenn wir den Willen da, wo ihn Niemand leugnet, also in den erkennenden Wesen, betrachten, so finden wir überall, als seine Grundbestrebung, die Selbsterhaltung eines jeden Wesens: *omnis natura vult esse conservatrix sui.* Alle Aeusserungen dieser Grundbestrebung aber lassen sich stets zurückführen auf ein Suchen, oder Verfolgen, und ein Meiden, oder Fliehen, je nach dem Anlass. — SCHOPENHAUER: *Welt als Wille*, II, 338.

In the natural world everything has a meaning. The mission of science is to ascertain that meaning. Without science and before science all is mystery. The motto of science is *nil admirari.* Among the mysteries about which philosophers have from time immemorial and with great ingenuity and enormous labor busied themselves, but for which the new science of biology has found an explanation wholly different from any proposed, much more simple, perfectly rational, and in harmony with all the facts, is that of the origin of pain, or in more dignified but less accurate phrase, the origin of evil. At the same time that it explained pain, however, it also explained pleasure, which, though more complicated and remarkable, had, nevertheless, never been regarded as a mystery, but as something that ought to exist in the nature of things. The fact is that neither pain nor pleasure exists essentially or in the nature of things. Neither is necessary, and the universe is easily conceived as destitute of both. The only sense in which they can be regarded as necessary is that in which whatever is, is necessary. In any other sense they are accidental.

To illustrate what I mean by saying that pleasure and pain are not inherently necessary, the recent announcement, one might almost say demonstration, of Prof. August Weismann, that death is not necessary is precisely in point. He has shown that the duration of life in different kinds of animals is not fixed in any such way as is popularly supposed, but has been brought about in each case by the coöperation of certain factors, especially the rate at which the species can multiply and the danger to life to which it is subjected in its normal habitat. These two causes working together determine the rate of reproduction, and the duration of life is adjusted to this so as to secure the requisite number of offspring per pair to insure the certain continuance of the species. But for these agencies the life of man, for example, might have been twice or ten times as long as it is, or might have been cut down to a score of years or less. Indeed there would be no necessary limit, and a gnat might live a century. Not only so, but from this truth as a basis Weismann works out with wonderful skill his doctrine of the continuity of the germ-plasm, and actually maintains that the least of all living things, the very germs of life, are in very truth "immortal," and that in the latest product of organic nature there exist elements that have never ceased to live since life was introduced into the world!

It is in exactly this sense that pleasure and pain are not necessary, but are products of certain conditioning phenomena belonging to the infinite chain of cause and effect which constitutes the actual universe. As a general proposition embodying this truth it may be stated that *pleasure and pain are the conditions to the existence of plastic organisms.* Organisms that are not plastic, such as most plants, have their existence secured by other conditions — the solid stem or trunk, deeply imbedded and protected roots, multiplied appendicular organs, etc. But plastic organisms, such as most animals, require different conditions of existence, and the one with which we find them provided is a sensitive organization, — that is, they are *sentient*.

Except by a degree of refinement greater than is necessary to our present purpose the origin of life is a different problem from the origin of mind, and as a fact in cosmic history probably antedated it by eons of time. Mind dates from the dawn of the sentient property. This property belongs to plastic motile beings, and as above stated, is the condition to the development of such beings. However faint it may be conceived to be in the most lowly of them they must all be assumed to be capable of feeling. And for the purpose for which feeling was created it must be supposed to consist of pleasure and pain. Indifferent feeling, such as was described as the basis of objective psychology, could have been of no possible use in insuring the life of inchoate plastic organisms. Whether we conceive them as possessing incipient nervous systems or merely channels in apparently unorganized protoplasmic masses, the sensations which led them to obtain nourishment and escape danger must have belonged to the intensive class. In the higher metazoans and all the developed beings that people the earth this property is distinct and manifest, and in the highest, where alone we are in the habit of observing it, it does not differ in any appreciable respect from what we experience in ourselves.

We have seen that the cerebro-spinal system of the higher animals and man supplies sensori-motor nerves to all exposed organs, and we know that those not thus provided are incapable of feeling. The proof is adequate that it is the purpose of these nerves to warn the system of danger to such organs. It is a legitimate inference from abundant induction that the purpose and function of pain is protection from injury. From the biological standpoint it has no other object, and but for the necessity of such protection the whole animal world might far better have been incapable of pain. Nor is there any doubt that in the absence of this necessity such a quality as sensitiveness to pain would not and could not have been developed. Remove this quality and sentient life would quickly disappear. The hostile environment would close in upon it and ruthlessly crush it. But pain in and of itself is evil — the only evil. Yet viewed in the dry light of science it is good if there is any good, for it is the sole guaranty of life itself. This then is the origin of evil and forever closes the great debate, while at the same time it furnishes the ultimate answer to pessimism, asceticism, orientalism, and all the 'isms that bewail the sufferings of the world.

If we look at the other side of the case we find a parallel series of facts. Plastic organisms exist by virtue of what physiologists call *metabolism*. Their substance must be constantly renewed by assimilation of the materials of which they are composed. Not to speak of growth, they are perpetually consuming it by the vital processes of existence. This consumption of tissue or normal waste of organic substance must be incessantly supplied from without. It could never be done without an adequate stimulus or motive for doing it. The replenishing of wasted tissues is nutrition, and to insure nutrition some inducement must be provided to perform the acts that will accomplish it. No other motive can be conceived than that of agreeable sensation. To this end every organism is provided with a nervous apparatus adapted to render the nutritive act pleasurable. In the lower forms it is some degree of agreeableness in the contact of the absorbent tissues with the nutritive substance. In the higher it becomes taste, to which the sense of smell is directly ancillary. Nor is this sufficient. To it is added the pain or "pangs" of hunger only appeasable by renewal of the supply. And if the term nutrition is taken in ts broad sense of supplying all the elements that make up the organic body, since the greater part of all organisms consists of water, thirst must be added with its intolerable effects driving the creature to the source from which it may be slaked. These however may be transferred to the side of pleasurable sensations by considering the intense satisfaction that attends these acts of nutrition.

Finally, in most of the higher organisms in which this supreme end is not otherwise attained, the procreative pleasure has been added to prevent such races of beings from perishing for lack of renewal.[1] The fact that this is absent from so many living creatures makes it easy to conceive of its being absent from all, and furnishes an excellent example in illustration of the accidental character of sentiency in general, and of what is meant by saying that pleasure and pain are not necessary, but are simply conditions to the existence of beings organized as plastic organisms are.

We thus see that pleasure and pain have their origin not in the nature of things but in the nature of plastic organisms, without which the latter could not have existed, and that their sole function is to conserve life, either by insuring escape from the dangers of a necessarily hostile environment, or by constituting the motive to nutrition and reproduction. From this fundamental truth the corollary flows that the so-called evil of the world is a mere incident of the complicated conditions under which life exists. To what extent it is necessary and to what extent it is avoidable are questions that belong to the second part of this work.

Several prevalent errors are also capable of removal by this view of the subject. It is commonly supposed that pleasure and pain are opposites. This is seen not to be the case.

[1] According to Weismann it is not renewal or *reproduction* that nature aims at in developing the sexual instinct, but *variation* through the union of different hereditary tendencies. It amounts to nearly the same thing, however, since without such variation organic life would have been very low and simple even if it could have been maintained through purely asexual reproduction.

They are practically independent of each other. There is no opposite to pleasure except it be the absence of pleasure, and there is no opposite to pain except it be relief from pain. They are physiological states arising from the condition of the appropriate nerves. These nerves are for the most part specialized[1] for producing either the one or the other, and the parts that yield pain-sensations are incapable of yielding pleasure-sensations, as instance the senses of feeling and of taste and smell. Feeling, as has been remarked, is essentially a pain-sense, and all the cerebro-spinal plexuses attending exposed parts of the body are susceptible to pains only. And although flavors or odors may be agreeable or disagreeable this is the only sense in which they may be called opposite. The same is probably true of the emotional sense, but so complicated and involved are these internal phenomena that it is unprofitable to speculate upon them.

A kindred error is that pleasure is the positive and pain the negative element. Both are positive and very unlike. There is nothing more positive than pain, although of the two, as will be seen, it is the one whose absence or elimination can be most easily conceived. Neither is it to quite the same extent the normal condition, and those philosophies which are based upon the postulate of necessary pain, or of the essential predominance of pain, are the products of an unhappy social state rather than of a clear grasp of natural truth. But this much is clear, that, to use the current teleological forms of speech, Nature has no concern whatever for the degree of pleasure or of pain, but only for the preservation and perpetuation of the beings she has evolved.

While, as above stated, there is a sense in which pain may be said to be a good, the scientific view here presented is nevertheless wholly opposed to that other philosophy which would seek to make it a desirable end of life. Created for the

[1] See foot-note to page 47. The broader application here made of this principle will, I believe, be borne out by further research.

purpose of warning the sentient being against dangers to life, unless it heeds that warning its function fails and it were better it had not been created. The principle taught by Bain and Spencer, and long before by Spinoza,[1] that pleasure leads to life and pain to death, that the pleasurable is the good and the painful is the bad, and that the duty of life is to pursue the former and avoid the latter, is thus seen to rest upon a fundamental truth of organic development as well as to reflect the simplest dictates of common sense ; and the opposite doctrine is one of those deductions of the rational faculty which so frequently lead the world astray when not proceeding from a sound basis of acquired knowledge. As remarked in Chap. V, there is nothing more untrustworthy than the legitimate deliverances of the ignorant or error-laden intellect. But as showing that even those who would court pain and "mortify the flesh" themselves recognize the higher claims of common sense it is noteworthy that their philosophy is the outcome of a religion which teaches a future state of infinite misery or unlimited bliss, and that it is the belief that present pain will insure future pleasure in an increased degree which underlies their teachings, so that when this is remembered it is seen to be after all the maximum pleasure that they are seeking, and there is no essential difference in their general theory from that which science and common sense unite in enjoining.

[1] Lætitia directe mala non est, sed bona ; Tristitia autem contra directe est mala. — SPINOZA : *Ethica*, Pars IV, *Propositio* XLI.

CHAPTER VIII.

NATURE OF THE SOUL.

Biology has overthrown the anthropocentric theory as astronomy has the geocentric, and every creature lives in and for itself and shares with man to some degree the sublime attributes of mind and soul. — *Course of Biologic Evolution*, p. 26.

Angelangt an dieser äussersten psychologischen Consequenz unserer monistischen Entwickelungslehre begegnen wir uns mit jenen alten Vorstellungen von der Beseelung aller Materie, welche schon in der Philosophie des DEMOKRITOS, SPINOSA, BRUNO, LEIBNIZ, SCHOPENHAUER einen verschiedenartigen Ausdruck gefunden haben. Denn alles Seelenleben lässt sich schliesslich auf die beiden Elementar-Functionen der Empfindung und Bewegung, auf ihre Wechselwirkung in der Reflexbewegung zurückführen. Die einfache Empfindung von Lust und Unlust, die einfache Bewegungsform der Anziehung und Abstossung, das sind die wahren Elemente, aus denen sich in unendlich mannichfaltiger und verwickelter Verbindung alle Seelenthätigkeit aufbaut. 'Der Atome Hassen und Lieben,' Anziehung und Abstossung der Moleküle, Bewegung und Empfindung der Zellen, und der aus Zellen zusammengesetzten Organismen, Gedankenbildung und Bewusstsein des Menschen — das sind nur verschiedene Stufen des universalen psychologischen Entwicklungsprocesses. — ERNST HAECKEL: *Die heutige Entwicklungslehre im Verhältnisse zur Gesammtwissenschaft*, p. 14.

The night has a thousand eyes,
  And the day but one;
Yet the light of the bright world dies
  With the dying sun.
The mind has a thousand eyes,
  And the heart but one;
Yet the light of the whole life dies
  When love is done.

FRANCIS W. BOURDILLON: *Light.*

In view of the fact that the word *soul*, like the word *will*, is a popular and not a technical one, and that all the elements that it can be shown to possess are known by other special names and can be referred to their proper places in a system of psychology, some are disposed to drop the term altogether in all attempts to treat the mind scientifically, as liable to lead to confusion rather than contribute to clearness. But I think its retention can be justified as supplying a place which no other term in use now supplies, and in thus avoiding the necessity of introducing a new one. It is true that it expresses a complex conception whose elements may be separated and are specifically named, but there is need of a term to embrace these elements in combination, and thus frequently obviate a circumlocution, besides having the advantage of conveying a crystallized idea and familiarizing it. The English word has, indeed, many vague and unscientific associations from which it is difficult to liberate it, but the corresponding German word *Seele* seems to be freer from these and is used by scientific writers in substantially the same sense that will be given here to the word soul.

It is hardly necessary to say that this sense has little in common with that given this term by religious writers and by the medieval or modern Christian writers. This latter sense, however, is not noticeably different from that of the New Testament (ψυχή in the Greek and *anima* in the Latin Vulgate), and no complaint is made of its use by these writers. Neither does it differ essentially from the earlier Greek usage or from that of Scipio the younger, Cicero, and others who, long anterior to Christianity, speculated upon immortality if they did not teach it. That doctrine, as shown by Tylor, was not such a stranger to other nations as it was to the Hebrews, and the distinctive characteristic of Christianity was the engrafting of this foreign tenet upon Judaism in which it was previously unknown.

But by none of these writers, whether pagan or Christian, was there ever any attempt to analyze the soul or to look upon it philosophically as a part of the mind. The conception was purely ontological, and by most the existence of *a* soul in man was simply taken for granted, while concern was only manifested for its future destiny after the corporeal part should have returned to its elements. There is, however, one important respect in which this conception harmonizes with the scientific one, and that is the uniform investiture of it with the capacity for enjoying and suffering. In whatever language and from whatever standpoint the soul has ever been mentioned it has always been identified with pleasure and pain and made to embody the deepest expression of sympathy and feeling.

If therefore we define the soul as *the feelings taken collectively* we do but echo the common sentiment of all mankind in all countries and all ages. Still, this definition falls short in one particular of expressing the full conception as it presents itself to the mind, and it is necessary to add to it the notion contained in the workings of the conative powers, as set forth in Chap. VI. The full definition of the soul therefore becomes : *The collective feelings of organic beings and their resultant efforts.*

No subject can be thoroughly understood without prolonged investigation, and profound reflection. Down to the present century the soul, notwithstanding the amount of time and energy expended upon it, had never been the subject of any such critical study. A great amount of keen analysis and ingenious speculation had been given to the thinking and knowing faculty, and it must be admitted that the real knowledge of the objective side of the mind had been considerably advanced. But the philosophers who were capable of doing this studiously avoided turning their attention to the soul, doubtless from a vague apprehension that should they do so it might prove capable of analysis whereby its ontological oneness would be destroyed and the supposed foundations of religion and hopes for the future would be put in jeopardy. On the other hand theologians and religious writers possessed no such powers of analysis, and accepting their alleged knowledge of the soul from sacred writ, had no disposition or inducement to make it the subject of speculative inquiry. Although laboring directly for a state of infinite happiness for the soul they would resent any insinuation that this was equivalent to seeking the maximum pleasure, and although hoping eventually to attain to a condition of the most exalted feeling they would deny with warmth that feeling was in any sense a proper end to pursue. All men vied in their efforts to degrade the feelings and by constantly measuring all feelings by the lowest succeeded in fastening a stigma upon most terms employed to describe them, as witness the words *sensual* and *sensuality*. Even the wealth of the German language in its vocabulary of attributes of the mind was incapable of furnishing such a master of it as Kant with a term for the subjective psychic phenomena which should be free from these implications, and he was driven to use for this purpose the word *Sinnlichkeit* in an altogether new and technical sense, the popular one implying something even more gross or specialized than its English analogue sensuality. Thus tabooed, the animated feelings, or true soul, could not be expected to receive that penetrating criticism which alone could yield a true conception of its nature, and the whole subject remained, philosophically and scientifically speaking, a *terra incognita*.[1] It was given over entirely to other agencies, to art, literature, religion, and government, all of which proceeded blindly and added nothing to its extent or fruitfulness.

But with the introduction of the scientific method and its all-exploring spirit, so fertile a field could not longer remain uncultivated. As the body began to be made the theater of research and the brain and nervous system to be studied, the functions of these organs attracted more and more the attention

[1] But the grievous lack of generally accepted results is most apparent in the domain of feeling. The discussion of feeling in most manuals is very meagre and unsatisfactory. . . . It is obvious, then, on the most cursory review that very little has been accomplished in the pure psychology of feeling. Here is a region almost unexplored, and which, by reason of the elusiveness and obscurity of the phenomena has seemed to some quite unexplorable. — HIRAM M. STANLEY in *Science*, Oct. 7, 1892, Vol. XX, pp. 203–204.

of physiologists; and a new psychology was introduced which, naturally enough, has no sympathy or patience with the old. But by a sort of induction in the varied approximate electric thought-currents the students of pure mind began to feel the new impulse and unconsciously to change the base of their speculations. This change of base consisted chiefly in overcoming the former aversion to the study of the subjective side of mind, and taking the bare hint thrown out by Kant, to subject the feelings and conative faculty to the cold glance of reason. In a future chapter (Chap. X) I shall dwell especially upon one such philosophical system and endeavor to show some of the results which this movement, as yet scarcely begun, promises for the future. This revolution is proceeding from the intellect to the feelings and tending to transfer the working basis of philosophy from the reason to the soul.

The birth of the soul was the dawn of the psychic faculty. It marks an era in the cosmical history of the earth. Dimly and imperceptibly it worked through the primordial ages in the Silurian mollusk, the Devonian fish, and the Mesozoic reptile, producing scarcely any modification in the normal course of biologic evolution. During all these vast eons of time the only organic products of beauty or utility were such as nature in her objectless march chanced to produce. But with the advent of the highly developed insects in late Cretaceous and early Tertiary time the psychic factor began to react upon the plant world and, as I have several times pointed out,[1] flowers were the direct product of a growing esthetic faculty — the response to the demands of a true soul-force in nature. Later the same agency working in bird life and mammalian life

[1] The relation between insects and plants, and the consensus in animal and vegetable life. *The American Entomologist,* Vol. III, New York, March, 1880, pp. 63–67; April, 1880, pp. 87–91. See especially, p. 87.

The Course of Biologic Evolution, Annual Address of the President of the Biological Society of Washington, delivered January 25, 1890. Proceedings, Vol. V, Washington, 1890, pp. 23–55. See especially, pp. 46–48 (pp. 24–26 of separately paged reprint).

ushered in the rich, showy and nutrient fruits of the forest and the bread-yielding grains of the meadow and the marsh. The wonderful revolution wrought by this same growing soul in the relations of the sexes among the creatures last mentioned has also been dwelt upon [1] and might fittingly form the theme of the future poetry of science. In human society, as I shall presently endeavor to show, the soul is the great transforming agent which has worked its way up through the stages of savagery and barbarism to civilization and enlightenment, the power behind the throne of reason in the evolution of man.

[1] In later parts of the address last cited.

CHAPTER IX.

THE PHILOSOPHY OF DESIRE.

The state which prompts the organism to seek any object whatever is properly, though to limited degrees of intensity, a state of pain. But the inclination to seek an object is desire, and thus desire is psychologically a painful state. Desire may, therefore, be called ***negative pain***, being the disagreeable state experienced from a lack of the means of fulfilling a normal function, as distinguished from ***positive pain***, which is the disagreeable state experienced from having been deprived of such means previously possessed. — *Dynamic Sociology*, II, 149.

Cupiditas est ipsa hominis essentia, quatenus ex data quacunque ejus affectione determinata concipitur ad aliquid agendum. — SPINOZA : *Ethica*, Pars III. *Affectuum Definitiones*, I.

Id unusquisque ex legibus suæ naturæ necessario appetit vel aversatur, quod bonum vel malum esse judicat. — SPINOZA : *Ethica*, Pars IV, *Propositio* XIX.

La concupiscence et la force sont la source de toutes nos actions : la concupiscence fait les volontaires ; la force les involontaires. — PASCAL : *Pensées*, I, p. 220.

Desires are ideal feelings that arise when the real feelings to which they correspond have not been experienced for some time. — HERBERT SPENCER : *Principles of Psychology*, I, p. 126.

There are pains arising from states of inaction — pains we call them, since we here use the word as antithetical to pleasures ; but they are best known as discomforts or cravings, from having a quality in which they are like one another and unlike pains commonly so called. — *Ibid.*, p. 273.

When there come to be cases in which two very similar groups of external attributes and relations have been followed in experience by different motor changes ; and when, consequently, the presentation of one of these groups partially excites two sets of motor changes, each of which is prevented by their mutual antagonism from at once taking place ; then, while one of these sets of nascent motor changes and nascent impressions habitually accompanying it, constitutes a *memory* of such motor changes as before performed and impressions as before received, and while it also constitutes a *prevision* of the action appropriate to the new occasion, it further constitutes the *desire* to perform the action. — *Ibid.*, p. 481.

Alles Wollen entspringt aus Bedürfniss, also aus Mangel, also aus Leiden. Diesem macht die Erfüllung ein Ende. — SCHOPENHAUER: *Welt als Wille und Vorstellung*, I, 230–231.

Der Wunsch ist, seiner Natur nach, Schmerz: die Erreichung gebiert schnell Sättigung: das Ziel war nur scheinbar: der Besitz nimmt den Reiz weg: unter einer neuen Gestalt stellt sich der Wunsch, das Bedürfniss wieder ein: wo nicht, so folgt Oede, Leere, Langeweile, gegen welche der Kampf eben so quälend ist, wie gegen die Noth. — *Ibid.*, 370.

Jede Befriedigung nur ein hinweggenommener Schmerz, kein gebrachtes positives Glück ist. — *Ibid.*, 443.

Sed dum abest quod avemus, id exsuperare videtur
Cetera; post aliut, cum contigit illud, avemus
Et sitis aequa tenet vitai semper hiantis.
LUCRETIUS: *De Rerum Natura*, III, 1082–1084.

Nihil enim æque gratum est adeptis quam concupiscentibus. — PLINY THE YOUNGER: *Epist.* XV.

It has been a thousand times observed, and I must observe it once more, that the hours we pass with happy prospects in view are more pleasing than those crowned with fruition. — GOLDSMITH: *Vicar of Wakefield*, I, 337.

It was shown in Chap. VI that intensive sensations normally give rise to immediate movements towards the pleasure- and from the pain-producing object. With the simpler or presentative sensations, feeling, taste, and smell, this is usually possible since the object is already present and in contact with the nerve. The hand shrinks from the hot iron; the mouth closes more and more upon the savory morsel or quaffs the pleasant beverage. But with sensations at all remote, that is, with those which are in any degree representative, the movement may be in whole or in part prevented. If, for example, the food or drink be merely seen at a greater or less distance, even if a movement toward it is immediately begun, time is required to reach it, and should obstacles intervene it may be brought to rest. So if danger be reported by sound or sight, and flight from it be impeded by confinement or chains, motion does not result. Nevertheless the sensation thus representatively produced exists and the state of consciousness endures for a longer or shorter period. This state of consciousness is a *desire* either to approach or to retreat.

Representative sensations are necessarily derivative. The first organic being, though it were of a high type of structure, would be incapable of desire. Desire presupposes a psychic apparatus built up by the psychic process. Its essential prerequisite is the registration of impressions and the continuity of conscious states. In short, desire presupposes *memory*. A representative sensation is a remembered sensation, and desires are the recorded and remembered pains and pleasures of sentient beings.

The simple presentative sensations, though common enough, are little noted and comparatively unimportant. The more complex representative ones are constantly arising and in the higher forms of life become the dominant states of consciousness, absorbing attention and making up the greater part of the life of all sentient beings. The examples given are among the simplest. The principal cases are those residing in the internal emotions. In man these latter assume supreme importance and overshadow all others. The entire being is a theater of multiplied desires seeking satisfaction through appropriate action, but checked in a thousand ways and encountering innumerable obstacles. There results a perpetual *striving* to attain the objects of desire. The full significance of the conative faculty cannot be comprehended until this truth is clearly grasped. It is the principle of effort or exertion (*conari*, to endeavor) constantly in active operation, leading to all forms of action. It is this too that rounds out the conception of the *soul*, and without which it possesses little meaning.

I use the word *desire* in a highly generic sense, broad enough to embrace every inclination to act in obedience to intensive representative feelings of whatever class. These "springs of action" are manifold and may be variously classified. The primary conception is that of *appetence*, and under this are included all *appetites*. Most imperative of all are the desires that conduce to self-sustentation, *hunger* and *thirst*. Including with these the other indispensable needs of the body, such as clothing and shelter for man in cold climates, we have a congeries which can be conveniently grouped under the general term *want*. Next in degree of essentialness, if it does not hold an equal or higher rank, is that which demands the perpetuation of the species, the sexual appetite, and this, when viewed from the human, social standpoint, clothed with all the secondary attributes which civilization has given it, and refined and spiritualized by the moral elevation of intelligence and culture, becomes expanded into a lofty sentiment and may be characterized by the general term *love*. To these must be added the social, esthetic, moral, and intellectual cravings, the yearning after the beautiful, the good, and the true.

Even this sweeping classification falls far short of conveying an adequate conception of the conative powers, or soul-force in nature. Every emotion belongs to this faculty and helps to swell the vast tide of surging passion that propels the ship of sentient life. All animated nature is burning and seething with intensified desires. On the one hand, we have attractions, charms, allurements, and enchantments ; hopes, aspirations, longings ; determination, zeal, ambition ; and on the other hand we have fear, dread, apprehension ; avoidance, aversion, abhorrence ; disgust, hate, envy ; rivalry, jealousy, anger ; rage, fury, and despair. In another direction are seen grief, sorrow, sadness, repentance and remorse, as the expressions of the unattained, misdirected, or irretrievably lost. Even satiety, surfeit, tedium, and ennui become intolerable demands for the exercise of normal physical functions.

So widely varying, complex, and recondite are these affective phenomena of mind that it is not surprising that their common bond of union should have been usually lost sight of, and the general truth ignored that they represent a single great fact, *conation* — the universal struggle for the satisfaction of desire. And so different do the manifold desires appear to be, that only by giving the subject the closest attention is it possible to arrive at a general conception of their true nature. One truth at least seems to have been clearly grasped and adequately recognized, and that is that desire in its essential nature is a form of pain. It is true that there are some desires that it is customary to associate with pleasure, and many confound them with pleasures, but when closely studied it will always be found that this is due to the difficulty in separating the desire from its appropriate object. It is often almost impossible to concentrate the attention upon the purely conative state and disregard entirely for the time being the end which it seeks to attain. This difficulty does not exist in such desires as hunger, where the acknowledged painful state receives the special name of *pangs*. Similarly with thirst, but with love, even in its primary form, the pleasurable end becomes intimately associated with the instinct. It needs, however, only to be conceived as never attaining its object to bring out its painful nature in clear light. Not so the more involved states of that passion in refined natures. Such love is conceived to be a joy and a great good. But here again it is requited love that occupies the foreground, and the constant presence of the one loved is the thing thought. Remove this associated idea and think only of love itself, the object toward which it is directed being wholly left out of the mind, and conceive this state to continue indefinitely, as when that object is dead, permanently absent, married to another, or incapable of returning any part of the sentiment. No one, I think, will deny that under any of these circumstances it were better not to love. Ergo, love is pain. Even the other forms of love in which sex takes no part, as parental, filial, fraternal love, or merely warm friendship that takes that name, — any of these in the permanent absence of the object is painful. In case of death it becomes grief, often inconsolable, and even temporary separation causes anxiety, longing, and sadness, which are certainly not pleasurable feelings. And so we might go through the list and show that in every case desire pure and simple, in and of itself, is pain.

But the final and crucial test of the question consists in the patent fact that all the effort that is put forth in obedience to desires is in the direction of *satisfying* them. And to satisfy a desire is simply to allay it, i.e., to terminate it. In other words, the unpleasant nature of desires is proved by the fact that we always seek to end them. Correctly understood, all the enormous exertions of life are made for the sole purpose of getting rid of the swarm of desires that goad and pursue every living being from birth to death. Too much has not been made of this fact by a certain class of writers who have laid stress upon it, and the better it is understood the clearer will be the true conception of the subjective nature of mind. No one need be afraid to face this truth. Those who shrink from the corollaries that have been drawn from it, need not shrink from the truth itself. I shall endeavor to show that some of these corollaries do not legitimately flow from it. I shall also hope to make clear that other corollaries that have never been drawn, do, and must necessarily follow, and that these latter are of the utmost importance and promise the greatest results for the future welfare of man.

This much, at least, has been learned, that desire is the all-pervading, world-animating principle, the universal *nisus* and pulse of nature, the mainspring of all action, and the life-power of the world. It is organic force. Its multiple forms, like the many forces of the physical world, are the varied expressions of one universal force. They are transmutable into one another. Their sum is unchanged thereby, and all vital energy is conserved. It is the basis of psychic physics and the only foundation for a science of mind.

It should, however, be added that the parallel between physics and *psychics*, as thus defined, fails at one point. While, so far as is known, there has never been any loss of psychic energy, it is certain that there has been an immense increase of it. Indeed, time was when none existed. It has developed or been evolved with all organic nature, and has increased pari passu with the increase of mind and the development of brain. Complete analogy between the organic and inorganic forces is not reached until it is recognized that the former are derived from the latter, and that vital and psychic forces are simply additional forms of the universal force. The soul of man has come from the soul of the atom after passing through the great alembic of organic life.

While all desire is pain all pain is not desire, except in the sense of an inclination to escape it. Ordinary pains are not the desires themselves but causes of action. They are more or less peripheral and direct, whereas, as above shown, desires usually arise from within, are representative, and more or less emotional. These fall under two classes : those which shun pain, and those which seek pleasure. It is when we study these two classes of desires that we perceive most clearly the essential difference between pain and pleasure psychologically viewed. It has already been shown that they are not opposites. It remains to be shown that they are essentially dissimilar psychological factors. Pain is the more simple, is less capable of analysis. Developed for the purpose of protecting the organism from destruction, it consists simply in a disagreeable sensation giving rise to instantaneous effort to move from the object producing it. The simultaneity of contact and movement allow no interval of time for the occurrence of a desire, at least the time is only so long as it requires for the nerve currents to perform their function, which is too short to be taken into the account. Such is the nature of all direct or presentative pains, i.e., of all pains other than desires, and little more can be said of them. They admit of no further analysis.

Presentative pleasures are much more limited. They are practically restricted to the senses of taste and smell. In these, as in pains of the same class, no desire intervenes between the contact and the pleasure. The latter is immediate. In order to make all possible exclusions, it is necessary to admit that agreeable sounds and objects agreeable to the eye usually give rise to the corresponding pleasures directly without the intervention of anything that can be properly called a desire. Possibly other cases of this class may exist. Grouping all these under the head of presentative pleasures, there remains the great class of representative pleasures, forming by far the larger part of all enjoyments.

If now we limit attention to this class of pleasures, and agree that by pleasure only representative pleasure shall be understood, we may appropriately inquire what pleasure really consists in. To this at once the answer and the proper definition of pleasure, must be: *the satisfaction of desire.* That is to say, the predominant class of pleasures consists in the *termination* of the predominant class of pains. As already argued, pleasure is not the desire itself. It is the satisfaction of that desire. Although desire is of the nature of pain, and is pain in every proper sense of the word, still it is very unlike the simple direct pains of the external parts. If we seek among these latter for its analogue the nearest we find to it is probably the phenomenon of itching. We must class this phenomenon among painful states, because it calls forth an effort to terminate it as quickly as possible, and yet the act necessary to put an end to it yields what all probably recognize as a pleasure. Itching, therefore, may be called a direct physical desire. If allowed to continue it becomes intolerable, and is therefore a pain. If the act which it prompts is performed the desire is *satisfied* and at the same time terminated. The act itself of satisfying it is a pleasure. If all these steps be admitted, the analogy with all other desires is complete. Desire is essentially prurient in its nature. It is this which makes it so effective. Every one knows how much more bearable pain proper is than itching. Unsatisfied desires become unbearable, they charge the batteries of force till they can contain no more; the discharge produces a shock and performs extraordinary feats, whether for good or evil.

The desire satisfied and terminated, what follows? Restoration of equilibrium. Whatever may have been accomplished upon surrounding objects by the discharge of conative energy the only effect upon the subject is the termination of the unpleasant conscious state. True, the desire was satisfied and the act of satisfying it produced the pleasure sought, but after that, nothing! Not only is the pain gone, but the pleasure is also gone. Equilibrium is restored and the subject is again in the same condition as before the desire arose. Just here lies the question upon the answer to which the truth or falsity of pessimism depends. That doctrine will recognize nothing between the existence of a desire and its termination. Admitting that desire is pain, it sees only pain and the relief of pain. The satisfaction of desire, it says, is simply the termination of it. After that nothing remains. The popular association of pleasure with the satisfaction of desire it declares to be a delusion and a self-deception. Can this doctrine be successfully refuted? It is not enough to dogmatize against it. It has been exhaustively elaborated by some of the greatest scholars and deepest thinkers of the world, and their arguments must be squarely met.

CHAPTER X.

THE WILL OF SCHOPENHAUER.

Nicht allein in denjenigen Erscheinungen, welche seiner eigenen ganz ähnlich sind, in Menschen und Thieren, wird er als ihr innerstes Wesen jenen nämlichen Willen anerkennen; sondern die fortgesetzte Reflexion wird ihn dahin leiten, auch die Kraft, welche in der Pflanze treibt und vegetirt, ja, die Kraft durch welche der Krystall anschiesst, die, welche den Magnet zum Nordpol wendet, die, deren Schlag ihm aus der Berührung heterogener Metalle entgegenfährt, die, welche in den Wahlverwandtschaften der Stoffe als Fliehen und Suchen, Trennen und Vereinen erscheint, ja, zuletzt sogar die Schwere, welche in aller Materie so gewaltig strebt, den Stein zur Erde und die Erde zur Sonne zieht, — diese alle nur in der Erscheinung für verschieden, ihrem inneren Wesen nach aber als das Selbe zu erkennen, als jenes ihm unmittelbar so intim und besser als alles Andere Bekannte, was da, wo es am deutlichsten hervortritt, *Wille* heisst. — SCHOPENHAUER: *Welt als Wille*, I, 131.

Es giebt in der letzten und höchsten Instanz gar kein anderes Seyn als Wollen. Wollen ist Urseyn, und auf dieses allein passen alle Prädicate desselben: Grundlosigkeit, Ewigkeit, Unabhängigkeit von der Zeit, Selbstbejahung. Die ganze Philosophie strebt nur dahin, diesen höchsten Ausdruck zu finden. — SCHELLING: *Werke* I, 7, S. 350.

Wille, die eigentliche geistige Substanz des Menschen, der Grund von Allem, das ursprünglich Stoff-Erzeugende, das Einzige im Menschen, das Ursache von Seyn ist. — SCHELLING: *Werke*, I, 10, S. 289.

Wie Kant der grösste Philosoph ist, der über den Kopf geschrieben hat, so ist Schopenhauer der grösste Denker, der über das Herz philosophirte. — MAINLÄNDER: *Philosophie der Erlösung*, p. 465.

Dies [Schopenhauer's doctrine of the will] war ein glänzendes geniales Aperçu, und ich befürchte nicht, mich einer Uebertreibung schuldig zu machen, wenn ich sage, dass es eine Revolution auf geistigem Gebiete eingeleitet hat, welche ähnliche Umgestaltungen in der Welt hervorrufen wird, wie die vom Christenthum bewirkten. — MAINLÄNDER: *Ibid.*, p. 466.

Great thinkers are condemned, not for their theorems, but for their corollaries, and further analysis often proves that the latter do not logically flow from the former. It was so with Hume, so with Voltaire, so with Comte, so with Thomas Paine, and it was so with Schopenhauer. The two great philosophical heresies of Schopenhauer were his idealism and his pessimism. Both these he believed to follow from his two basic conceptions, his *Satz vom Grunde* and his *Wille*. The former was the first philosophical establishment of the law of causation in nature, now recognized as the foundation of all science. The latter was the first enunciation of the unity of psychic and physical force, the highest and most involved example of the law of the conservation of energy, formulated much later by the physicists. If, as most persons believe, truth really is to "prevail," then, when pessimism and idealism shall have become historic curiosities, Schopenhauer will be universally recognized as the philosopher who created two epochs.

With the first of these philosophic fundamentals we have here nothing to do. It belongs to cosmology and has received universal acceptance. The second is the essence of our present theme, and is scarcely known, much less understood, even by those who devote themselves to philosophic psychology. It is the practice, whenever Schopenhauer's name is pronounced, to throw up the hands and exclaïm, Pessimist! Those who read his books skim over everything else till they reach his pessimism and hang spellbound over this alone. The more it is condemned the more greedily it is devoured. Yet those who denounce it most vehemently are those who have not read it. On the other hand, it is receiving a wide acceptance in certain quarters where the hard conditions of existence seem to give it special countenance. I have already intimated that it does not logically follow from Schopenhauer's doctrine of the will, and this view will be more fully substantiated in the next chapter. But first let us inquire into the real meaning of Schopenhauer's will.

We may begin by saying that, so far as sentient beings are concerned, the will of Schopenhauer is nothing more nor less than the generalized conception defined in the last chapter and denominated *desire*. It is the universal soul-force operating under the inexorable law of the sufficient reason or mechanical causation, which constitutes the only basis for the real science of mind. It is the underlying cause of all the efforts and activities of animated nature. It is purely subjective. In and of itself it has nothing whatever to do with the rational faculty. In calling it *unconscious* Schopenhauer simply means this. It is blind impulse (*blinder Drang*). All exertion, all interest, all strife and struggle represent the assertion of the will to live (*Bejahung des Willens zum Leben*). This great truth is forced home with all the power of the German language, so rich in synonyms and so forcible in construction.[1]

Schopenhauer realized that he had found in this conception of the will the true basis of mind, and he proceeded to endow it with objective reality, even raising it to the dignity of being the long sought *Ding an sich*, or thing in itself. As such it was declared to tower in importance far above the reason and the intellect. From one point of view he was correct, for this it is which constitutes the dynamic basis of mind without which reason and intellect would have nothing to work upon.

He also rightly perceived that the will had priority in point of time over the thinking faculties, and so firmly did this truth take possession of him that he was wont to belittle the latter and exalt the former. Thus he declared, and not without sound reason, that the intellect was merely an accident, a late graft as it were upon the full-grown tree of mind; that the will was the primary trunk of that tree. It is true, as shown in a previous chapter, that the soul-force itself, when considered as a development from the original elements of life,

[1] Among the many terms employed by Schopenhauer to compass this widely generic conception of the *Wille* the following may serve as samples: Wollen, Wunsch, Suchen, Versuchen, Sehnen, Sehnsucht, Bestreben, Bestrebung, Streben, Trieb, Drängen, Drang, Begierde, Begehren, Anstrengung, Drücken, Stoss, Jagd, Neigung, Reiz, Regung, Leiden, Quälen, Lieben, Hassen, Hoffen, Fürchten, Leidenschaft, Angst, Ueberdruss, Leere, Langeweile, Reue, Wuth, Zorn, etc.

is in this same sense an accident and a late graft, but whether we look at it from the actual standpoint of geologic history or from the broader standpoint of structural development, the organ and function of thought is something extremely modern, while the conative system is old. Their relative antiquity is somewhat like that of the glacial epoch when compared with the Eocene, which to a geologist has a tremendous significance.

The preëminent service which Schopenhauer has rendered to philosophy has been that of turning the current of thought out of the old and hopeless channels of objective psychology into the new and promising channels of subjective psychology. Here, and here alone, is there hope for a science of mind.

CHAPTER XI.

REFUTATION OF PESSIMISM.

Alle Befriedigung, oder was man gemeinhin Glück nennt, ist eigentlich und wesentlich immer nur negativ and durchaus nie positiv. Es ist nicht eine ursprünglich und von selbst auf uns kommende Beglückung, sondern muss immer die Befriedigung eines Wunsches seyn. Denn Wunsch, d. h. Mangel, ist die vorhergehende Bedingung jedes Genusses. Mit der Befriedigung hört aber der Wunsch und folglich der Genuss auf. Daher kann die Befriedigung oder Beglückung nie mehr seyn, als die Befreiung von einem Schmerz, von einer Noth. — SCHOPENHAUER : *Welt als Wille*, I, 376.

Uebrigens kann ich hier die Erklärung nicht zurückhalten, dass mir der Optimismus, wo er nicht etwan das gedankenlose Reden Solcher ist, unter deren platten Stirnen nichts als Worte herbergen, nicht bloss als eine absurde, sondern auch als eine wahrhaft ruchlose Denkungsart erscheint, als ein bitterer Hohn über die namenlosen Leiden der Menschheit. — SCHOPENHAUER : *Ibid.*, 384–385.

Ainsi nous ne vivons jamais, mais nous espérons de vivre ; et nous disposant toujours à être heureux, il est inévitable que nous ne le soyons jamais. — PASCAL : *Pensées*, II, 41.

Man hat mich immer als einen vom Glück besonders Begünstigten gepriesen ; auch will ich mich nicht beklagen und den Gang meines Lebens nicht schelten. Allein im Grunde ist es nichts als Mühe und Arbeit gewesen, und ich kann wohl sagen, dass ich in meinen fünfundsiebzig Jahren keine vier Wochen eigentliches Behagen gehabt. Es war das ewige Wälzen eines Steines, der immer von neuem gehoben sein wollte. — GOETHE : *Eckermann's Gespräche*, I, 106.

Ich bin nicht geschaffen, um Familienvater zu sein. Ausserdem halte ich das Heirathen für eine Sünde, das Kinderzeugen für ein Verbrechen.

Es ist auch meine Ueberzeugung, dass derjenige ein Narr, noch mehr : ein Sünder ist, der das Joch der Ehe auf sich nimmt. Ein Narr, weil er seine Freiheit damit von sich wirft, ohne eine entsprechende Entschädigung zu gewinnen ; ein Sünder, weil er Kindern das Leben giebt, ohne ihnen die Gewissheit des Glücks geben zu können. Ich verachte die Menschheit in allen ihren Schichten ; ich sehe es voraus, das unsere Nachkommen noch weit unglücklicher sein werden, als wir, — sollte ich nicht ein Sünder sein, wenn ich trotz diesen Ansichten für Nachkommen, d. h. für Unglückliche sorgte? —

Das ganze Leben ist der grösste Unsinn. Und wenn man achtzig Jahre strebt und forscht, so muss man sich doch endlich gestehen, dass man Nichts erstrebt und Nichts erforscht hat. Wüssten wir nur wenigstens, warum wir auf dieser Welt sind? Aber Alles ist und bleibt dem Denker räthselhaft, und das grösste Glück ist noch das, als Flachkopf geboren zu sein. — HUMBOLDT: *Memoiren*, I, 365–367.

Whoever was to be born at all, was to be born a child, and to do before he could understand, and be bred under laws to which he was always bound, but which could not always be exacted; and he was to choose, when he could not reason, — and had passions most strong, when he had his understanding most weak, — and was to ride a wild horse without a bridle, — and the more need he had of curb, the less strength he had to use it; and this being the case of all the world, what was every man's evil, became all men's greater evil; and though alone it was very bad, yet when they came together it was made much worse; like ships in a storm, every one alone hath enough to do to outride it; but when they meet, besides the evils of the storm, they find the intolerable calamity of their mutual concussion, and every ship that is ready to be oppressed with the tempest, is a worst tempest to every vessel, against which it is violently dashed. So it is in mankind, every man hath evil enough of his own; and it is hard for a man to live soberly, temperately, and religiously; but when he hath parents and children, brothers and sisters, friends and enemies, buyers and sellers, lawyers and physicians, a family and a neighborhood, a king over him, or tenants under him, a bishop to rule in matters of government spiritual, and a people to be ruled by him in the affairs of their souls; then it is that every man dashes against another, and one relation requires what another denies; and when one speaks, another will contradict him; and that which is well spoken, is sometimes innocently mistaken, and that upon a good cause produces an evil effect; and by these, and ten thousand other concurrent causes, man is made more than most miserable. — JEREMY TAYLOR: *Works*, IX, 316.

Youth is a blunder; Manhood a struggle; Old Age a regret. — DISRAELI: *Coningsby*, p. 118.

There's not a joy the world can give like that it takes away. — BYRON.

Pessimism is the negation of pleasure.[1] It was shown in

[1] Both Schopenhauer and Hartmann recognize the reality of pleasure, and spend much time in seeking to prove that it is greatly exceeded in amount by pain. But

Chap. IX that in the normal case the satisfaction of a desire terminates it and leaves the subject in the same condition psychologically as before the desire arose. This is clear from the habitual use of the word *satisfy* and the universal admission of its appropriateness to express the fact. For nothing can be more than satisfied. Enough has no comparative. This is expressed with force and euphony in the German proverb: *Satter wie satt kann man nicht werden.*

This much settled, the question recurs: Does anything intervene between the desire and its satisfaction? Is the painful state called desire continuous up to the time when it ceases altogether and the mind reverts to the antecedent state? A negative answer to this question would deny the existence of pleasure, relegate happiness to the limbo of delusions, and make pessimism the only true philosophy.

The answer to pessimism comes from psychometry. It comes from the experimental demonstration that all psychic phenomena consume time. If the act of gratifying a desire were absolutely instantaneous there would be no answer to the pessimist. We should, as he claims, have all the great struggles of life with no other reward than that of putting an end, one after another, from childhood to old age, to the intolerable scourges that successively beset every life. Experience teaches that such is not the case, but it has been proved that in matters relating to the mind experience is not a reliable guide. The hallucinations of the rational faculty are among the best known of psychic phenomena. Scarcely less common and well attested are those of the senses themselves. How much more deceiving must be those emotional states that belong to the most derivative and involved of mental phenomena. Moreover, there is an especial reason why these latter should

Schopenhauer expressly declares that it consists simply in relief from pain, and this is probably also Hartmann's idea. This is a mere negative state and does not deserve to be called pleasure. It therefore remains true that pessimism denies the existence of positive pleasure. It does this logically at all events, irrespective of the views of these philosophers.

be illusive. It has been seen that they were developed to preserve existence. Nature has no concern for them as ends. They are for her purely means to the great end of continued and increasing life. It is to this end that every being is made a magazine of hopes. The reason is perpetually called upon to subdue extravagant expectations. Even in man those individuals are rare whose judgments are of any value against their interests. Prediction of results is in most cases nothing better than betrayal of preferences. Men as a rule believe that that will happen which they wish to happen. Optimism is only a higher expression of desire. It is the assertion of the will to live. No one is capable of balancing the profits and losses of life. The lower in the scale of intelligence the more complete this incapacity. The same innate sentiment which prompts the pursuit of pleasure and avoidance of pain makes every creature cling to life and fly from death, no matter how intolerable life may be or what relief death would give. The soul is the *fons et origo* of all illusions, purposely planted there, so to speak, to lure unhappy beings on to continue and multiply life. Fear of death is itself an illusion, since it is only pain and not death that is terrible. Faith, hope, buoyancy, enthusiasm, all are born of this instinct of preservation. Temperaments indeed differ, but viewed in this light all are sanguine. Men are all Micawbers in varying degrees. It follows that in this great battle for life, this the real struggle for existence, truth and fact are wholly without influence in determining opinion and action. It is easy to conceive that enjoyment itself, which is the ostensible goal of it all, might be a complete delusion and have no existence. Much of it is, we know, purely imaginary, and why might it not all be so?

In view of all this it behooves those who teach the reality of pleasure and happiness to prove their existence by something more than common experience. To attempt this it will be necessary to revert for a moment to direct or presentative sensations. So long as we consider only the indirect or representative ones we are liable to be led astray by the all-powerful optimism of every mental constitution. But in this lower form we are once more on the firm ground of sense, and all philosophers, though admitting the fallibility of the senses, nevertheless regard them as the absolutely highest criteria of truth. And in this they are speaking of perception, which is the second step in the psychic process. We are here concerned with sensation, which is the first step, and as such one remove nearer still to the citadel of truth. If simple sensation cannot be relied upon there is no certainty anywhere.

If I place a lump of sugar on my tongue, I experience a sensation. If normally constituted I can declare that sensation to be agreeable, and no one will assume to gainsay that declaration. If I do not know it myself, then there is nothing that I can claim to know. As compared with Descartes' dictum its sanction is immensely greater. There is no *ergo* in it. It is the simplest possible proposition: I experience an agreeable sensation. With those who would dispute it it would be unprofitable to argue, although, if I were to say at any given moment: I am happy, there might be valid ground for questioning it on account of the complex nature of the sensation and the deceptive character of all the emotional states.

The second fact to be observed is that the sensation produced by the sugar is not instantaneous or brief, but continuous, lasting as long as the sugar lasts, though diminishing in force from an apparent gradual exhaustion of the capacity of the nerve to respond to the stimulus. Still it endures. Without multiplying illustrations the question may at once be asked: Is there any reason in the nature of things why the nerves that govern the emotional centres should not also possess the power of more or less prolonged response to their appropriate stimuli? And is it not a natural supposition that the act of gratifying a desire, which is nothing more nor less than responding to a stimulus, may be one which consumes more or less time? The new experimental psychology leaves this no longer in the field of supposition. It demonstrates it as certainly as the problems of electricity are demonstrated. It is known that in psychics as in physics no phenomenon can take place except in time, and the velocity of nerve-currents, though varying greatly in different cases, are ascertained approximately in many instances. They are very much less than those of most physical media, and in general it may be said that molecular motion is much slower in organic than in inorganic bodies. All this is highly favorable to the view that the nerve activities and vibrations taking place in the act of satisfying a desire may be considerably prolonged or in certain cases almost indefinitely continued. As to the exact physiological nature of this process it is not necessary here to inquire. Whether there is actual continuity, or whether, as is more probable, the sensation of pleasure in all cases, presentative as well as representative, consists in a series of more or less rapid vibrations or molecular discharges along the nerve from the point affected to the brain, so rapid as not to be separable in consciousness, and yet distinct from one another, is clearly of no consequence to the argument. To all intents and purposes the mental state is a continuous one.

In the higher emotions the duration of the pleasurable state is greater than in the lower ones. While in the primary physical form of satisfying love it is only momentary, in the secondary spiritual form it seems to be indefinite in time. That is, so long as the object is present the pleasure abides. It would seem that the sentiment takes such complete possession of the individual, so thoroughly permeates the appropriate nerve centers, plexuses, and fibers, that they are set into a constant state of harmonious vibration throughout which renews itself momentarily and reverberates in moderate pulsations of agreeable molecular activity so long as the stimulus remains. These words may be wholly unscientific but they are the best that can be used in the present state of knowledge respecting these deep, inner processes.

What is true of love is true also of other permanent pleasures and enjoyments. They are real at least to the subjects of them, and there is every reason to consider them objectively real. And this is the refutation of pessimism. It simply aims to prove that pleasure is an objective reality and not a psychic illusion. It does not pretend to deal with the great indictment against the woes of life. I look upon it as a mark of healthy mental development that there should have arisen philosophers whose rational powers are keen enough to pierce the fogs of optimism in which the rest of the world is wrapped and who have been bold enough to announce that life is so largely made up of pain. Only by recognizing it can any mitigation of it be expected. But the despairing view that Schopenhauer and Hartmann take, borrowed from the philosophy of India, is based upon the supposed necessity of this state of things. With them it is the will perpetually driving its victims on toward some supposed goal of relief which is never attained, or if attained in the sense of the pain being simply ended, another and new scourge is applied, and so on indefinitely. Therefore they see no hope except in denying the will, resisting its power, abandoning all hope of happiness, refusing every proffered good, and letting every function cease until, with the cessation of life itself relief shall at last come through non-existence.

The answer to this side of the pessimistic philosophy is of a very different character from the last. It would be to anticipate my theme to undertake it here, but that final answer may be foreshadowed by reverting to the origin and function of pain as set forth in Chap. VII. The woes of mankind must be looked upon as the voices of nature telling him how hard they are being pressed by their environment, and how they are growing out of adaptation to it. Pessimism is the product of a hostile social state. Its answer is the substitution of a friendly social state. If this can be done it will disappear. The greatest problem that science has before it is that of overthrowing pessimism in the only way in which it can be overthrown — by the amelioration of the social state. The philosophy that stands opposed to pessimism and must ultimately triumph over it is not optimism, which is the gospel of inaction, but ***meliorism,*** which is scientific utilitarianism, inspired by faith in the law of causation and the efficacy of well-directed action.

CHAPTER XII.

HAPPINESS.

It is quite remarkable that utilitarianism should have been most strongly defended by English-speaking writers, whose language is notably deficient in terms by which to convey the delicate shades of meaning required for its adequate elucidation. The need of a milder substitute for *happiness* has been seriously felt, and no doubt serves to obstruct the progress of rational views on this subject. That the defect is in the language and not in the conceptions is evident from the fact that most other languages possess better words. The French "*bonheur*" or the German "*Glückseligkeit*," had they their counterpart in English, would afford a delightful relief.— *Dynamic Sociology*, II, 147.

Glückseligkeit ist die Befriedigung aller unserer Neigungen.— KANT: *Kritik der reinen Vernunft*, p. 532.

Thus recognizing, at the one extreme, the negative pains of inactions, called cravings, and, at the other extreme, the positive pains of excessive actions, the implication is that pleasures accompany actions lying between these extremes.— HERBERT SPENCER: *Principles of Psychology*, I, p. 276.

The idea that happiness is something different from pleasure probably requires no serious refutation. It prevailed formerly because there was supposed to be something essentially bad about pleasure, while happiness was regarded as morally permissible. Now that we know that pleasure is the original good of the sentient world and the essential condition to vital existence, there is no room for anything bad in it, considered in and of itself.

But some will maintain that the idea of pleasure is associated more especially with the sensual feelings, while that of happiness connects itself with the higher emotional ones, and therefore requires special explanation. This is to some extent true, but it is perhaps more correct to define happiness as a condition of continuous or constantly recurring pleasures of whatever class, predominating largely over pains. It has various degrees from mere contentment to intense enjoyment. Giving the subject an analytical glance, happiness may be seen to require several conditions. The first of these is health. Unless the functions of the body are in harmonious operation nothing worthy of the name happiness can exist. And yet there is an immense difference in the power of different parts of the system to diminish happiness by their derangement. Consumptives are often happy, even buoyant, to the last moment of their lives, while dyspeptics are proverbially wretched, even when their ailment is so slight as to carry no serious menace of death. There seems to be no doubt that the reason for this wide difference lies in the fact that the lungs are supplied from the cerebro-spinal, while the stomach and intestines are supplied from the great sympathetic nervous system. Again, the extreme nervous suffering of women whose uterine systems are out of order is explicable in the same way, while persons suffering severe pain upon some external part, as the finger, may still enjoy much of what life otherwise affords.

It has been maintained that all that the most perfect health can do is to furnish the negative form of happiness known as contentment. But there are reasons to believe that the complete and harmonious performance by all the organs of the system of the normal functions assigned them possesses so great a volume of sustained satisfaction that it amounts to positive happiness in and of itself. The manner in which this takes place must be that described in Chap. VI (p. 32), where it was shown that the great ganglionic centers that preside over the so-called vegetative functions of the animal body are not wholly irresponsible to the supreme ganglion or brain, and that along with the proper regulation of the lower ganglia, plexuses, and specialized nerves, there goes a continuous gentle molecular discharge to the brain, notifying it, as it were, that all is well. It is only of this that the subject is conscious, and these health reports, as they may be styled, are gratefully received and conduce to a general sense of well-being. Contentment pure and simple, as distinguished from happiness, would represent the condition of a healthy body in the absence of this intercourse between the great ganglionic centers and the brain.

The second condition to happiness to be noted is freedom, more or less complete, from pain. To some extent this condition coincides with that of health. For even if we refer to ill-health the accidental external pains due to injury or local diseases, there still remains the most important class of emotional pains — grief, disappointment, worriment, fear, regret, remorse, anxiety, etc., etc. In fact, this list of woes lies only just outside the boundaries of that vast ocean of prurient pains described in Chap. IX under the general name of desires. If any of these remain permanently unsatisfied, happiness is well nigh impossible.

This forms the natural transition to the third and last condition to happiness that need be specially insisted upon, viz., the means of satisfying desire. This is by far the most important of all conditions, because health and freedom from pain are the normal states and their opposites belong to pathology. Their occurrence to a greater or less extent is unavoidable, and we have only nature to blame. This third condition, on the contrary, is, in any state that man has yet attained, comparatively rare, whereas inability to satisfy desire is the almost universal estate of man, and moreover, it is only to a limited extent the fault of nature, and is in the main the fault of social surroundings.

But this needs many qualifications. If only the desires to eat, drink and reproduce were considered, it would indeed be untrue that the means to them were generally wanting. From vast numbers even these are more or less withheld, but such must perish, therefore those that live must possess these primary means of satisfying want. But such satisfactions constitute the lowest grade of happiness, and if the term were not here used in a broad generic sense they would be excluded entirely. Happiness in the popular restricted sense is the experiencing of the higher emotional pleasures afforded by the gratification of social, esthetic, moral, and intellectual tastes. It is the means of doing this that render a person, a community, or a nation happy. And these are constantly arising. New wants of the spiritual nature come thick and fast upon one another as soon as the coarser necessities of existence are fully supplied. It is really true, as the pessimists claim, that there is no possibility of satisfying all desires, for if they could all be once conceived to be satisfied new ones would immediately arise demanding satisfaction. Yet the degree of happiness depends upon the relative proportion of them that can be silenced, and upon the nature and refinement of the tastes that can be gratified. Therefore, provided the means of supplying wants can be secured, the greater the number and the higher the rank of such wants, the higher the state of happiness attainable. The problem of social science is to point out in what way the most complete and universal satisfaction of human desires can be attained, and this is one with the problem of greatest happiness.

CHAPTER XIII.

FEELING, FUNCTION, AND ACTION.

The two *functions* absolutely essential to life are nutrition and reproduction. To these correspond in all sentient beings two classes of desires. These may be denominated the *gustatory* and the *sexual* appetites. By the former, the sustenance necessary for replenishing the tissues is attracted to its proper place in the system; by the latter, the reproductive act is rendered agreeable, without which it would not be performed.

Against these objects of nature may be set the corresponding objects of the organism, or, confining ourselves to the human race, they may be called the objects of man. The end of nature is the preservation and perpetuation of life; that of man is the satisfaction of desire.—*Dynamic Sociology*, I, 468–469.

The satisfaction of desire taken in its broadest sense involves three wholly distinct things, feeling, function, and action. The first of these has been already considered at length, and needs only to be set down in its proper place in relation to the other two. As the condition to the existence of plastic organisms, its sanction is of the highest order, but from the standpoint of nature it is, as the formula implies, simply a means, and has no value in itself. The end to which it is the means is, from this standpoint, function.

In what has been aptly and appropriately called "evolutionary teleology"[1] the broadest conception that can be formed of the true object or end of organic life is that of transforming inorganic into organic matter. Many have conceived this ultimate end to be perfection of structure, but when closely studied it becomes apparent that perfection of structure is only one of the means to that end. Wherever it occurs it actually accomplishes this purpose, and wherever this purpose can be better accomplished in other ways it is not resorted to. Others have supposed that the great purpose of organic life was evolution,

[1] Asa Gray, Darwiniana, New York, 1877, Chap. XIII.

that is, the production of an ascending series of higher and higher types; but it is too well known that the actual series is not always ascending, and that wherever survival and multiplication can better be secured through degeneracy that takes place. If evolution is seen to have been the prevailing condition it is because the great end of increasing the quantity of organized matter is better subserved thereby than by any other means. This is exemplified in the higher types of both plants and animals. Even man, although far from the largest of animals, sustains this law, since by the possession of that most highly organized of all substances, the sapient brain, he is able to multiply his numbers and expand his faunal area far beyond the limit allotted to any other creature, and the combined mass of organized matter in the bodies of all the individuals of the human species would greatly exceed that of any other one species of animal on the globe.

The application of all this to the subject in hand lies in the fact that in the animal world this end is secured through performance of those functions which are the necessary consequences of the satisfaction of desire. Feeling impels to function, and function secures .protection, nutrition, growth, preservation, reproduction, multiplication, and perpetuation.

Feeling and function are distinct things. They have no physiological relation to each other. The gustatory and nutritive organs are in different parts of the body. The seat of sexual appetite is remote from that of gestation. It is not death and the extinction of the species that prompts to flight from danger, but only fear of pain. And yet the satisfaction of the desire to eat results in the preservation of the individual from starvation, the gratification of the sexual instinct results in the continuance of the species, and the escape by flight or other mode of action from the pain that enemies would inflict, results in safety to life. The two are essentially unlike and it is only by a sort of preëstablished harmony that they are so adjusted as to become in fact cause and effect. But this harmony is really not preëstablished, it is simultaneously established through the laws of selection and survival, and in this respect does not differ from a multitude of harmonies now familiar to naturalists under the name of adaptations.

At the beginning of Chap. XI it was said that the satisfaction of a desire left the subject in the same condition psychologically as before the desire arose. The word *psychologically* was used advisedly. In many cases it does not leave the subject in the same condition *physiologically*. This is because it results in function. The satisfaction of the desire to eat supplies the nutrient material, fills the stomach, sets the organs of digestion and assimilation to work, enriches the circulation, and may make a lean animal fat or a weak one strong. The reproductive desire passes into function only in the female, but in her it works a great and wonderful series of changes, resulting in new beings of the race to which the parents belong. The function of pain is simply protection ; i.e., it is negative, and although no physiological change is wrought by its escape, the change which would have been wrought had it not been escaped is prevented. When it comes to the higher emotional desires and their satisfaction the function is more obscure, but that it often exists there can be no doubt. Here it takes the form of the growth, strengthening, or development of the physiological centers, the general increase, expansion, and refinement of the capacity to enjoy. The law of improvement through use, so well attested in all other psychological processes, holds equally in the more subtile processes of the inner being, and the esthetic tastes, moral sensibilities, intellectual pleasures, and social attributes are, as all know, capable of cultivation and elevation as well as of intensification and multiplication. And through all this the great end of organic life is attained, since, as already remarked, structural perfection renders higher organization possible and insures survival and increase in the general sum of materials that have been withdrawn from the inorganic, and permanently added to the organic world.

All this would be irrelevant to the present work if it were not so intimately connected with another view of the subject. Too great stress cannot be laid on the fact that *function is the object of nature*, in order to bring it into sharp contrast with another somewhat new and startling fact, yet not less a fact, that *feeling is the object of the sentient being*. Still using the language of evolutionary teleology, it may be truly said that Nature never intended this to be so. Nature looks upon feeling simply as a means to function. She is utterly indifferent to both pleasure and pain. This is seen in the animal world where one half devour the other half and cruelty and torture are heartlessly practised. It is seen in the human race, half of which is so sunk in hopeless misery that they ceaselessly pray for utter annihilation, and even in the other half there flourishes a philosophy which teaches that to live is to suffer (*leben ist leiden*) and finds no loftier theme than the misery of existence (*Elend des Daseins*).

But in creating pleasure by which to compass her ends Nature, as it were, o'erreached herself. By this act there was brought forth at once the despair and the hope of the world. Designed as a means it at length became an end, and during the last half of the earth's history there has gone on a struggle between Nature and Life for the attainment of their respective ends. Wherever these proved incompatible the end of Life must fail or Life must cease, but in a great number and variety of cases compromise was possible, and the most remarkable consequences ensued. Passing over for the present the sub-human phases of the subject which can be better treated a little later, we come to the human stage, and here we find much more clearly defined than ever before this great antithesis between the object of Nature and the object of man. The careful student of man and of human history easily reaches the generalization that the great drama of human life, like the little drama of each individual life, has for its sole theme the satisfaction of desire. The *dramatis personæ* are all seeking to attain some end, to carry some point, to further some scheme, to accomplish some purpose, to gratify some ambition, to realize some aspiration. Or else they are seeking to escape some impending evil, to thwart some vile plot, to defeat some nefarious scheme. There is no end of purposes, some good, some bad, some high, some low, but there is always a purpose. And from the narrow standpoint of self these purposes are all good ; that is, they are good for the agent, or, at least, are believed to be so. But this is nothing more than to say that in accomplishing them the agent expects to secure some benefit or escape some injury, i.e., to attain pleasure or avoid pain, or at least, in the ultimate analysis, to realize a balance of pleasure or happiness over pain or misery. For the sake of brevity, then, this one universal end of human action and sole object of man may be said to be happiness. The conclusion is thus finally reached that *the object of Nature is function while the object of man is happiness.*

The above will serve as a preparation for considering the third something involved in the satisfaction of desire, which, for want of a better term, has been called *action.* Totally distinct in its nature from both feeling and function, it nevertheless invariably accompanies these and mediates between them as the direct consequence of the former, and the necessary condition to the latter. In itself, and except as such consequence and condition, it is utterly useless both to Nature and to the organism. To the former it is simply a mechanical means, to the latter it is a costly burden. Of what use then is it? What intrinsic value has it? To what is it in and for itself an end?

To the answer to these important questions a separate chapter must be devoted, but their full consideration may be anticipated in so far as to premise that for the subhuman world of life, if utility can be predicated of this soul-activity at all, the only beneficiary that can be conceived of is organic progress or evolution. In the human stage, however, this beneficiary assumes a more concrete form and may, without any forced interpretation and in a true and literal sense, be called *Society*.

The threefold truth therefore to which the foregoing considerations growing out of subjective psychology in general and the philosophy of desire in particular have led, is, if we do not descend to the subhuman stage of existence, that:

1. The object of Nature is Function.
2. The object of Man is Happiness.
3. The object of Society is Action.

CHAPTER XIV.

THE TRANSFORMING AGENCY.

The social forces, in the sense in which they have been here spoken of, are those influences which impel man to action. They are qualities residing in men which determine and control their physical activities. They have their seat in the nervous system, and are what inclines the body and limbs to move in any particular manner. We call them *desires*. They are the monitors which prompt us as to the demands of the system, and propel us toward the object demanded. Now it is human activity which has exerted the great influence upon society that has resulted in making it what it is. It is action which has worked out human civilization. — *Dynamic Sociology*, I, 663.

This new force, manifesting itself in at least three prominent ways at almost the same time in the earth's history, and producing such astonishing revolutions, was the psychic force beginning to respond to a long process of cephalization, or brain-enlargement, in the animal world. It represents the birth of the soul in nature; it was the response to a demand for the satisfaction of wants, of instincts, of tastes; it was the first expression of purpose and of will. For these are the attributes which led the bee to seek the nectar from the flower, the bird to visit the brilliant cluster of fruit, or the female of the higher creatures to choose the most beautiful male for its mate. And these are psychic qualities and represent the subjective half of of the world of mind — the great heart of nature. — *Course of Biologic Evolution*, p. 31.

The profound modification accomplished by this agency [cross fertilization] was not confined to size, color, fragrance, and the secretion of nectar. The forms of flowers underwent in many cases a complete change, and an infinite number of wonderful irregularities appeared, varying from the slightest differences in the petals to the amazing abnormalities of the orchids, all calculated to adapt plants to the useful ministrations of insects, sometimes, as in the yucca, to those of a single species of insect, without which reproduction is impossible. — *Ibid.*, p. 25.

In that branch of philosophy designated in Chap. I by the name of cosmology, the most important law, notwithstanding the recent date of its full conception and acceptance, is that of evolution. In the organic world this law as frequently goes by the name of development. The history of organic development has been made the theme of a great number of the most important modern contributions to biology. To it, Darwin, the Newton of biology, devoted his life, producing a distinct epoch in that science and a revolution in human thought. His eminent contemporaries in all the advanced nations of the world, especially in England, Germany, France, and America, have grandly seconded the great movement, until the literature of the subject has become voluminous and it is still rapidly accumulating. Every conceivable problem growing out of this fertile principle has been attacked, and one would suppose that there could remain no new point of view from which the general subject could be contemplated. Notwithstanding the intense activity so long manifested in this field, the thoroughness of its treatment at the most competent hands, and the wealth of substantial contribution to the general subject of evolution and especially to the department of organic development, there is one phase which has been neglected the importance of which to the problem now in hand demands attention in this place.

The agencies that have coöperated in the production of the higher types of life are divisible into two distinct classes. Those of the first of these classes may be called normal or legitimate, those of the second extra-normal or illegitimate agencies. Normal or legitimate agencies give rise to characters or modifications which are of obvious utility to the organism. Extra-normal or illegitimate ones result in changes which are only indirectly beneficial, or they may be of doubtful utility and even in the end injurious. Usually though apparently useless they prove ultimately of the highest value. It is the special characteristic of extra-normal influences to give a new direction to development, to create unexpected and otherwise impossible modifications, landing the organism upon an entirely new plane of existence and completely changing the future course of development.

Looking more closely into the subject, it is perceived that all progress below the stage at which, in the sentient world, the nervous system begins to call forth marked activities in the direction of satisfying distinctly felt wants is the result of normal causes. This, of course, permanently excludes the entire vegetable kingdom. It also relegates to this stage of organic history, the whole of the Primary or Paleozoic period of geology, and probably all but the latter portion of Mesozoic time. Further, it rules out of the domain of extra-normal development all the lower types of animals, but the line here is not drawn at the beginning or end of any of the great structural series. No other kind of structure has any weight in determining it except nerve-structure, but this necessarily determines it irrespective of skeletal or any other type of structure. In fact, although it may be dimly perceived in some other creatures both lower and higher in the accepted scales of zoölogical classification, it first clearly manifests itself in insect life. It then comes out broadly into view in bird life, still more prominently in mammalian life, and most decidedly in human life.

The reader will be quick to perceive that this extra-normal agency thus described corresponds in all respects with what was defined in Chap. VIII as the Soul, and it remains to show that it is this that constitutes the great transforming agency in nature. Hitherto it had been chiefly the environment in interaction with the mere vegetative processes of life that had brought about modifications of structure and determined evolution. Now it is chiefly the organism acting in response to internal promptings of definite kinds that forces change and causes transformation. The two classes of evolution, therefore, may be regarded as respectively objective and subjective, and subjective evolution is the first chapter in the science of subjective psychology. It begins with the birth of the soul in nature, the initial recognition of creature wants, the origin of desires, and the beginning of that great crusade whose achievements are recorded in Chap. IX.

The influence of the transforming agency was sometimes felt upon the environment, sometimes on the organism, but whatever it touched yielded to its power and became molded into harmony with the ends of the agent. These ends were always the satisfaction of desires. The immediate means was *action* in the sense defined in the last chapter, and in this sense action constitutes the transforming agency itself, and subjective evolution is the product of the combined workings of this agency along a number of very different lines. It will be profitable to pause and consider for a moment a few of the most striking and characteristic of these transformations in the sub-human stage before rising to the important consideration of the relations which the subject sustains to man and society.

Among the most remarkable, and at the same time primitive and characteristic phenomena of this class is the influence of the insect world upon the plant world, Down to the close of Jurassic time the vegetation of the globe consisted exclusively, so far as now known, of cryptogamic and gymnospermous plants, i.e., of plants whose reproductive organs were inconspicuous and had no other attribute than that of performing the normal function of such organs. This was accomplished either by some kind of close fertilization, or if the sexes were separate, by the wind or water or some other mechanical and more or less accidental agency, and usually was only made certain by the production of a vast quantity of spores or pollen-grains adapted to easy transportation. It is known that during the Cretaceous epoch the class of plants which now bear true, often showy and fragrant flowers, was introduced, although no remains of the flowers themselves have as yet been discovered at this early date.[1] Toward the close of this same epoch and especially during early Tertiary time, it is also known that insects resembling the present Hymenoptera, Coleoptera, and

[1] Dr. J. S. Newberry in February, 1886 (Trans. N. Y. Acad. Sci., vol. V., p. 137), announced the discovery of the flowers of a helianthoid plant in the Amboy Clays (Lower Cretaceous) of New Jersey, for which one month later (Bull. Torr. Bot. Club, vol. XIII., March, 1886, p. 37) he proposed the name *Palæanthus*.

Lepidoptera made their appearance. So it is now known that the sole purpose of showy and fragrant flowers is to attract insects and secure cross fertilization. It seems to be a legitimate scientific deduction that these were entirely due to the agency of insects and developed pari passu with the higher types of these latter during the close of Secondary and beginning of Tertiary time. Only the botanist can fully estimate the sweeping character of this great transformation wrought by the spirit of life passing into mind, embodied in these humble creatures, and moving over the face of nature.

A similar epoch was inaugurated a little later when bird life began to react upon its vegetable surroundings. Hitherto, though showy and fragrant flowers may have been borne on herbs, shrubs, and trees which insects had created, all fruits may be supposed to have consisted of dry capsules or other vessels containing chaffy innutritious seeds. But bird mind proved capable of transforming these into pulpy berries or drupes, or nutritious grains stored with life-giving albumen. The fruit-trees with their showy and luscious pomes and drupes were the result, while the grasses came into existence yielding the bread-products of the world.

I never accepted this determination on account of the now well-established fact that the Gamopetalæ were of late development and the Compositæ probably the most modern order of plants. But not having seen the specimens and no figures having been published, I have thus far refrained from any expression of opinion on the subject. Now, however, that I have recently had an opportunity to examine both the specimens and Dr. Newberry's drawings of them I do not hesitate to say that his claim is not sustained by the facts. The forms are probably related to those obtained from the Potomac formation on the James river at the Dutch Gap Canal by Prof. Wm. M. Fontaine and myself, which Prof. Fontaine refers to Williamsonia, usually regarded as belonging to the Cycadaceæ.

This paragraph was written in February, 1892, and may be allowed to stand but early in April collections of fosil plants were made by Dr. Eugene Smith, State Geologist of Alabama, and myself from two very favorable localities in that state belonging to the Tuscaloosa formation, which is of nearly the same age as the Amboy Clays of New Jersey, and in the material from both these localities I have found objects which closely resemble flowers of three different kinds. In two of these cases either sepals or petals seem to be represented, but of course it is impossible to say whether they were colored to attract insects or not.

There is reason to believe that while mammalian life contributed somewhat to the results last noted it performed the further service of accelerating and directing, if not of initiating the development of nut-bearing trees, in which, however, bird life may have coöperated. And all this is not mere fanciful speculation, but is based on what is actually known of the interrelations of animal and plant life. Only the special details are not claimed to be exact, but it is probable that if the whole truth could be known it would be far more wonderful than the imagination of the naturalist is likely to depict it, checked by the caution which all scientific study inspires. It is practically certain that but for this psychic agency in the animal world the vegetation of the earth would not only have been very different from what it is, but would have lacked so much of what now contributes to the sustenance and enjoyment of man as to render the globe scarcely habitable for him.

Let us next consider one of the more important of those transformations which have affected the animal organism. In the lowest forms of life reproduction is asexual. The differentiation of the two sexes was a normal process of evolution and early took place. At first reproduction scarcely differed from nutrition, of which even in the highest it may always be regarded theoretically as one of the modes. But the earliest forms of distinct bisexuality consisted of a fertile individual supplemented by an accessory fertilizing agent or adjunct, which latter had no importance or use except to serve in this one capacity of dualizing or crossing the germ to prevent its vitality from becoming exhausted.[1] Although this in most cases relatively diminutive, and, except for this one purpose, wholly insignificant organism might with propriety be called the male, and the other primary and only real substance of the race or species might be called the female, still it is clear that the latter constituted the main trunk, and for all other than the

[1] Or, as Weismann would say, to insure variation through which alone natural selection can act.

one purpose mentioned, really was the organism. As further enforcing this truth, many cases exist in which the services of the fertilizer are only occasionally necessary and the main organism is capable of reproduction without its aid, at least up to a certain point. It is therefore obvious that from Nature's standpoint the female is the organism and the male only a sometimes useful, sometimes necessary adjunct or incident. With further development a nearer approach to equality between the two sexes was attained, but in nearly all invertebrate life and in a considerable part, especially the lower forms of vertebrate life, the superiority of the female is manifest. In many even of the higher insects the male is of little importance except as a fertilizing agent, often short-lived and without organs of nutrition in the imago state. In spiders we have the now familiar fact that the male is often exceedingly diminutive and is sometimes made the prey of the female while paying his court. In the mosquito the world knows nothing of him, and when seen he is not supposed to belong to the same type of insects. In bees he is the drone and has only the fertilizing function to perform. In many fishes there is a great disparity in size between the sexes, and even in some birds, as the hawks, the female is larger than the male.

From all this and much more that might easily be adduced it appears evident that from the standpoint of nature, and according to the normal processes of evolution, the female is the principal sex and constitutes the main trunk of development, she alone continuing the race, except that in the higher forms she usually requires the aid of a fresh element derived from the male to cross the stock and renew the vitality of the offspring. But for the intervention of some extra-normal influence, therefore, female superiority would have been found to be universal in the animal kingdom. The fact that in most birds and mammals the opposite is the case becomes an anomaly and requires explanation. This explanation is found in the law we are here seeking to illustrate. We perceive that, as in the cases of extra-normal development already considered, this phenomenon began to manifest itself in early Tertiary time, the precise period when the soul-force began to react upon the vegetable world. Though a very dissimilar phenomenon in itself it nevertheless is seen to have a very similar cause. The former movement was due to the development of those faculties which aid in securing supplies of nutriment to sustain life, in the heightened powers of scent, taste, and vision ; in the new-born pleasure derived from nectar, fragrance, and even from beauty ; in a word, it came with the dawn of the esthetic faculty, its first appearance in the world, and yet scarcely different from what we find it in man, who, before he learned the new truth (and how far has he learned it ?) was so vain as to claim that the beautiful and fragrant flowers, the delicious fruits, and the nutritious grains were created for him ! The phenomenon now under consideration was also the result of the growing esthetic faculty. It had nothing to do with the coarser reproductive instinct, but was the product of a sharpened sense of beauty, a romantic choice of partners by the females of the higher types of animal life. These heartless coquettes condemned to perpetual celibacy the meaner and uglier suitors for their charms, and only admitted to the privilege of parenthood those which by superior prowess, physical beauty, size, or other attracting qualities, were able to win their title to it. Heredity did the rest, and the product is the proof that this was the method, and it enables us to form a definite conception of the exact nature of those esthetic sentiments that prompted these selections. Again we find that they were practically identical with the higher tastes of man, since he regards the beautiful feathers of birds and the branching antlers of the deer and elk as among the most pleasing objects that can appeal to the eye.

There is much reason for regarding the faculty of cunning as one of those passports to female favor of which we have been speaking. While it may not have been so manifest among birds and among those mammals of which mention has been made, it may have constituted a leading factor in the life of the ancestors of man during their presocial and prehuman period. We know that nothing more readily captivates the human female than the display of brilliant mental qualities, and it is easy to conceive that the female Anthropus of the African or Lemurian forest may have been more attracted by male sagacity and success in circumventing rivals than in any other quality. If this be so it explains many difficulties in the path of the student of man. It explains especially the relatively small brain of woman and places the large brain of man on the list of secondary sexual characters. Many of these are known to be partially developed in both sexes, and thus may be understood the fact that man has become a being with enormously developed cerebral hemispheres.

There is one aspect of this question which possesses especial interest. It was shown in Chap. X that the intellect as compared with the soul is of recent date, not seeming to have appeared until late in Tertiary or even in Quaternary time. If the above hypothesis could be sustained it would furnish a remarkable confirmation of Schopenhauer's claim that it is a mere "accident." Not only is it a newcomer, branching off in modern times from the time-honored psychic trunk represented by the feelings, but it is an accident in the sense that it was produced by what have here been called extra-normal or illegitimate agencies in evolution, so that had Schopenhauer been acquainted with the laws and course of evolution he would doubtless have branded it as the bastard product of unholy alliances. Let us rather regard it as a natural child, not responsible for its origin, and, as among human beings, all the more likely to display high qualities and possess sterling worth.

Having glanced at the results accomplished in the subhuman stage by the transforming agency which is the universal concomitant of desire seeking satisfaction, we would naturally rise next into the field of human and social life and note its workings there, but although it will be necessary for the sake of completeness to furnish grounds for the assertion that it is here that this law may be seen in its fullest operation, still, for many reasons it will be advantageous to postpone the full discussion of this subject until the second part of the work is entered upon when all the preparatory considerations will have been disposed of. It will, therefore, for the present suffice to remark that nearly all the activities, and especially the substantial achievements of man fall under this head. The great variety and intensity of human desires, all finding expression in those actions which are intended to secure their satisfaction, has, thus incidentally but with marvellous effect, wrought changes in man's environment far greater than those produced by the animal inhabitants and greater than it would be possible for any irrational creature to effect.

CHAPTER XV.

THE DYNAMICS OF MIND.

The relation which the mind-force bears to these sense-forces is similar to that which the rudder operated by the pilot bears to the sails operated by the wind. Desire uninfluenced by intelligence is a true natural force and obeys the universal law of dynamics. Bodies acted upon by a normal force always tend to move in straight lines either from the impelling or toward the attracting body. If they move in curves or irregular lines, it is because a plurality of forces, having different directions, are operating upon them. It is precisely so with organisms impelled by desires only. They move as directly toward the objects of desire as do the objects of magnetic attraction toward the attracting magnets, or falling bodies toward the earth's center. — *Dynamic Sociology*, I, 486–487.

The pressure of hunger is an actual force — a sensation implying some state of nervous tension; and the muscular action which the sensation prompts is really a discharge of it in the shape of bodily motion — a discharge which, on analyzing the mental acts involved, will be found to follow lines of least resistance. Hence the motions of a society whose members are impelled by this or any other desire, are actually, and not metaphorically, to be understood in the manner shown. — HERBERT SPENCER : *First Principles*, p. 244.

All the sciences of the hierarchy deal with forces. Whether it be called gravitation, as in astronomy and barology, or heat, light, electricity, magnetism, etc., as in those branches of physics, or elective affinity, as in chemistry, or the vital force, as in biology, there is in all cases a dynamic agent determining the phenomena of every subdivision of knowledge which is entitled to be called a science.

The sterility of the old psychology, so long known as metaphysics, was due to the fact that it was without any such dynamic agent. As such it was essentially lifeless. It dealt exclusively with the intellect, and, as will be shown in Part II, the intellect is in no proper sense a force. Metaphysics possessed no animating property, no vitalizing or vivifying principle. It therefore soon degenerated into platitude and inanity. For centuries it consisted in the threshing of old straw, pulverizing it, until it choked itself with the very dust that arose from beneath its flail.

Mind only becomes a science when grasped in its entirety. The dynamic agent resides in the feelings. The mind-force is the soul. The psychic power inheres in the emotions. The propelling energy of the world is the "Will" of Schopenhauer. The active principle of sentient nature is desire. In the language of romance and of popular speech the emotional side of life is called the *heart*. Some physiologists have been disposed to attribute this to ignorance, but there is a sense in which it is more than half true, even from the standpoint of physiology. It is not supposed to refer to blood-currents, but to nerve-currents, and if there is any nerve center that is entitled to be called the seat of the emotions it is the great cardiac plexus of the sympathetic system, and the strongest emotions can be definitely located in that region of the body. But there is another point of view from which popular language can be defended, always remembering that we are not dealing with literal facts, but with analogies. The physiological heart is, more than any other organ, the engine of the living body, the force-pump of the life-current, and the seat of vital power. Behind it and impelling it is the system of nerve fibers, plexuses, and ganglia storing and transmitting the nerve-currents that constitute the power itself. But it is this same power, only ramifying throughout the system and controlling every organ of the body, that impels, by its rhythmic pulsations, every bodily movement and every act of life, the conscious and rational actions, as well as the involuntary and vegetative functions. And it is not, therefore, a mere figure of speech, but in a certain correct sense the expression of a scientific truth to call the feelings, as they are here treated, the great heart of nature, in contrast with the rational faculties, which constitute the head of nature. Both together form the subject of a true science dominated, like all other true sciences, by its peculiar form of the universal force, and therefore capable, like other sciences, of exact treatment, and of yielding with such treatment beneficial results. Feeling is the basis of a philosophy of action, and whether viewed from the standpoint of achievement and progress or from the standpoint of ethics and happiness, it constitutes the only real foundation for a science of mind. Subjective psychology puts a heart and soul into philosophy, gives it life and meaning, makes it practical and utilitarian, furnishing a key alike to past history and to future progress.

Thus viewed it can be seen what an important fact feeling is in the world and how worthy it is of all attention and honor. That maudlin sentimentality that would banish it from philosophy as unworthy a place by the side of its great grandchild, the intellect, must be overcome if psychology is to become a science, and the equal dignity and nobility of the emotions, nay, even of what it pleases us to call the baser passions, must be recognized and their true position in the scheme of philosophy assigned them. When this is done not only will much that is regarded as bad be seen to be good, but much that is false in the habitual mode of reasoning will yield its place to true conceptions of nature and life.

As a single illustration coming under this last head may be taken the popular estimate of the worth of woman. Because she does not possess the power of abstract reasoning to the same degree as man, his attitude toward her, however it may be expressed, and often most clear when unexpressed, is that she possesses little relative importance in the world beyond her function of continuing the race. While she could reply that there was a period in his phylogenetic history, when, as shown in the last chapter, he was literally of no use except for that function, and perhaps not necessary even for that, and when she was in very truth the race itself, she can also with even greater effect reply that her emotional nature, in which he concedes her superiority, is not only far older in the history of development, but far grander in its essential nature and more useful in the economy of man and society, than his modern faculty of speculation. Whatever she may have lost by the action of those illegitimate agencies which have been described, she has not lost that greatest of all possessions, her heart, which still beats with undiminished force and regularity in unison with the pulsations of the great heart of nature of which it is a part.

The central and all-important truth toward which all that has been said thus far in this work has tended, is that *desire is a true natural force*. There is not the least, figurativeness, metaphor, or analogy in this formula. It is the expression of a literal truth. The psychic force conforms to all the established criteria of the nature of a force and is capable of an unlimited number and variety of concrete illustrations. It obeys the Newtonian laws of motion. An animal body like a physical body, acted upon by a single force will move in a straight line in the direction in which that force acts. If acted upon by two forces that are equal and opposite, a condition no rarer in the animal than in the physical world, it will remain stationary. If the two forces be neither equal nor opposite, it will move on the line of the resultant of the two. But as in the animal the forces are always continuous, the effect is commonly that of constrained motion and the corresponding curve is described.

Of all the known forms of force or modes of motion, that of magnetism is the one to which the psychic force approaches most nearly. This has long been perceived. The most typical of all the desires is love, and in the French language the present participle of the verb to love is the word for magnet. There is however an important apparent difference. Whereas the magnet seems to attract the object, in desire it is the object that attracts the subject. But in reality the attractions of the magnet and the object are strictly mutual, as in gravitation of which magnetism seems to be a special form, and in the magnetic properties of objects there are all degrees. The psychic force may also be likened to electricity. The animal body may be regarded as a battery which it is the function of life to keep constantly charged. The attachment is to the muscles, and locomotion is analogous to that of an electric car. Again, the nervous system is analogous to a telegraphic or telephonic system, the fibers representing the wires. But it is not in these analogies that the proof of the dynamic character of the subjective phenomena lies. It is in the nature of the phenomena themselves and the results produced. These, as has been shown and as will be more fully shown in future chapters, are indistinguishable from other natural phenomena under the operation of recognized forces.

CHAPTER XVI.

SOCIAL ACTION.

All objects on the surface of the earth, though supposed to consist of multitudes of molecules which are moving among themselves, and though known to be undergoing secular changes, and destined to manifest, sooner or later, wholly different forms without human agency, may nevertheless, so far as man's daily dealings with them are concerned, be regarded as in a state of repose or inertia. The forces of gravitation and chemical reaction have reduced them to a state of equilibrium. Though differing immensely in properties, in form, size, consistency, etc., they are most of them in so far tangible that they allow their relations to be changed at the hands of man. In short, they neither escape him, nor resist him, nor refuse to be subdivided, modified in form, or transported in space. Before the active efforts of man the materials of nature are wholly passive. The condition which they have naturally assumed is the statical one. The free forces of nature have already played upon them in antecedent dynamic states until they have at last been reduced to their present state. This is the one in which they are capable of producing the least effects upon surrounding objects. While their matter has been integrated their motion has been dissipated, until the matter and force of the universe — at least, of the part of it which man occupies — have, as it were, become separated or divorced, and exist and manifest themselves independently — such is the apparent, and, so far as human action is concerned, the practical condition.

Now, it would be reasonable to suppose that, since natural objects have been constantly borne down until they have been brought to assume the greatest degree of stability of which they are capable in the existing condition of the universe, any attempt to disturb that condition would remove them more or less from that stable state and render them less inert and less indifferent to the influences of the free forces still playing upon them. Such is, in fact, the case, and it is an indisputable truth that the great results achieved by man in operating upon the material objects of the earth have consisted in removing these objects from the still folds of material death in which he has found them, and so placing them that the surrounding influences which had consigned them to this state can again set up changes in them and, as it were, reanimate them. In scientific phrase, it is by the transfer of material objects from the statical to the dynamical state, from a condition of molar equilibrium to one of molar activity, that human civilization has been enabled to originate and to advance. — *Dynamic Sociology*, II, 379–380.

The history of man, if it should ever be written, would be an account of what man has done. The numerous changes that have been made in the position of certain imaginary lines on the earth's surface, called political boundaries, and the events that have given rise to such changes, would be recorded, but instead of making the bulk of human annals as they now do, they would occupy a very subordinate place. Such changes and their conditioning events are temporary, superficial, and unimportant. They leave no lasting impress and are soon swept by time completely from the real record of man's achievements. The major part of a true history of man would be devoted to the reproduction of this real record. Although it is written on the face of nature by the events themselves, very much as the cosmical history of the earth is written in the rocks, still the history of man needs to be studied from these natural records, interpreted by the facts there observed, and described in writing and by graphic representation as much as the history of the earth needs to be thus treated by the geologist. Human phenomena, or, as they are popularly called, social phenomena, differ in these respects from geological and other phenomena only in the nature of the forces which produce them. In these it is the psychic forces, as described in the last chapter. Man is the instrument through which these forces operate, and the immediate cause of the phenomena is human action. As man has been a social being during the greater part of his history, and as the principal results of his activities have been brought about by some form of social coöperation, it is customary and proper to designate such action as social action. The laws and principles of such action belong to social science, or sociology, and it thus becomes clear that sociology rests directly upon psychology, and especially upon subjective psychology.

Subjective psychology is a philosophy of action. Looked at retrospectively and from the standpoint of natural history it is seen that all the changes that have taken place either in the organism or the environment have been due to the action of the former under the influence of the psychic or vital forces, and that from the time that conscious desires began to determine action great transformations have taken place and are still going on. Not dwelling on the subhuman stage, it is obvious that man is the being that has most notably displayed this transforming power. An animal of rather inferior physical strength, endowed with few natural weapons of either offence or defence, lacking the powers of nocturnal vision, keen scent, fleetness in pursuit or escape, flight, or special skill in swimming, by which to aid him in migration, he has nevertheless almost completely changed the appearance and character of everything above ground over half the land surface of the earth and established himself supreme over all else in all the habitable parts of the globe. All this is commonly and properly attributed to mind, and it will be shown in Part II. in what special ways mind has produced these results. But the present point of view is that of insisting that the motive power of mind has been his multiplied and ever-increasing wants, to supply which perpetual effort has been put forth and ceaseless activity has taken place. This purposeful activity is the middle term of the threefold psychologic succession, mediating between desire and feeling and the necessary condition to the satisfaction of the former in attaining the latter. Here more than anywhere else pleasure or happiness has been made an end, though only intended by nature as a means. But neither did the transformations wrought by man's activity constitute in any sense the purpose of that activity. The sum total of these transformations constitute what is meant by material civilization, but man never made civilization an end of his efforts. In so far as this has been a gain the sole beneficiary of that gain has been society, as shown in Chap. XIII.

There are those who maintain that civilization can only be achieved through the action of the individual, unconscious of the end, doing that which will conduce to the end. The present state of progress is adduced as proof that this is the necessary result. But while it is admitted that this has resulted in some parts of the world and in past history, it must be denied that the effect has been beneficial in all parts of the world or wholly so in any part, and also that any guaranty exists that it will continue indefinitely to be so, even where the actual benefits have been greatest. It can also be legitimately argued that much greater benefits might be secured if society were the conscious agent and had its improvement for its clearly perceived end. But this is an anticipation. This much needs however to be said, that in predicating action as the object of society the time has not yet come when it can be said to be conscious of its end. Society has not yet begun to seek its end. It has not reached the stage of psychic development attained by the Cretaceous insect, the Eocene bird, the Miocene mammal, or the Quaternary man, when conscious desire began to inspire activity in securing its satisfaction. The soul of society is not yet born. Yet none the less is society the beneficiary of the direct results of human action in so far as they are beneficial, albeit that action is directed solely toward the attainment of the object of the individual man, viz., happiness.

It is the essence of the doctrine of individualism that what is good for the individual must be good for society. This is based on the admitted fact that society exists only for the individual. Society is only an idea — a Platonic idea, like species, genus, order, etc., in natural history. The only real thing is the individual. And it is argued: Why strive to benefit that which has no feeling and therefore is incapable of being benefited? The argument is plausible. Only it proceeds from a misconception of what social reformers really mean when they talk of improving society. There are none so simple as literally to personify society and conceive it endowed with wants and passions. By the improvement of society they only mean such modifications in its constitution and structure as will in their opinion result in ameliorating the condition of its individual members. Therefore there is nothing illogical in their claim, and to answer them it must be shown in each case that the particular supposed reform that they are advocating will not as a matter of fact result in the alleged amelioration of the individual members of society. Arguments of this class are legitimate.

It would also be legitimate to argue that no possible alteration in the existing status of society can produce beneficial effects as thus defined, but I am not aware that anyone has ever taken that position. It is too obvious on the most superficial view that the evils that individuals suffer are often due to the constitution of society which entails them. This results from the constant changes that are going on in every direction through the activities of individuals seeking their ends, and from time to time causing the needs of the mass to outgrow the restrictions which society under very different previous circumstances was obliged to impose. So that if a state of perfect adaptation of the individual to society could be at any given moment conceived to exist it would not remain so very long, and new internal transformations would soon again throw the individual units out of harmony with the social aggregate. It is this inertia of society and its inability to keep pace with the growth of the living mass within it that gives rise to social reformers who are legitimate and necessary, nay, natural products of every country and age, and the ignoring of this fact by conservative writers who lay so great stress on the word *natural*, is one of the amusing absurdities of the present period.[1]

[1] "*Laissez faire* is 'translated' into 'blunt English' as meaning 'mind your own business,' and this injunction he drives home to almost every one who has ever done anything except to write about 'what social classes owe to each other'; the salutary reservation of Sir Joseph Porter, 'except me', seeming to be constantly kept in mind. . . .

"Again in his severe condemnation of the 'friends of humanity', as he sneeringly calls all who believe in the attainment through human effort of a higher social

So long, therefore, as society remains the unconscious product of the individual demands of each age, so long will the organized social state continue to be found out of accord with and lagging behind the real spirit of the age, often so intolerably so as to require more or less violent convulsions and social revolutions. But if ever an ideal social organization shall come to be a clearly defined conscious individual want, it will be possible to establish one that will have elements of flexibility sufficient to render it more or less permanent. But here, as everywhere else under the dominion of the psychic forces, the end of the individual or object of man, happiness, or some improvement in his personal condition, must be put vividly before him as the loadstone of desire and motive to action.

state, he seems to forget that these very troublesome persons are merely products of society and *natural*. To hear him, remembering his premises, one would suppose that these men either had invaded the world from some outer planet or had artificially created themselves. But they belong to society as much as the hated paupers and worthless invalids whom he would turn over to nature. Why then not let them alone? Why meddle with the natural course of things? In fact what is the *raison d'être* of this earnest book that wants to have so much done? On his own theory, the author should let his deluded victims alone, should *laisser faire* — we omit the 'translation.'" — Review of Prof. W. G. Summer's book, entitled: What Social Classes Owe to Each Other. *Man*, Vol. IV; New York, March 1, 1884.

CHAPTER XVII.

SOCIAL FRICTION.

Ethical principles are a growth of the social system. The members of society are literally bound by them, not by an ideal bond, but by positive constraint. The prevailing idea is, that any one might conduct himself immorally if he preferred, and that pure *principle* is all that prevents the majority of mankind from doing so. Such ideas legitimately follow from the free-will doctrine and other kindred errors that pervade the moral teaching which we all receive. The truth is, that men are compelled to conduct themselves according to the established standards of propriety. This is the condition upon which society has been enabled to develop. The few who attempt to break over these restrictions quickly come to grief. They drop into the criminal classes, and find their way into the penitentiaries ; or they are stamped as monomaniacs, fanatics, "cranks," and rigidly guarded. They are driven from the centers of culture, and find for brief periods the means of continuing their licentious course on the expanding borders of civilization. Here they are known as "roughs" and "desperadoes," and flourish until compelled to succumb to the summary justice of "vigilance committees," which are merely the rude guardians of moral law in such communities. For there is really no hard-and-fast line which can be drawn between criminality and the less heinous forms of immorality. But even the least deviation from the path of rectitude is, in developed social centers, a signal for ostracism, the withdrawal of esteem, systematic avoidance, and all the other forms of punishment which render life intolerable, and demonstrate the completely compulsory character of the ethical code. It is a code which enforces itself, and therefore requires no priesthood and no manual. And strangely enough, here, where alone *laissez faire* is sound doctrine, we find the *laissez faire* school calling loudly for "regulation."—*Dynamic Sociology*, II, 372–373.

The great object of action is to *do* something. Conduct only aims to *avoid doing*—either to avoid interfering with the "pursuits of ends" by others, or to prevent others from pursuing such ends, or to do some benefit for another, whereby he is prevented from doing the necessary acts for rendering an equivalent, or to do him an injury whereby he is prevented, to that extent, from pursuing his natural ends. It is all through a negative proceeding, interfering at every point with the normal course of action. Conduct is a *guidance* of acts so as to prevent or to occasion conflicts in normal actions.—*Dynamic Sociology*, II, 376–377.

Moral conduct, instead of being, as usually represented, conduct in a right line, is in reality conduct in a very irregular line. The path of *rectitude* is a crooked path, and the distance lost in following it counts heavily against the progress of the world, yet less heavily than would the jars and collisions which a failure to follow it would inevitably produce.

The remarkable fact to be noted is, that it is this class of human action, aiming simply to avoid such conflicts of interest, insignificant as it is in comparison with the main current of human action, that has been the subject of all the ethical teaching and ethical writing which have flooded the world from the earliest historic periods. — *Dynamic Sociology*, II, 377–378.

From the sociological point of view, then, Ethics becomes nothing else than a definite account of the forms of conduct that are fitted to the associated state, in such wise that the lives of each and all may be the greatest possible, alike in length and breadth. — HERBERT SPENCER: *Data of Ethics*, p. 133.

Our vices thus are virtues in disguise,
Wicked but by degrees, or by surprise.
POPE: *Essay on Man*, Epistle II.

Thus spite of all the Frenchman's witty lies
Most vices are but virtues in disguise.
POPE: *Ibid.* (another version of the above).

If any one were to write a book professing by its title to set forth the value of machinery and its usefulness to civilization, and were to confine himself exclusively to the subject of friction, pointing out in great detail the importance of reducing it to the minimum, describing the most effective kinds of journals, gudgeons, and bearings for this purpose, and treating exhaustively the subject of lubricating oils, the case would be closely analogous to that which exists with respect to the treatment by all writers of human or social action. Unquestionably the most important subject that can engage the attention of the human mind, its laws, principles and methods, as well as its substantial results have been ignored and volumes by thousands have been written on the mere friction which it engenders, its interferences and conflicts and how they may be lessened. This insignificant field of investigation has been dignified by the high-sounding name of ethics, or sometimes even by the more grandiloquent one of "moral science." These voluminous reports of the Circumlocution Office upon "the art of perceiving how not to do it" are of a piece with the traditional schoolboy's composition on pins setting forth their usefulness in saving men's lives by their not swallowing them.

That unthinking persons, theological writers, and authors of sentimental homilies should extol morals and regard it as the chief end of life is not perhaps to be wondered at; but that philosophers of breadth and penetration should have so uniformly failed to assign it its proper and natural place in their systems, will always remain one of the curiosities of the human mind. It would at least be supposed that where one of these latter was also a professed teacher of social science, and as such to have been forced to make the most careful study and analysis of all the different kinds of social action, he could not help seeing the subordinate rank and incidental character of those negative phenomena which alone belong to ethics. It is all the more surprising, therefore, to find Mr. Herbert Spencer making this subject to form the cap-sheaf and crown of his great system of synthetic philosophy, and speaking of that part of his system as the one to which he regards "all the preceding parts as subsidiary."

While sociology deals with all human actions and, therefore, includes ethics, the latter deals only with the limited class of actions which are properly included under the word *conduct*, and which, as said above, constitute the conflicts that occur in normal action. They are not only unimportant from their limited scope, but from their essentially negative character. Their tendency, as in mechanical friction, is to impede, and to their full extent, to prevent the regular operations of society. They are therefore wholly non-progressive. Any one who from moral considerations acts in any respect differently from what the psychic forces within him normally impel him to act, to that extent lessens the effect of his action. Of course this is far from saying that it is not very frequently necessary and in all respects best to do this, it is merely to insist that there is nothing so wonderful and exalted about moral acts as is commonly supposed, when viewed from the broadest philosophical standpoint. If one sees the question only from the standpoint of social progress, which consists in producing the maximum permanent improvements in man's material surroundings, all hindrances to this consummation are bad, and those acts which are morally good are in most instances socially bad.

It may be admitted that the subject of interferences among human actions and of their avoidance is a complex and difficult one, nevertheless it has been so long and exhaustively studied that it seems impossible to add anything of value. All the great moral precepts are as old as human records. The "golden rule" of Christ was laid down independently by Hillel and Confucius and never practised by any one. Among the best maxims are those of the Brahmins, while Antoninus and the Stoics have furnished as pure and lofty conceptions of duty as any modern moral science writer could wish. Mr. Spencer laid claim to finding a "scientific basis" for ethics. One volume of his Principles of Ethics is now out and I am unable to see that he has sustained that claim if by "scientific basis" he means anything else than the old basis. What he says that is new is no part of ethics. The doctrine that pleasure is the good and pain the bad, and that happiness is the end of action, while "scientific" is not ethical. It is a corollary dimly seen by Spinoza and others, growing out of the principle set forth in Chap. VII, which is a principle of psychology, or, one may say, of biology. And as to his "Justice" the subject does not belong to ethics, but to jurisprudence. As treated by him it is a partisan defence of extreme individualism, amounting to practical anarchism.

However important moral conduct may be in itself, and there is no difference of opinion on this point, there are many reasons, in its overdone condition already referred to, why it should not be made to absorb so large a share of the attention of thinking persons. The moral precepts observed at any time and in any country are the effect and not the cause of the moral condition of those who observe them. If there is any mutual interaction between ethical teaching and moral conduct by which each influences the other and tends to cause the advance of both it is very slight. Certain it is that the former can be and frequently is pushed so far that the moral sense is more or less blunted and deadened by the iteration of moral injunctions. It would probably be better for personal morality if ethics were only taught historically and philosophically.

Another serious evil results from the erroneous belief that moral character can be improved by ethical teaching. Many persons, and especially teachers, habitually labor under such a load of responsibility for the moral character of those who come within the circle of their influence that they become paralyzed for usefulness in life. No one dares to say what he thinks. All originality is screened out of whatever is produced. Teaching, that noblest of all vocations, degenerates into pedantry. This has now reached such a stage that the utterances of professors in colleges have assumed a stereotyped form and the sagacious student knows in advance what is going to be said. Or, if any one of these should chance to say anything original, he feels obliged immediately to recant it, or to add a saving clause to the effect that he meant something else. And it is getting to be the practice in set papers, orations, and scholastic addresses in which the mind has been allowed some freedom to expand, to close with a "protest," as the Catholic writers call it, namely a disclaimer of everything that could be construed to be injurious to morals. Frequently, after stating an important scientific truth, it is deemed necessary to explain to the reader, as the judge does to the jury, how much of it it will do to believe and what conclusions it will not do to draw from it. University lectures become infected with this true moral cowardice, until the lecture-room style can be recognized and readily distinguished from the independent exposition of the original investigator. The same difference is seen in the books produced by the two classes, in the cringing fear that animates the one, contrasted with the manly courage characterizing the other.

Along with the dwarfing effect of this state of things, there goes the further demoralizing influence of egotism and conceit. For the idea of continually guarding the character of others begets an inordinate conception of personal importance, and this is always seen grotesquely mixing itself with pretended humility. A form of this sometimes takes possession even of truly great minds, and unless checked by wholesome influences from without they are apt to merge into a state in which they vastly overestimate the effect their labors are to produce. It was so with Auguste Comte, after long practising his "*hygiène cérébrale*" of reading nothing and conversing with no one, but evolving his system out of his inner consciousness, until he fancied himself the high priest of a new dispensation and even fixed the time for its universal acceptance. And do we not see some trace of this enlarged personality in Mr. Herbert Spencer when, in the preface to his Data of Ethics, he explains his haste to lay before the world his ethical system before any serious evils should result from its delay? For it is in this connection that he says: "Few things can happen more disastrous than the decay and death of a regulative system no longer fit, before another and fitter regulative system has grown up to replace it." Under such a weight of responsibility he ought at least to be consoled by the view expressed in this chapter and to congratulate himself that the morals of the world may still be safe even if he should not live to complete his Principles of Ethics.

To all this may now be added the further law that the moral state is a product of social evolution and a condition to the existence of society. The moral code only differs from the legal code in taking cognizance of cases that society will adjudicate without the aid of the courts. Society will not tolerate an incorrigibly immoral member. To be in society at all and out of jail he must practice the moral virtues of his age and country. Great latitude there no doubt is in these matters, but his treatment by his fellow men will depend upon the degree to which he conforms to popular conceptions of right, and though he may keep within legal rules, if he persists in violating moral rules he will be ostracized and deprived of the means of gaining a livelihood, and ultimately made to perish and make room for those who will conform. Therefore there is no need to preach morality. It is self-regulating. Society literally compels its members to observe its moral laws.

To the statement that ethics merely represents the social friction it may be objected that this is to take too narrow a view of the subject, that there are departments of ethics that are not covered by this definition. I have tried to discover such and thus far failed, although there are some cases in which this is apparently true. It may be said that ethics need not necessarily relate to others, but may relate wholly to self. One may do an immoral act to himself wholly irrespective of any other individual. For example he may be intemperate and thus abuse his own nature. To this it may be replied that if he were alone in some vast wilderness and his act were unknown to any other human being this would be a case in point. But it is merely a hypothetical case which could practically never occur, and if it should occur it would have no importance, because such a life would be socially useless. But the moment he is brought into society his immoral practises begin to react on others and in various ways to increase the friction of the social machinery.

It is also true that this view relates primarily to normal or egoistic conduct and only secondarily to supra-normal or altruistic, better named *supererogatory* conduct. At least beneficence, benevolence, philanthropy, charity, etc., do not directly result from conflicts in normal action. But we have only to analyze the motives to these to perceive that they are at least the indirect consequences of such conflicts. Taking charitable acts as the generic type of the whole supererogatory class, it is obvious that they presuppose the prior existence in society of serious obstructions to the normal course of action. They exist only because there is a class in society who are in some way more or less deprived of the means of subsistence. How came such a class to exist? Clearly through some form of interference with their normal actions. There is an abundance of food. The benevolent class possess a large enough surplus to sustain the indigent class, and they are but a handful compared with the non-benevolent class who possess a surplus. Those who have nothing, were they free to act, would proceed to supply themselves with the surplus. Something prevents them from doing so. It is not to the purpose to inquire here what the nature of these barriers is, it is only necessary to point out that they exist. But this is only to say that action has been interfered with, arrested, clogged, choked, and hence objects of charity exist in society. An act of charity is, therefore, from our present standpoint, simply a mode, usually only a temporary one, of relieving pressure upon this class, of clearing away the obstructions to life, in a word, of overcoming the social friction.

The above is independent of the ethical nature of this kind of social friction and also of that of charitable action in general. It is fashionable now-a-days to animadvert upon all charitable work from the supposed fundamental and scientific standpoint that it interferes with the law of the survival of the fittest in society. The argument proceeds from a superficial analogy between animal life and human life, and is neither scientific nor sound. But this much is true and is the basis of the popular error, namely that under the law of parsimony, i. e., that an individual will always seek the greatest gain for the least effort, it is easy to create a pauper class by injudicious charity. This class then becomes in society the strict homologue of the degenerate parasite so well known in almost every department of biology.

There is, however, a really fundamental and scientific objection to charity, but this I have never seen stated. It is that charity is really the giving by the benevolent class, not to the indigent class, but to the non-benevolent class. To illustrate this let us take the case of waiters' "tips" and porters' fees. All who have ever given the subject a moment's thought know that to tip a waiter or fee a porter is simply to give so much money to a hotel keeper or a railroad company. Its effect is to encourage these to continue to keep down the wages of these employés to the point of dependence upon the public, and the more generous the public the lower will be the wages. If all would resolve to cease tipping and feeing altogether, these employés would be paid regular wages like other employés. Charity and alms-giving do not differ in principle from this giving of tips and fees. It is true that in the latter case it is definitely known from whom the money should be taken as an act of justice, while in the former case the ones who should pay it are a large ill-defined class. But there is no doubt that the ones who have the wealth of the world have included in it the share of those who have none. The only escape from this conclusion is to say, as many are ready to do, that those who have nothing have no right to exist in society. If the indigent class were coextensive and identical with the criminal class there would be some ground for this position. But those who assume it generally argue that the poor are more moral than the rich, and it is probably true that the percentage of criminals from the wealthy classes is greater than that from the indigent classes. The only argument remaining is that poverty is due to idleness and profligacy. Yet if the percentage of idle and profligate rich could be compared with that of the idle and profligate poor, it would make a far worse showing for the former than that of the comparative criminality of these two classes. The conclusion therefore remains unassailable that the means of subsistence is justly due to the indigent class from the opulent class, and no amount of patchwork on the part of a few benevolent persons can ever balance this great account with society. Its effect is to increase the surplus of the non-benevolent in the sums contributed by the benevolent.

The several considerations above brought forward are merely samples of the short-sighted and superficial character of nearly everything that is said or done with relation to ethics. This is because in the nature of things there cannot be any logical and fundamental treatment of that subject. The moment logic and scientific principles are applied the problem ceases to be an ethical one and becomes a sociological one. The ethical and sociological standpoints are the opposites of each other. The former looks to the curbing, the latter to the freeing of social energy. Any philosophy that has for its object the hemming and cribbing of a great natural force can have no permanence. As well try to dam the waters of a river and hope for final success.

This thought introduces the fundamental truth with which this treatment of social friction must conclude. It is that the whole subject of ethics is essentially provisional and the stage to which it belongs is a merely transitional stage. There are those who by devoting their whole lives to doing good conceive of the life of future blessedness as one in which there shall be no other occupation but that of doing good. They forget that they have been taught that in that life there will be no one to need their ministrations. Could they realize such a state it would appear a wretched one. The only thing they enjoy they would be deprived of. I have known saintly beings of this class who seemed so to long for an opportunity to do good, that they could not conceal a secret joy at the occurrence of an unfortunate accident which promised to furnish such an opportunity. Were all suffering abolished the occupation of such persons would be gone. And yet Mr. Spencer and other ethical writers do but reflect a wide-spread popular sentiment in regarding ethical conduct as the climax of human achievement and ethics as the goal of philosophy.

The idea that there must always be a field for ethical action is only a part of the more general idea that all things must always be what they now are. And both of these ideas prevail in the face of the fact that the most radical changes have actually many times taken place within the narrow limits of human history. "The poor always ye have with you" is supposed to express a necessary social truth. It is doubtless as true now as it was two thousand years ago, but that is far from giving warrant for saying that it will continue to be true two thousand years hence. There are many who think that it will have ceased to be true two hundred years hence. But if it shall thus cease it will not be ethical teaching but improved social organization that will have produced the change. And so one might take up one by one all the social facts that make ethical conduct possible, and theoretically conceive of their ėlimination. It will, of course, be said that such an idea is visionary and utopian. Grant this and it still remains true that if any of the existing evils can be removed the domain of ethics is to that extent circumscribed. Deny that this is possible and the utility of all ethical work is given over. Admit that it is possible and there is no place to stop short of a reclamation of the whole field.

But is this claim wholly utopian? Has there been no moral progress? If not why continue to inculcate moral principles? As a matter of fact there has been great moral progress. Let any one read the history of England, even the meager account of its kings and their exploits which is called history, and compare the acts of the men of the 12th to the 16th centuries with those of the men occupying relatively the same national and social positions to-day, and see whether there has been any moral progress. Not even in Russia which we call despotic is there anything to compare with the immorality that openly stalked abroad three hundred years ago over all Europe. The subject need not be enlarged upon. The other point to be noted is that none of this real moral progress has been due to the enforcement and inculcation of moral precepts. It has been wholly due to the march of events, such as the growth of scientific ideas, the spread of letters, the influence of commerce, the establishment of universities, the invention of printing, and the introduction of machinery and manufactures ; in general to the progress of intelligence, laying bare the enormity of the abuses formerly practised and creating a new code of morals which society literally enforces. Men could not be as cruel and immoral as they once were if they would. The power of public sentiment crushes every display of it. In other words as already stated, the modern improved morality is a condition to the modern improved state of civilization and the latter is the cause of the former, not the reverse as ethical expounders teach.

The effect of social friction is always painful, therefore moral progress, which consists in reducing this friction, is restricted in its popular acceptation to the lessening of pain i.e., to the mitigation of suffering, the decrease of misery, and the removal of unhappiness in general. In short it is negative in its character, and such it really is in the main. But there may be a positive moral progress consisting in the increase of pleasure, the heightening of enjoyment, and the broadening and deepening of human happiness. Just as social friction is painful so social action is pleasurable. All desire is for the exercise of some function, and the objects of desire are such only by virtue of making such exercise possible. Happiness therefore can only be increased by increasing either the number or the intensity of satisfiable desires. It has in fact been greatly increased in both these ways. Without elaborating this principle I will simply point to the very modern date of two of the highest sources of man's present enjoyment in civilized countries, the enjoyment of music and the enjoyment of what may be called beauty in the amorphous — in the landscape, the cloud, the sea, the rocks, and the mountains. No faculty for appreciating either of these sources of delight seemed to exist in what we call ancient times, and it is practically wanting in all but modern civilized races. At least it cannot be sufficiently developed elsewhere to make up any considerable part of their enjoyment of life, which is the present point of view. Yet its germs doubtless exist in all races and have existed at all times, capable of development through civilization.

The highest ideal of happiness, therefore, is the freest exercise of the greatest number and most energetic faculties. This must also be the highest ethical ideal. But it is clear that its realization would abolish moral conduct altogether and remove the very field of ethics from a scheme of philosophy. To remove the obstacles to free social activity is to abolish the so-called science of ethics. The avowed purpose of ethics is to abolish itself. The highest ethics is no ethics. Ideally moral conduct is wholly un-moral conduct. Or more correctly stated, the highest ideal of a moral state is one in which there will exist nothing that can be called moral.

Whether we look at the subject from the standpoint of social progress or from that of individual welfare the liberation of social energy is the desideratum. The sociologist demands it because it increases the progressive power of society. The moralist should demand it because it increases happiness. For activity means both, and therefore the more activity the better. True morality not less than true progress consists in the emancipation of social energy and the free exercise of power. Evil is merely the friction which is to be overcome or at least minimized. This cannot be done by exhortation. It must be done by perfecting the social mechanism. The tendencies that produce evil are not in themselves evil. There is no absolute evil. None of the propensities which now cause evil are essentially bad. They are all in themselves good, must necessarily be so, since they have been developed for the sole purpose of enabling man to exist, survive, and progress. All evil is relative. Any power may do harm. The forces of nature are good or bad according to where they are permitted to expend themselves.

The wind is evil when it dashes the vessel on the rocks ; it is good when it fills the sail and speeds it on its way. Fire is evil when it rages through a great city and destroys life and property ; it is good when it warms human dwellings or creates the wondrous power of steam. Electricity is evil when in the thunderbolt it descends from the cloud and scatters death and destruction ; it is good when it transmits messages of love to distant friends. And so it is with the passions of men as they surge through society. Left to themselves like the physical elements they find vent in all manner of ways and constantly dash against the interests of those who chance to be in their way. But like the elements they readily yield to the touch of true science, which directs them into harmless, nay, useful channels, and makes them instruments for good. In fact human desires, as defined in Chap. IX, seeking their satisfaction through appropriate activity, constitute the only good from the standpoint of sociology. They are the *Social Forces*.

CHAPTER XVIII.

THE SOCIAL FORCES.

All beings which can be said to perform actions do so in obedience to those mental states which are denominated desires. . . . Desire is the essential basis of all action, and hence the true *force* in the sentient world; and consistency as well as truth requires us to predicate this equally of man and of all things lower in the scale of animal life. . . . The classification of the forces operating in the department of animated nature will then be equivalent to, and, in fact, the same thing as, the classification of animal desires; and, as what is true of all must be true of a part, this will likewise constitute a classification of the social forces. — *Dynamic Sociology*, I, 468.

The following table will exhibit at a glance the classification of the social forces as already sketched:

The Social Forces are:

- Essential Forces.
  - Preservative Forces.
    - Positive, gustatory (seeking pleasure).
    - Negative, protective (avoiding pain).
  - Reproductive Forces.
    - Direct. The sexual and amative desires.
    - Indirect. Parental and consangiuneal affections.
- Non-essential Forces.
  - Æsthetic Forces.
  - Emotional (moral) Forces.
  - Intellectual Forces.

Dynamic Sociology, I, 472.

Only when it is seen that the process is in all cases similarly determined by forces, and is not scientifically interpreted until it is expressed in terms of those forces; — only then is there reached the conception of Sociology as a science, in the complete meaning of the word. — HERBERT SPENCER: *Study of Sociology*, p. 329.

No psychologist has yet devoted himself to make, or has succeeded in making, a complete analysis of the emotions, by resolving the complex feelings into their simple elements and tracing them back from their complex evolutions to the primitive passions in which they are rooted; this is a promising and much-needed work which remains to be done; but when it is done, it will be shown probably that they have proceeded originally from two fundamental instincts, or — if we add consciousness of nature and aim — passions, namely, that of self-preservation, with the ways and means of self-defense which it inspires and stimulates, and that of propagation, with the love of offspring and other primitive feelings connected with it. — MAUDSLEY: *Fortnightly Review*, April 1, 1874, Vol. XXI (New Series, Vol. XV), p. 470.

Demgemäss füllt die Sorge für die Erhaltung jenes Daseyns, unter so schweren, sich jeden Tag von Neuem meldenden Forderungen, in der Regel, das ganze Menschenleben aus. An sie knüpft sich sodann unmittelbar die zweite Anforderung, die der Fortpflanzung des Geschlechts. Zugleich bedrohen ihn von allen Seiten die verschiedenartigsten Gefahren, denen zu entgehen es beständiger Wachsamkeit bedarf. — SCHOPENHAUER: *Welt als Wille*, I, 368.

While all wealth is not originated by labor, all labor originates wealth. Man toils, not because labor necessarily preceeds wealth, but because wealth necessarily follows labor. The possession of want-satisfying products is what the laborer seeks, and desire is the moving force in the whole process. Labor is not to be conceived of as the *vis a tergo* that pushes wealth forward; but wealth is to be conceived of as the siren that lures labor onward. Wealth is always the cause of labor; labor is not always the cause of wealth. . . . Nature subjected and appropriated is wealth; man's subjection of nature is labor. — J. B. CLARK: *Philosophy of Wealth*, p. 25.

In view of the thoroughness with which the subject of the social fôrces was elaborated in Dynamic Sociology, it is of course no part of the purpose of the present chapter to enter into it exhaustively. As stated at the beginning of the present work the social forces constitute one of the two primary doctrines of dynamic sociology, scarcely perceived by any other writer and as yet almost completely neglected even by those who are favorably disposed toward the general system of philosophy outlined in that work. I am far from anxious about the recognition of this or any other principle merely because it was practically original with me, and should be glad to learn that some one before me had developed it even more fully than I have done, especially if that would lead to its general recognition, because I regard it as an exceedingly fertile principle, and one which, though, like most great truths, it may seem to some, after fully comprehending it, to be little more than a truism, lies at the foundation of social science and without which there can be no such science. To the objection of its simplicity it may be answered that nearly all important truths are simple and easy to understand, but this has not prevented most of them from remaining long unperceived, nor has it rendered them any the less effective agencies in revolutionizing thought when once recognized and applied. On the contrary it is usually this quality of simplicity and reasonableness that has made such a use of them possible.

I am not therefore disposed to believe that the failure to recognize and apply this principle to the great problems of society and economics has been due in any great degree to the humble source from which it was put forth, or to the fact that its announcement was not made *ex cathedra*, and I prefer to attribute it to causes more worthy of the able and earnest class of workers in these fields. Much of it is doubtless due to the fact that the large work in which it was incorporated was necessarily addressed to a small class of readers, is a heavy tax upon the busy brain of active investigators, contains much else to divert the attention, and has not made its way into the curriculum of colleges or lists of indispensable reading matter of most writers and teachers.[1]

It has also grown more and more apparent to me as the years have passed that notwithstanding the direct manner in which this principle appeals to the understanding and to the reason, still, so cautious has the rigid scientific method of the time made the investigators of every subject that many may have felt that, in the treatise referred to, it was not sufficiently substantiated to be accepted in the form presented. So forcibly was I struck with it at that time, so impressed by its simplicity

[1] The work is now in use in the postgraduate courses of the University of Chicago, the University of Indiana, Cornell University, and Colby University.

and obviousness, that from a desire to avoid the possible charge of seeking to demonstrate an axiom, I refrained from presenting the philosophic grounds on which the principle itself rests, and contented myself with its simple announcement as a truth apparent to all. The treatment that followed was confined exclusively to the elaboration of the details that naturally flow from it. But since the appearance of that work in 1883 I have had many intimations that this part of the subject had been slighted. It is true that the general philosophy of desire was there treated from a psychological point of view in several places, particularly in chapters V, VII, IX, and XI, but the more I reflected upon it the more difficult it appeared, and the greater seemed the need of subjecting it to a thorough analysis as a basis for the doctrine of the social forces to rest upon. Plain and simple as the statement seems that the desires constitute the social forces, as soon as the attempt is made to go deeper and explain the nature of the desires great difficulties arise. The whole philosophy of feeling is opened up and the knotty problems of pleasure and pain, of the soul and the will, and the train of complicated antecedents to individual and social action must be probed to the bottom. Nor can one escape from the consideration of social friction which involves the vast lumber-strewn field of ethics. Those therefore who hesitate to accept the doctrine of the social forces, as originally presented, on the ground that it was not adequately supported by scientific proofs, seem to me to be much nearer right than those who discard it because it is too elementary. For the former class I have great respect, and this I have endeavored to show by the present attempt to elaborate the groundwork of that principle. To do this I have found it necessary to dwell almost exclusively in the domain of psychology, and to show that one great neglected department of that science underlies this principle, and forms the only secure basis for the whole science of sociology. Here at last the mind that seeks for causal relations can rest with a sense of satisfaction.

But in this search for the foundations of sociology we seem, as it were, to have stumbled upon a true science of mind. Both sciences have their roots far down in the beginnings of sentient life and we find ourselves, whether we will or no, feeling our way in the morning twilight of the soul of nature. We assist at the birth of a great transforming agency, and we follow this new-born power to its maturity in the social forces. In Chap. XV it was seen that desire is a true natural force and the basis of dynamic psychology, which accounts for the transformations that have taken place through the activities of the higher animals and of man. It is obvious that it is no other which is the motor of social change, and the truth comes forth that the social forces are essentially psychic. It is this that has made it imperative that the foundations of sociology be sought in psychology. I wish to lay special stress on this because it certainly has not been sufficiently insisted upon, and writers on sociology have seemed rather to be trying to base the science upon biology and to find its dynamics in the vital forces.

Although I have used the expression *dynamic sociology* in a somewhat special sense, fully explained in the work by that title, and to be, if possible, still more clearly brought out in the second part of this work, still, I have never lost sight of the primary sense, in which society is looked upon as a theater of active forces, its phenomena explained as due to those forces, and its condition at any time or place interpreted as the result of the former action of those forces. It is only in geology that the word *dynamic,* in precisely this sense, has been regularly adopted and is constantly used to mark off a distinct department of that science. But there is no reason why it should not be introduced into all the sciences,[1] since all must have, in order to be sciences at all, their dynamic department. The

[1] This chapter was written early in March, 1892, since which date Prof. Simon N. Patten of the University of Pennsylvania has published a work entitled : *The Theory of Dynamic Economics.* Publications of the University of Pennsylvania, Political Economy and Public Law Series, Vol. III, No. 2, Philadelphia, 1892.

other departments of most or all, sciences are chiefly the historical and the descriptive, or some may be restricted to the latter alone. The dynamic department of the other sciences, except geology, either have not been specially named or they have been called by other names. In astronomy that department is usually called the mathematical, and if we exclude sidereal astronomy, which as yet scarcely possesses a dynamic department, i.e., is as yet scarcely a science, this is the most exact of all the sciences. In physics no special name has been given to this department because it embraces so nearly the whole of the science. In chemistry it includes everything that relates to elective affinity and reagency, and leaves little else except the description of chemical substances and the history of their discovery. In biology there was no recognized dynamic department until the time of Darwin. Lamarck and a few others had founded this department and thus erected it into a science, but their views were rejected. It now has a definite dynamic department, and its phenomenal progress since Darwin simply shows what a vivifying power this principle possesses whenever it is applied ; shows, in a word, the power of the scientific treatment of any subject.

The old psychology was wholly devoid of a dynamic department. It was not a science but mere metaphysics, i.e., beyond nature, as the word implies, and transcendental, as the metaphysicians admitted. Objective psychology in and of itself is essentially so. Psychology does not become a science until its subjective phenomena are considered, because it is in these that its forces lie.

With regard to sociology, although Comte, who founded and named it, dimly perceived that it possessed a dynamic department and treated both social statics and social dynamics at some length, and although Spencer wrote an early work entitled Social Statics, implying the existence of social forces, it remained, I am bound to affirm, without a clearly recognized dynamic department until the appearance of Dynamic Sociology in 1883. This is not because there was not an attempt on the part of both Comte and Spencer to establish such a department, but because these authors both made the mistake of supposing that the social forces were vital instead of psychic forces. They both perceived the analogy between society and an organism, and the latter has worked out this analogy to its minutest details. Although much too competent a biologist not to perceive that it was only an analogy, and that society is not a literal organism, he still treats the development of society essentially and persistently from the biological standpoint, and calls in as its conditioning instrumentalities the biologic laws and principles that he had so ably expounded in his Principles of Biology.

I hasten to disclaim, however, that in the above is meant to be implied a complete failure on the part of all writers to recognize the existence of the true social forces as I define them, or of the fact that desires are true forces. There is no important truth established by scientific investigation which poets and seers such as Goethe, Shakspeare, and Emerson, have not foreshadowed in their vague but comprehensive forms of diction. Of the older philosophers Spinoza, Hobbes, and Bacon have given adumbrations of the true position of hunger, and love as mainsprings to human action. Among moderns Maudsley clearly perceived the social power of love distinct from its physiological function. But it must also be admitted that both Comte and Spencer have perceived and repeatedly referred to these underlying causes of social phenomena and recognized their fundamental nature. Indeed, what philosopher, nay, what thoughtful person could fail to see that hunger, love, and want in general drive men on in a great struggle with nature and absorb the energies of the greater part of mankind? It is true that the popular notion is that "money" is what all the world is seeking, or, as some keen-sighted, coarse natures more fully and accurately state it, "money or women"; and the vulgar newspaper heading that there was "a woman in the case" shows that love is also recognized as a universal power in society. But all this is not philosophy. It is the mere glimpse which the masses catch of principles that no one could formulate. These principles are not established by the fact that popular writers crystalize these glimpses in neat epigrams or weave them into romances. All know with what immense labor every great truth has had to be brought forth and really born. A few university lectures, laboratory experiments, or even carefully prepared memoirs in the Philosophical Transactions would not have established the law of gravitation. It required the labor of a lifetime culminating in the Principia for the world really to possess this truth. To establish the law of organic development Darwin must write at least five volumes packed with facts and weighted with arguments. Cosmic and organic evolution could make no headway until a Synthetic Philosophy was put behind it. And so it is with all great conceptions. Littré embodied the idea in its application to Comte's Positive Philosophy when in his introduction to the edition of 1869, he said: "Il n'est point de grande doctrine sans grand livre." And so I presume that the conception of a dynamic sociology will require much more than two thick volumes fairly to launch it into the world. And the 132 pages devoted to this one of the two cardinal principles of that doctrine needs to be supplemented by half another volume setting it squarely upon its psychologic base, so that there shall not remain the least chance for it to fall or a single brick wanting to threaten its permanent connection with the whole fabric of nature below it. Upon biology it can only rest unconformably and precariously, since it is felt that there is a causal hiatus between them, but upon psychology it rests naturally and safely, since, as has been shown, the dynamic department of psychology becomes also that of sociology the moment we rise from the individual to society. The social forces are the psychic forces as they operate in the collective state of man.

The present work, therefore, is only intended to be complementary of the previous one. In that the social forces were defined, their laws established, and their action and effects set forth, but their origin, nature and cause were not treated. The foregoing pages are intended to supply this deficiency and to place the doctrine itself of true natural forces in society upon a scientific footing.

CHAPTER XIX.

RECAPITULATION.

The several steps that lead up through the labyrinth of mental phenomena to the full conception of social forces may now be briefly summarized with profit.

The phenomena of mind in its widest sense belong to two distinct classes, viz., those embraced under feeling and those embraced under intellect, both these terms being expanded to include both preliminary or initial, and supplementary or derivative stages. The department of feeling is subjective psychology, that of the intellect is objective psychology.

The impression of an object on the nerve of sense through its appropriate medium produces a sensation, and invariably must do so, although in certain senses the organism as a unit or ego is not conscious of this sensation. Sensations thus produced may be classified as follows :

1. Intensive { Pleasurable, Painful,
2. Indifferent { Conscious, Unconscious.

A sensation consists in the transmission of the impression in the form of some little understood molecular change in the nerve fiber of the afferent nerve to the sensorium and back along the efferent nerve to the point impressed. Whether the sensation be intensive or indifferent will depend upon the force of the impression, strong impressions producing intensive, feeble ones indifferent sensations. Subjective psychology relates to intensive sensations and their subsequent phenomena. Objective psychology results from indifferent sensations. A sensation which, though distinct, is so slight as to produce neither pleasure nor pain conveys to the brain a notion of the nature of the object producing it. This notion is called a perception, as is also the act of receiving the notion. Perceptions are impressions made by nerve-currents transmitted to the cortical layers of the brain. Such impressions are registered so as to be to a considerable extent permanent. This makes it possible for the brain to possess a large number of perceptions, and through the incessant activity of all brain substance by the aid of innumerable connecting fibers these perceptions are combined, grouped, compared, and classified. Every object has numerous qualities, and when a number of such have been perceived, the mind, by the process described, combines these into a conception of the whole object. Conceptions are compared in like manner and their agreement or disagreement becomes a third psychological unit called a judgment. Judgments are subjected to similar processes and there result all the different forms of reasoning and thinking. Memory, imagination, and artistic creation result from the fact that all psychological operations are more or less permanently registered in the brain substance and may be used in any desired way at any time. This entire process, however far it may be carried, constitutes objective psychology or the phenomena of the intellect.

The phenomena of feeling constituting subjective psychology are wholly different from those of intellect constituting objective psychology. With the sensor apparatus there is always connected a motor apparatus. To an intensive sensation there is always a response along a motor nerve connecting with the appropriate muscles, and their contraction results. If the sensation is painful, those muscles will contract which will tend to remove the organ or the whole organism from the pain-producing object. If the sensation is pleasurable the opposite set of muscles will contract, and the organ or organism will approach the object and seek to continue or increase the sensation.

Besides the five external senses there is a sixth or internal sense, which may be called the emotional sense. Like the sense of touch and unlike the other four, it is diffused throughout the body, having no single local seat, but having, nevertheless, a number of regions of special sensibility due to extensive nerve-plexuses. The emotional sense is located chiefly or wholly in parts of the body that are supplied with fibers from the great sympathetic nervous system. The special distinguishing characteristic of the emotional sense is that it is not affected by material objects either directly or through any medium of communication, but receives its impressions only through nerve currents transmitted from the brain. The objects producing sensations are therefore chiefly psychologic, the products of brain action as above described. Such action is sometimes called ideation, and these products, ideas. It is these ideas which produce emotional sensations. This sense and this class of sensations are of primary moment to subjective psychology, although they depend upon the phenomena of objective psychology.

Pleasure and pain are the conditions to the existence of plastic organisms, pleasure leading to those acts which insure nutrition, and reproduction, and pain to those which will insure safety. Both were developed under the laws of natural selection or survival of the fittest, and present no special biological anomalies or difficulties. It was because it secured these ends that the nervous system acquired its motor apparatus accompanying its sensor apparatus, and that intensive sensations always result in the movements called forth by the nature of the objects producing them.

In the animal world there has gone on under the laws of evolution a gradual process of cephalization, by which the power of combining perceptions of the qualities of objects into conceptions and remembered mental states has been increased. The remembrance of an agreeable sensation and its attendant circumstance gave rise to the representation of pleasure not presently experienced. This mental state reacted upon the emotional sense producing a special form of sensation, intensive, and essentially painful in its nature, but unlike the primary form of pain. This sensation is called desire. Desire may be called secondary or representative pain in contradistinction to that produced by the too violent direct contact of objects, which is primary or presentative pain. Desire is prurient in its nature, and this pruriency is satisfied by the attainment of an appropriate object which is to yield the pleasurable sensation represented. Like other sensations it is attended by motor effects, and the muscles contracted are those which impel the organism toward the object desired. The attainment of the object not only satisfies and terminates the desire, but it yields the pleasure represented. As desire can only result from an idea of the pleasure-giving quality of the object, it must have developed pari passu with the organ whose function it is to generate ideas, viz., the cortical layers or cerebral hemispheres. Hence cephalization had for its earliest result the development and increase of conscious desires.

As a consequence of this process of cephalization and increasing desire in the animal world activity increased, and this activity became a transforming agency. The leading desires were for nutrition, protection, and reproduction. These are the ends of Nature and her only ends, but since the satisfaction of desire in addition to securing these ends, also yielded pleasure to the organism, this pleasure constituted an end and was the only end the organism sought. To attain the end of the organism, pleasure, was to secure the end of Nature, function. But in pursuing solely the first of these ends, certain important results were brought about which had no relation to either pleasure or function, and which wrought great changes in the constitution of organic life and in its surrounding conditions. The most important of these changes below the human stage of development, were the creation of a flower and fruit bearing vegetation, the transfer of physical superiority from the female to the male, and probably the development of the primary directing faculty of the brain known as sagacity or cunning.

The transforming agency was neither the desire nor the pleasure of satisfying it, still less the function thereby subserved, but the activities resulting from the efforts put forth in the attainment of these ends. The changes wrought were no part of the purpose either of Nature or the organism, but were purely incidental. They were not always beneficial, but have thus far been in the main progressive. They have marked great epochs in evolution. Therefore the true beneficiary of their effects is evolution or general organic progress. With respect therefore to the general subject of desire, it may be said that:

1. The object of Nature is Function,
2. The object of the Organism is Pleasure,
3. The object of Evolution is Activity.

Considering activities as motions, the forces producing those motions are the desires, and we have a science which may be called mental physics or *psychics*. It constitutes the dynamic department of psychology and may also be called the dynamics of mind.

Rising to the human stage, while no change is perceptible in the nature of the principle considered, the coöperative habits of the human animal resulting in what is known as society gives this principle greatly increased importance. Animated, the same as the lower animals only more intensely, by desires, seeking those higher and more generalized pleasures which collectively go by the name of happiness, man has, almost as unconsciously as the lower animals, put forth varied, multiplied, and incessant efforts, attended by universal, continual, and restless activity, and resulting in wide-spread, radical, and colossal changes in all his surroundings. Not always useful, any more than were those of the humbler creatures, these changes in his environment have nevertheless been upon the whole progressive, and constitute, taken together, what is known as civilization. Not themselves the object of either Nature or Man, their true beneficiary, in so far as they have resulted in benefit, has been society, which is with respect to them as impersonal and unconscious as Evolution must be conceived to be of the results of animal activity. The conclusion is thus again reached, as at the close of Chap. XIII, that:

1. The object of Nature is Function,
2. The object of Man is Happiness,
3. The object of Society is Action.

Treating human action as social motion, the forces producing this motion are the desires, and we have a science which may be called social physics. It constitutes the dynamic department of sociology or *dynamic sociology* in the primary sense of that term, the department which treats of the social forces.

PART II.

OBJECTIVE FACTORS.

The only means by which the condition of mankind ever has been or ever can be improved, is the utilization of the materials and the forces that exist in nature. — *Dynamic Sociology*, I, 18.

Ohne wissenschaftliche Beobachtung, ohne Versuch und ohne gesunde Theorie ist in der Technik stetiger Fortschritt undenkbar. Er beruht nothwendig auf bewusster Benutzung der in ihrem gesetzmässigen Wirken durchschauten Naturkräfte. — EMIL DU BOIS-REYMOND : *Culturgeschichte und Naturwissenschaft*, p. 19.

What thin partitions sense from thought divide! — POPE : *Essay on Man*, Epistle i, line 226.

CHAPTER XX.

THE OMITTED FACTOR.

Taking a retrospective view of the entire field of evolution and bearing in mind its uneven course as I have sought to depict it, there may be discerned, standing out prominently above all the minor fluctuations, a few great cosmic crises or epochs, in which the change appears so abrupt and so enormous as to suggest actual discontinuity. Three such cosmic epochs belong to the history of life on the globe. The first was the origin of life itself. The second was the origin of soul or will in nature. The third was the origin of thought or pure intellect. While I do not say that any of the factors producing these epochs came suddenly into existence, or that any definite lines exist separating life from soul or soul from intellect, theoretically speaking, the general fact remains that they are practically distinct principles, having diverse effects, originating at widely different periods in the earth's history, and succeeding one another in the order named. — *The Course of Biologic Evolution*, p. 32.

Denn der Intellekt ist uns allein aus der animalischen Natur bekannt, folglich als ein durchaus sekundäres und untergeordnetes Princip in der Welt, ein Produkt spätesten Ursprungs: er kann daher nimmermehr die Bedingung ihres Daseyns gewesen seyn, noch kann ein *mundus intelligibilis* dem *mundus sensibilis* vorhergehn; da er von diesem allein seinen Stoff erhält. Nicht ein Intellekt hat die Natur hervorgebracht, sondern die Natur den Intellekt. — SCHOPENHAUER: *Ueber den Willen in der Natur*, p. 39.

At the close of Chap. V reference was made to a neglected faculty or intellectual process which it was proposed to call *intuition*, or the *intuitive faculty*, and to make the subject of special treatment and the essential basis of the discussion in Part II. This omitted factor is a quality of mind, and, singularly enough, belongs to the department of objective psychology, i. e., to that department of mind which was first studied and which has received almost exclusive attention. Still more strange, it is the quality within that department which not only was first developed, but has been chiefly useful to those beings that possessed the higher class of mental attributes. Although belonging to the intellect, the operations of which have been so carefully investigated, its operations have not been described, and notwithstanding the rich terminology that has long been in use for the intellectual faculties, this faculty has not been named.

While this remarkable omission added much to the sterility of the old philosophy of mind, chiefly due, as stated in Chap. XIV, to its failure to recognize the psychic forces, it is equally fatal to the current social philosophy in lowering it to the plane of biology and divesting it of its only characteristic attribute, its essentially human or anthropic character. It is this that was the vice of the old political economy as embodied in the teachings of Ricardo and Malthus, and the sociology of Herbert Spencer and his adherents is simply an extension of the Ricardian and Malthusian doctrines. Malthus discovered a law of biology, but applied it to man to whom it is inapplicable on account of this omitted factor. Darwin, who admits that he was inspired to his great labors by the writings of Malthus, saw the application of this law to the animal world and worked it out to its logical end, making an epoch in biology. Notwithstanding the failure of Malthusianism at all points, the impression prevailed, and still prevails, that it is a fundamental law of society, and the current sociology is based upon it. Although the whole trend of social events is directly against this doctrine, so much so that the latest utterances of its advocates have assumed the tone of a general wail at the alleged reckless and headlong tide of things, still it is not perceived that this tide is due to a wholly neglected element in the current philosophy, and that when that element is taken into the account there is not only nothing reckless nor headlong in it, but it is the normal and healthy result of natural and legitimate causes.

The fact is, thanks to this omitted factor, that man and

society are not, except in a very limited sense, under the influence of the great dynamic laws that control the rest of the organic world. Dynamic biology is a department distinct from dynamic sociology. The dynamics of society is, in the main, the antithesis of the dynamics of animal life. The psychic element referred to, supplants "nature" by *art.* If we call biologic processes natural, we must call social processes artificial. The fundamental principle of biology is natural selection, that of sociology is artificial selection. The survival of the fittest is simply the survival of the strong, which implies and would better be called the destruction of the weak. If nature progresses through the destruction of the weak, man progresses through the protection of the weak. And so it is throughout. The terms are all reversed.

It would be wrong to say that modern scientific philosophers take no account of so important a matter as brain development and human intelligence. They only fail to see the radical change of base which these have effected. Imbued with usually safe uniformitarian principles they naturally shrink from sensational speculations about cataclysmic changes. But it is possible to carry this method too far. For while it is true that nature makes no leaps, while, so long as beginnings only are considered, all the great steps in evolution are due to minute increments repeated through vast periods, still, when we survey the whole field, as we must do to comprehend the scheme, and contrast the extremes, we find that nature has been making a series of enormous strides, and reaching from one plane of development to another. It is these independent achievements that the true philosopher must study. Not to mention the difference between a nebula and a solar system, or between a ball of fire and a habitable planet, the origin of life, through the development of a substance in which life inheres, was a *saltus* that finds no parallel. In Chap. XIV was portrayed the wonderful transformation wrought by the appearance of what I have defined as the soul in nature, the date of which appearance can be geologically fixed with considerable precision. And now we have to contemplate a third cosmic epoch in the history of life, the birth of the intellect, developed in obedience to the same laws and for the better attainment of the same purpose — the satisfaction of desire.

The current sociology, it may be safely said, fails to recognize the full import of this psychic factor. Just as metaphysicians lost their bearings by an empty worship of mind, so modern evolutionists have missed their mark by degrading mind to a level with mechanical force. They seem thus ready to fling away the grand results that the doctrine of evolution cannot otherwise fail to achieve. I freely admit that the theologians commit a fatal error in treating the soul as independent of the body, but this enormous fallacy is scarcely greater than that of the modern evolutionist, who ignores the magnitude of the step which was taken when the soul acquired a directing agent. The enthusiastic student who climbs the Alps may climb to little purpose or come to grief unless he employs a guide. The great ship may sail beautifully in mid-ocean, but when she approaches a harbor she needs a pilot. Enthusiasm cannot help the one nor fair winds save the other. The course of biologic evolution has been exceedingly irregular, the biologic policy is extravagantly wasteful[1], so that nothing but enormous fecundity could prevent utter failure. Progress in nature was exceedingly slow under the rule of simple forces. All this was for want of a guide. Indeed it is this which makes all the difference between the animal and the man. It is a superficial view to suppose that the human form is essential to a human being. Form may help or impede, but no particular form could have prevented the general result. It is as easy to see defects as advantages in the actual human form. If we are thankful that man has a mouth and teeth instead of a toothless beak we may deplore his lack of wings.

[1] See Chap. XXXIII.

In either case and in any case the sapient brain would have made him the master creature.

But the temptation to descant upon the results of "brain development," upon the achievements of "mind," and upon the "rational faculties" has too often been yielded to and generally proves profitless because there is no attempt to show how it comes about that they are the causes of the observed effects, and it is not to be wondered at under such circumstances that the popular mind should as naturally ascribe these effects to the erect posture, the facial angle, the opposable thumb, and other anatomical differences that make the physical man, as to the more intangible qualities to which they are really and exclusively due. It still requires to be explained in a clear and intelligible way what the particular attribute of mind really is through which man's superiority has been reached and by what steps it has been developed and the vantage-ground gained. The study of the commonly accepted faculties of the mind does not accomplish this object. The processes of perception, cognition, conception, judgment, reason, thought, however well understood, throw no light on the problem. The facts of memory, imagination, creative power, wonderful and fascinating though they may be, lead us no nearer to its solution. The more we contemplate these things the clearer it becomes that these are not what have given man his advantage, and those who now possess them in the highest degree have no advantage over the rest of mankind.

CHAPTER XXI.

INTUITION.

The second, or indirect, method by which conscious beings seek to attain desired ends involves an entirely new principle, and produces wholly different results. In the process of the development of the brain and the psychic faculties, a stage was ultimately reached at which the consciousness took on the attribute which enabled it to perceive a few of the general laws of phenomena, and thereby to predict from a given modification some of the secondary changes which would result. This is the simplest manifestation of the *intellectual* faculty, and it is this faculty that constitutes the new element required to form the transition from the direct to the indirect method. This transition constitutes one of the great leaps which nature has taken along its course of evolution, and the first break in that process since the development of protoplasm. Henceforth the possibilities of vital existence are to be multiplied, and the rate of organic progress enormously accelerated. For success in the sentient world is the ability to attain its ends, and the intellectual element is especially adapted to augmenting that power. By the direct method, action in this direction is restricted to cases which are within the muscular strength of the organism, and easily accessible without the intervention of obstacles. The utmost possible to be accomplished by it was measured by the energy actually expended. The least obstruction beyond the power of the individual to clear away by muscular force is an effectual bar to its access to the object of desire. By the aid of the new element all this is changed. Interposed barriers are evaded by circuitous routes of approach. Powerful natural forces are by appropriate adjustments made to do the work of overcoming resistance, and what is wholly unattainable in the present is, by the necessary adaptation, secured in the future. — *Dynamic Sociology*, II, 99–100.

The order of evolution was not from knowledge in any form to feeling, but the reverse, and we may suspect that in the completest analysis consciousness will still be found to obey its original law. If the rise of knowledge was at the instance of feeling, it is certainly unlikely that a fundamental order should be more than apparently reversed. — HIRAM M. STANLEY: *Philosophical Review*, July, 1892, Vol. I, p. 438.

Acknowleding the many blunders likely to be made in so broad a departure from traditions, I yet must declare this whole matter of the biological origin of mind to be one of the most promising sources of future psychological investigation. To me, also, it is a main avenue to the deeper secrets of the universe and of man's futurity. — Dr. HERBERT NICHOLS: *Philosophical Review*, September, 1892, Vol. I, p. 534.

Der Wille, als das Ding an sich, macht das innere, wahre und unzerstörbare Wesen des Menschen aus: an sich selbst ist er jedoch bewusstlos. Denn das Bewusstseyn ist bedingt durch den Intellekt, und dieser ist ein blosses Accidenz unseres Wesens: denn er ist eine Funktion des Gehirns, welches, nebst den ihm anhängenden Nerven und Rückenmark, eine blosse Frucht, ein Produkt, ja, insofern ein Parasit des übrigen Organismus ist, als es nicht direkt eingreift in dessen inneres Getriebe, sondern dem Zweck der Selbsterhaltung bloss dadurch dient, dass es die Verhältnisse desselben zur Aussenwelt regulirt. — SCHOPENHAUER: *Welt als Wille*, II, 224.

Diese Steigerung der Gehirnentwickelung, also des Intellekts und der Klarheit der Vorstellung, auf jeder dieser immer höheren Stufen, wird aber herbeigeführt durch das sich immer mehr erhöhende und komplicirende Bedürfniss dieser Erscheinungen des Willens. Dieses muss immer erst den Anlass dazu geben: denn ohne Noth bringt die Natur (d. h. der in ihr sich objektivirende Wille) nichts, am wenigsten die schwierigste ihrer Productionen, ein vollkommneres Gehirn hervor. — SCHOPENHAUER: *Ibid.* II, 315.

In giving the name *intuition* to the omitted factor just considered, at least to its earlier manifestations, I do so to avoid the introduction of a new term, and in the full knowledge that much has been said about intuition. I would not do so, however, if it did not seem evident that the application here to be made is really an extension of the commonly accepted meaning, even the popular sense of that term, nevertheless the application is a new one and few would probably recognize its appropriateness.

The discovery of the true dynamic principle in biology has not only revolutionized that science, but must equally affect those sciences which rest upon biology, viz., psychology and sociology. While the dynamic agent in biology is not the same as that of psychology the latter has been a direct outgrowth from the former. The key note to the whole series is the notion of *advantage*. It has been seen that the origin and growth of the soul-force in nature have taken place in response to the correspondingly increasing demand for opportunity to expand. To the organism the only *gain* consists in increased ability to satisfy desire; anything that secures that end becomes an object of effort. From this resulted the development of the conative power. It is the essential of sentient life to *strive*. Desire is the force that impels all activity, and by the multiplication of desires and the strengthening of their intensity, all was attained that the operation of pure psychic energy was capable of accomplishing. Whatever obstacles could be thus overcome were removed, and all the ends of being that would yield to the power of direct effort were realized. This is still the chief method employed by animals and the lower types of men in compassing their ends. In popular parlance it is described with tolerable accuracy as *brute force*.

But there were innumerable objects of desire that could not be attained by this method. Hence innumerable desires were doomed to go unsatisfied. The higher the development the more complex and varied the desires, and the greater the proportion of those that were unattainable by the primary method of direct effort. Just as in the realm of pure biologic law the stage of organization reached at any given epoch was capable of development only to a certain point, beyond which the organism could not progress, and at which it must stop and remain until some new and better structures could be developed that would admit of a new departure, so in the realm of psychic law the pure conative force was incapable of allowing the organism to advance beyond a certain stage, where it would have remained indefinitely but for the appearance of a new psychic faculty adapted to giving it a new impetus. This stage corresponds roughly with the summit of the animal series, although the new element began to be operative some time anterior to this period. Again, just as any new and progressive structure in biology, such as the trunk in trees, the floral organs that succeeded the spore-bearing state, the closed ovary, or the successive steps in the development of the floral envelopes, may be looked upon as so many devices of nature to secure the biologic end of increasing the mass of organic matter in the world, so each new psychic quality which secures the increased gratification of desire and thus fulfils in an increased degree the psychic end, enjoyment, may be similarly regarded as a device of nature adapted to its peculiar purpose. And yet each such step in organic evolution has a long history behind it, is the normal effect of antecedent causes, and was brought to any observed stage of perfection through the slow operation of developing influences. It is the general failure to recognize this truth that renders the current philosophy of the mind so unsatisfactory, and which, I fully believe, has led to such remarkable omissions as the one now under consideration. In biology it is becoming recognized that the beings inhabiting the earth, considered as material organic products, have been raised to their present estate through a prolonged series of developmental steps, but in psychology it is still the practice to deal with mind as something independent of the past, as if it had come forth, like its goddess Minerva, full-fledged from the brain of Jove.

Guided by the biologic principle of advantage, keeping in view the psychologic end, enjoyment, and considering the inadequacy of the primary psychic means to that end, direct effort or brute force, we are in position to penetrate into the intimate conditions which must have combined to give direction to developmental tendencies leading to the origin and genesis of a psychic faculty destined to usher in a new and higher epoch. Desire, as a true natural force, impels the organism in a straight line toward the attracting, or away from the repelling object. But obstacles intervene. At first, while activity is sluggish, the organism, like a material body similarly acted upon, simply comes to rest. Its force meets a counter-force, and equilibrium results. But later, when desire has grown stronger and activity more intense, while locomotion is checked by intervening obstacles, internal motion, or motility, continues, and the effort is unabated. Imagine it to be a winged insect. Its wings continue to vibrate the same as if no obstacle were in its way. Suppose the obstacle to be transparent and the goal to remain in full view. Against this obstruction the creature persists in buzzing, each vibration only serving to produce pressure against it. Fatigue at length causes the insect to yield to the force of gravitation. It falls below and perchance encounters an opening through which it immediately darts and secures the coveted prize. But should this not occur, a moment of comparative repose restores its energy and it resumes its efforts, this time moving irregularly and fortuitously over the surface against which it continues to press until it either accidentally rises above it, or shifts its position to its right or left margin, or to another opening through it, and thus succeeds. If we suppose an environment in which this, or a similar obstruction, impedes a large proportion of its efforts, an environment which remains more or less permanent through an indefinite number of generations of such a creature, the advantage derived from such persistent vertical and lateral movements would be such as to develop in the brain through the known laws of selection and survival, modifications of structure adapted to their regular and systematic execution. Those individuals in which this quality was best developed, would be the ones that would live longest and be most certain to leave posterity, until those devoid of it would have disappeared, and an organism would be developed possessing superior ability to satisfy its desires. This mental quality would at first take the form of an instinct, but all instincts are only partially so, and the faculty would soon be strengthened sufficiently to meet and overcome slight changes in the environment. In fact, the less instinctive it was, the greater would be the advantage, and it would continue to develop as long as such development possessed any advantage. This development would consist in the formation of cortical centers whose function it is to *guide* the activities of an organism to the performance of acts which in themselves have no direct effect in attaining the ends of its being, but by the aid of which alone, in a vast number of cases, it is enabled to attain them.

This step in the progress of intellectual development may be characterized as the stage of *exploration.* It is well illustrated by the numerous experiments actually made on frogs. This animal, before the vivisectionist has removed its cerebral hemispheres, has this faculty fully developed. Placed at the bottom of a tank of water with a bell-glass over it, it will soon require air and rise to the submerged surface of the bell-glass through which it sees the free open air and light above, which it cannot reach by this method. Instead of continuing to press against the bell-glass indefinitely until it drowns, it will immediately commence a series of movements, first about the upper surface, then round the sides, and finally back to the bottom. If space enough exists on any side under the lower edge of the bell-glass for it to escape, it will find it, and soon come up to the top of the water outside the glass. If, however, its hemispheres have been skillfully removed so as not greatly to injure the animal's vitality, as is easily done, it is remanded to the condition of our hypothetical insect before the development of the exploring instinct, and will remain as motionless under the roof of the bell-glass as do the bubbles it has generated, which latter act under the influence of purely physical laws.

The frog has doubtless passed the stage of mere instinctive exploration, and fairly entered upon the second stage, which may more properly be called that of *incipient intuition.* By the aid of the faculty it has acquired it is able to perceive that the indirect act will be the successful one. But even if it could see distinctly the opening below, so feeble is this faculty that it would probably first explore the interior of the bell-glass and not finally hit upon the right way until a large number of ineffective ways had first been tried. The third stage, or that of ***full intuition***, is not reached until the creature, after surveying its surroundings, is capable of perceiving from the outset that only by setting out in a direction different from that of the object to be attained, can it succeed. It will therefore undertake no explorations, but will proceed directly to the location of the means as if it were itself the end. A canary shut up in a room will fly against a closed window to escape, but a jackdaw will seek a small opening which leads out, although it may be so arranged as not to admit the light.

By considering a great variety of animals possessing different degrees of this attribute all gradations between the purely machine-like actions of the lower types and the highest stage reached in the subhuman world could probably be found. The display of this quality would be seen not to coincide exactly with the purely biological development, nor to depend upon physical organization entirely, although in the long run there is a rough correspondence of this kind. But some invertebrates are psychically higher than some vertebrates, and some birds than many mammals. It depends largely upon other conditions, such as environment, mode of subsistence, fecundity, etc. It will be higher in a hostile environment than in one where dangers are few; predatory animals have it greatly in excess of herbivorous ones, and a slow rate of breeding calls it forth as a substitute for numbers. This last is clearly exemplified in the contrast in these respects between rats and mice, though so closely related otherwise, yet in this case the larger size of the rat doubtless has much to do with it. A very late influence also comes in here and is now exceedingly potent with many other animals, viz., the fear of man. The tameness of animals on remote islands, as the Galapagos, has been much discussed, but many, like myself, have had opportunity to watch the progress of this principle in the game at points where population has rapidly increased. It may be doubted whether the time is here sufficient to assume an actual development of special cortical centers, though this may be more rapid than would be supposed, but it is probable that such centers already existing in such birds as the pinnated grouse (prairie-hen), for example, but previously developed for other purposes, have taken on this additional function vicariously, and have been quickly fitted up, as it were, for their new duties.

If we search the matter to the bottom we will find that not only are all these different manifestations virtually one and the same faculty, but that no other strictly intellectual faculty exists in the animals considered. It is the primary and original form that intellect assumes, and is, up to the highest stage thus far treated, the intellect itself. Unlike the so-called reflective faculties that have formed the subject of nearly all psychological investigation, this attribute is intensely *practical*, exists for a definite purpose, and is the means and secret of success to the beings that possess it in the great struggle for existence. It is simple and direct, and beyond the steps explained which led, as one may say, to its discovery through exploration, it is incapable of analysis or reduction to lower terms.

I have called this faculty intuition from the etymological accuracy of the word. It consists in a power acquired by the mind, of looking into a more or less complicated set of circumstances and perceiving that movements which are not in obedience to the primary psychic force are those that promise success. It may be called *psychic attraction*, or the faculty of converting means into ends and diverting the psychic force from the latter to the former. The means is made for the time being the object of desire, and as such is directly sought. But in order to this it must be first seen by the mind, which must possess a distinct motor apparatus for switching off the train of ideas from the track that leads to the end to the one that leads to the means. From another point of view this kind of intuition may be called a *perception of relations*. Perception proper, as defined in Chap. V, is an entirely different thing. It merely notes the nature of an object, either directly or through its appropriate medium, in cases where the impression produces an indifferent sensation. It is also different from my understanding of the German term *Anschauung*, which, as Kant says "relates immediately to the object," although this object need not, as in the case of perception, be material, but may be either time or space. This doubtless comes much nearer to the attribute in question and by a slight extension of the Kantian definition may be made to include it. But intuition as here used is always a *perception of relations*, not merely in time and space, but relations of resistance and direction. Moreover, I am not aware that Kant, although he translates the German word by the Latin *intuitus*, has ever applied it to the primary and practical quality of mind here described. It is with him a purely metaphysical conception, furnishing through the senses the objects of the mind in its complex processes of ideation, reason, and thought. The new intuition is of a higher order. It employs the senses but is not directly derived from them. It is a form of thought, is under subjection to the will, is the product of ever-pressing and constantly unsatisfied desire, and therefore has its origin in the emotional sense. It is much more closely linked to the great subjective psychic trunk of the mind than any of the so-called faculties treated in the books. It is, in fact the intellect itself in its fundamental form, is much older than the reason, and is the parent of all the later faculties of abstraction and reflection.

CHAPTER XXII.

INTUITIVE PERCEPTION.

It is only under the guidance of the intellectual faculty that the first step in this direction can be taken. The means necessary to be employed differ so widely from the ends that intellectual foresight can alone insure their adoption even in the simplest cases. The acts really required are so wholly unlike those which would be required if the end were directly sought, that a highly developed rational faculty is demanded in all beings that are capable of performing them. When a being, endowed with desires to be satisfied, is made acquainted with the existence of a desirable object, it is immediately prompted to move, or to put forth efforts, in the direction of that object. To such a being, another, desiring the same object, that should turn away from it and commence making adjustments in other objects lying about, would, to use the language of fable, appear extremely stupid. It would be an *unnatural* action, i. e., it would be an *artificial* one. If successful in securing the end, unattainable by direct effort, it would be an exercise of true art, and would involve an acquaintance with the principles of true science. — *Dynamic Sociology*, II, 380.

Τὴν δὲ πρώτην ὁρμήν φασι τὸ ζῷον ἴσχειν ἐπὶ τὸ τηρεῖν ἑαυτό. — DIOGENES LAERTIUS : *Zeno*, 52.

Nulla virtus potest prior hac (nempe conatu sese conservandi) concipi. — SPINOZA : *Ethica*, Pars IV, *Propositio* XXII.

Die Nahrung muss daher aufgesucht, ausgewählt werden, von dem Punkt an, wo das Thier dem Ei oder Mutterleibe, in welchem es erkenntnisslos vegetirte, sich entwunden hat. Dadurch wird hier die Bewegung auf Motive und wegen dieser die Erkenntniss nothwendig, welche also eintritt als ein auf dieser Stufe der Objektivation des Willens erfordertes Hülfsmittel, μηχανη, zur Erhaltung des Individuums und Fortpflanzung des Geschlechts. Sie tritt hervor, repräsentirt durch das Gehirn oder ein grösseres Ganglion, eben wie jede andere Bestrebung oder Bestimmung des sich objektivirenden Willens durch ein Organ repräsentirt ist, d. h. für die Vorstellung sich als ein Organ darstellt. — SCHOPENHAUER : *Welt als Wille*, I, 179.

Selbst der Verstand der Thiere wird durch die Noth bedeutend gesteigert, so dass sie in schwierigen Fällen Dinge leisten, über die wir erstaunen:

z. B. fast alle berechnen, dass es sicherer ist, nicht zu fliehen, wann sie sich ungesehen glauben: daher liegt der Hase still in der Furche des Feldes und lässt den Jäger dicht an sich vorbeigehen; Insekten, wenn sie nicht entrinnen können, stellen sich todt u. s. f. Genauer kann man diesen Einfluss kennen lernen durch die specielle Selbstbildungsgeschichte des Wolfes, unter dem Sporn der grossen Schwierigkeit seiner Stellung in civilisirten Europa: sie ist zu finden im zweiten Briefe des vortrefflichen Buches von Leroy, *Lettres sur l'intelligence et la perfectibilité des animaux*. Gleich darauf folgt, im dritten Briefe, die hohe Schule des Fuchses, welcher, in gleich schwieriger Lage, viel geringere Körperkräfte hat, die bei ihm durch grössern Verstand ersetzt sind, der aber doch erst durch den beständigen Kampf mit der Noth einerseits und der Gefahr andererseits, also unter dem Sporn des Willens, den hohen Grad von Schlauheit erreicht, welcher ihn, besonders im Alter, auszeichnet. — SCHOPENHAUER: *Welt als Wille*, II, 248–249.

It is the peculiarity of the main branch of the intellectual faculty, intuition, that it was developed under the spur of strong feeling or passion, i.e., of desire. It was a product of and outgrowth from this as the main trunk of the mind, of which intellect may be considered a branch. It came as a last resort to the assistance of the psychic force in its effort to secure the chief ends of being. As these chief ends are sustenance, safety, and reproduction, it is the desires which lead to these ends that are strongest and that therefore mainly call out this method for their satisfaction. The several stages attained in the development of this faculty, above those of mere exploration and simple animal intuition, go by different names. In speaking of their manifestation in animals the terms *sagacity* and *cunning* are commonly used, although both these terms are also applied to men. Among the definitions of "sagacious" in the Century Dictionary we find: "Keenly perceptive; discerning, as by some exceptionally developed or extraordinary natural power . . . having keen practical sense," etc. One finds no attempt to analyze these terms. They are regarded as simple, and are really well understood by every one. The intellectual act which they describe is as direct or unmediated as perception or *Anschauung*. It consists, as does the simpler intuition, of a perception of relations of resistance, direction, etc., implies cognition of properties and forces, and always connects these with utility, i.e., is always practical.

In the cases considered in the last chapter the properties and relations involved are those of inanimate objects, but in sagacity and cunning they are largely those of other organisms whose activities are conceived as uniform under like circumstances. Where this quality is exercised in the interest of safety, in escaping danger, the degree of penetration is usually, but not always, lower than when exercised in the interest of sustentation or reproduction. Creatures in which it is not developed have no means of insuring safety except in direct flight from the source of danger, but in some the modes of escape become indirect. When pursued by dogs certain birds, as the ruffed grouse (*Bonasa umbellus*), simply fly into trees, perceiving that dogs do not climb. They continue flying if flushed by men. The pinnated grouse habitually hides ("skulks") in the grass and displays great power of assuming invisible attitudes. I once saw one of these birds alight on an almost barren spot between two plowed areas. Proceeding to the place I searched during fifteen minutes in the immediate vicinity, scanning the ground carefully. At last the reflection of light from its eye betrayed it to my view, and I could then see that the entire bird was in plain sight and was so near that I killed it with my gun-barrel. I had stepped over it several times. Hares will pretend to follow a hedge, but finally go through it and return past their pursuers on the other side. The habits of various birds and animals of the gregarious kinds in appointing sentinels, flying in triangles, etc., are familiar examples.

The pursuit of food by herbivorous and granivorous animals usually calls this faculty very slightly into exercise, or not at all, but carnivorous animals display it in a high degree. They *know*, as we say, what their victims will do under given circumstances and devise means to prevent their escape. Stealth and slyness in approaching them, advantage taken of the time and place of attack, are among the commoner modes in which they manifest their cunning. The fox is usually taken as the type of such animals, and similar traits in men gain for them the name of being "foxy," while to this whole class of acts the term "vulpinism" is sometimes applied.

But it is in connection with the function of reproduction that this quality is probably called forth in the most effective manner. This may seem a surprising statement, but anyone who has read Darwin's chapters on sexual selection as an element in the "descent of man" cannot fail to realize its truth. Here it is no longer an effort to outwit other animals much inferior in this power. It is necessary to measure swords with others of the same species and the faculty is sharpened to the utmost extent. The rivalry of the males for the possession of the females is of the most intense nature. Not only must they understand the ways of their own sex, but they must cater to the caprices of the females. Only a small proportion can at best succeed. The greater number in most species are doomed to failure and celibacy. The instinct is the strongest of all passions. The prize is infinitely great and the effort correspondingly supreme. Every art is called into play. Every quality of attraction and fascination is displayed. Rivals must not only be discomfited in open battle, they must be *circumvented* in secret intrigue. Along therefore with the development of strength and weapons to overcome antagonists, and of size, beauty, and grace to charm the females there goes an especial and rapid development of psychic power to secure in indirect ways what is unattainable in direct ways. It is such facts that have led me to suspect, as stated in Chap. XIV, that brain development may be regarded as a true secondary sexual character, belonging primarily to males, like tusks, antlers, gaudy tail-feathers, and superior size, but reflected, as many such are, in a feebler manner in the female anatomy.

But in the females also, besides the same efforts as the males to obtain food, a certain mental power of an indirect kind is exercised in the course of these courtships. The forms of refusal are manifold and require skill. During the greater part of the life of any female animal the attentions of the males are intolerable while their desires are uninterrupted. Something more than brute force is required to prevent violence being done to nature. For this numerous arts are resorted to, and cunning devices contrived. But even at the proper time her preferences must be respected and unwelcome suitors must be successfully thwarted in their persistent efforts. To accomplish all this involves the practice of innumerable wiles and strategems. She becomes coy, artful, and deceptive.

To this may properly be added the influence of parental care in developing the intuitive faculty, and here it expends itself almost exclusively on the female. Usually, it is true, the mother knows no better way than direct open attack upon anything that threatens to harm her offspring and relies on violence and fury to frighten enemies even a hundred fold her match in physical strength. But this is usually accompanied by the device, aided by special muscular development, of assuming a formidable mien by the erection of hairs or the ruffling of feathers. The most important of these modes of protecting offspring, however, is the wholly indirect one of feigning. Almost all birds and many mammals habitually feign lameness on the approach of an enemy, and thus seek, usually with success, to decoy the enemy into a fruitless pursuit of themselves until far away from the spot where the young ones are being kept. There is great diversity in these evolutions of the female, and although, like most of the other acts of this general class among animals, they come at length to constitute true instincts, still their development has involved cerebral modifications in the general direction of cephalization and in the special direction of building up coördinating convolutions of the class now under consideration.

It is only in some of the mentally highest animals, especially domestic dogs, elephants, and a few horses, that the clearest cases of true sagacity are to be found. Anecdotes relating to such cases, often unreliable, but too numerous and common to be ignored, are familiar to everyone. How far the principle has been carried in other wild animals than the elephant it is not easy to learn. The following experience of my own may be recorded for what it is worth : In the summer of 1875 while making botanical collections in Rabbit Valley on Fremont River, Utah, the camp was several times invaded by coyotes (the common prairie wolf, *Canis latrans*) during the absence of myself and my assistant, and these animals would howl round us nights, sometimes approaching quite closely. I finally set my fowling piece, both barrels loaded with buckshot, in a gulch among the sagebrush a hundred yards from the tent, attaching a piece of fresh meat to a string twenty yards long, which at the opposite end passed round the stem of a bush and was tied to both triggers. The least jerk on the string would fire off the gun which was carefully aimed in the direction of, and a little over, the meat. The next morning tracks were seen all about the place, but meat, string, and gun were untouched. The second morning I found the meat gone and the string bitten off. The meat had been dragged six inches toward the gun, as shown by the mark it made in the loose alkaline soil, and the string was slack. The gun had not been discharged. I renewed the meat and reset the gun, and the third night I heard the report of the gun in the night. It was moonlight and I went to the spot as quickly as possible, but as no dead wolves were to be found I left matters till morning when I found that the operation of the previous night had been repeated, but that by some accident the string had been pulled and the gun discharged, probably without injury to the animal, as the string now lay out of range. I continued for several nights to repeat the experiment with somewhat varying results, but did not succeed in killing any wolves. The tracks showed that on the first night they had traversed the length of the string and around the gun, evidently exploring the situation thoroughly and acting upon the knowledge they possessed.

Quite recently I have had an almost equally interesting experience in trying to entrap a wary rat that found its way into my cellar. After my most ingenious devices had failed and I had nearly given up the attempt, I succeeded, as it would seem, by very lack of precaution, the animal perhaps going to the length of supposing that nothing that I made no attempt to conceal could be attended with danger.

The faculty of cunning or sagacity manifests itself in a variety of modes depending on the animal, the circumstances, etc., and language seeks to express these by numerous words with different shades of meaning. The terms most commonly applied to animals, most of them also applicable to men, are : sly, artful, knowing, wily, crafty, subtle, adroit, etc., besides the regular adjectives cunning and sagacious. The general homogeneity, however, of all these terms is obvious, and the central idea which they embody is that of *indirection.* They have a common object, that of successful effort to satisfy desire, and a common method, that of taking advantage of perceived relations. But the intellectual act is simple, and may at this stage be called *intuitive perception.*

It may now be studied at a slightly more advanced stage, as manifested by man. Without wishing to imply that there is any generic difference between animal and human intuition, but merely in deference to the prevailing opinion that man is especially a rational being, I will call the latter *intuitive reason.*

CHAPTER XXIII.

INTUITIVE REASON.

Under the law of Natural Selection, everything is an advantage which serves to protect individuals from destruction from outer enemies, both organic and inorganic, or which enables them better to secure the means of subsistence. A race of large apes living in the vast forests of Central Africa or tropical Asia, where lions, tigers, leopards, and many other large and ferocious carnivora abound, would be the constant prey of these beasts, and especially liable to have their young carried off and devoured, thus rendering the existence of the species precarious. Lacking most of the means of defense, as well as of escape necessary to prevent destruction from such creatures, the only substitute possible for these is increased sagacity or cunning in outwitting their enemies. But increased sagacity can only come of increased brain-mass in relation to size of body. These creatures must have constantly found themselves "put to their wits' end" to devise means of preventing such attacks, and we seem fully justified in supposing that, from the recurrence of such efforts, in which bodily efficiency was not, and mental efficiency was, solely relied on, the development of the cerebral lobes went on rapidly under the law of direct adaptation. But, from the increased protection thus rendered both to adults and to offspring, the number of the latter enabled to survive was increased, and these inherited the increased brain-power of their parents, and again transmitted it, with an additional increment, to their offspring.

In addition to this negative influence, which was perhaps the strongest, there was also the positive influence exerted in the same direction in the struggles of these creatures for the means of subsistence. The discontinuance of their arboreal habits put a vast amount of their natural food beyond their reach. The rich nuts that hung from the branches of tall trees, the dates and other delicious fruits of the palm, the plantain, and the banana, must now be watched till, ripened by time, they fall to the ground, if happily the lesser monkeys, the squirrels, and the bears have not already devoured them all. These losses must be made up. This can only be done by increased cunning; and here, again, the direct impulse to further brain-development is exerted. From these two influences acting in the same direction, aided by natural selection, the entire amount of cerebral increase, with its corresponding cranial enlargement, necessary to bridge over the chasm between the true ape and the true man, between the highest animal and the lowest human brain, can be readily accounted for without exceeding the time-limits within which geology requires this differentiation to have taken place. — *Dynamic Sociology*, I, 428–429.

Diesen letzten Schritt in der Ausdehnung und Vervollkommnung des Gehirns, und damit in der Erhöhung der Erkenntnisskräfte, thut die Natur, wie alle übrigen, bloss in folge der erhöhten Bedürfnisse, also zum Dienste des Willens. Was dieser im Menschen bezweckt und erreicht, ist zwar im Wesentlichen dasselbe und nicht mehr, als was auch im Thiere sein Ziel ist: Ernährung und Fortpflanzung. Aber durch die Organisation des Menschen wurden die Erfordernisse zur Erreichung jenes Ziels so sehr vermehrt, gesteigert und specificirt, dass, zur Erreichung des Zwecks, eine ungleich beträchtlichere Erhöhung des Intellekts, als die bisherigen Stufen darboten, nothwendig, oder wenigstens das leichteste Mittel war. Da nun aber der Intellekt, seinem Wesen zufolge, ein Werkzeug von höchst vielseitigem Gebrauch und auf die verschiedenartigsten Zwecke gleich anwendbar ist; so konnte die Natur, ihrem Geist der Sparsamkeit getreu, alle Forderungen der so mannigfach gewordenen Bedürfnisse nunmehr ganz allein durch ihn decken. — SCHOPENHAUER: *Welt als Wille*, II, 316–317.

For then they glorie, then they boaste, and cracke that they haue plaied the men in deede, when they haue so ouercommen, as no other liuing creature but onely man could: that is to saye, by the mighte and puisaunce of wit. For with bodily strength (say they) beares, lions, boores, wulfes, dogges, and other wild beastes do fight. And as the moste part of them do passe vs in strength and fierce courage, so in wit and reason we be much stronger than they all. — THOMAS MORE: *Utopia*, pp. 133–134.

If persons are helped in their worldly career by their virtues, so are they, and perhaps quite as often, by their vices: by servility and sycophancy, by hard-hearted and close-fisted selfishness, by the permitted lies and tricks of trade, by gambling speculations, not seldom by downright knavery. — JOHN STUART MILL: *Chapters on Socialism*.

L'esprit est toujours la dupe du coeur. — LA ROCHEFOUCAULD: *Maxime* 102.

While cunning and sagacity are attributes of both animals and men, shrewdness and tact are generally limited to the latter. They represent a somewhat higher stage of development of the same faculty of mind. They are usually, though not necessarily, applied to human acts that relate to sustentation, especially in its derivative forms. The pursuit of subsistence, which is direct in animals and the lowest human types, early becomes indirect in the social state. Instead of pursuing, seizing and devouring prey, or searching, finding, and eating the vegetable products of the earth, man soon acquired the habit of seeking opportunities for securing permanent supplies of subsistence, a step which is indeed taken through the aid of instincts by many animals. But with man in the social state, however primitive, foresight was exercised, which is itself a form of the intuitive faculty, and the habit of making *provision* for the future arose. This had the immediate effect to render his wants unlimited by his immediate appetite. The consequence was that his desire for the means of subsistence, instead of being periodical, became continous and the pursuit of this end was incessant. Other collateral wants also arose as the necessary concomitants of social existence, especially in varying degrees those of clothing and shelter. A crude esthetic sentiment must have also been very early developed, for no tribe of savages has yet been found so low as not to be fond of ornaments, however grotesque, and where clothing was not needed decorations were demanded and sought with zeal. Other objects of desire multiplied themselves and their possession became an end of effort. Slowly the notion of property came into being and in acquiring this, as history shows, the larger share of all human energy has been absorbed. The ruling passion has from a time long anterior to any recorded annals always been proprietary acquisition. Pari passu with the development of this passion there also proceeded the development of that faculty which was most potent in securing its gratification. Both the passion and the means of satisfying it were conditions to the development of society itself, and rightly viewed they have also been leading factors in civilization. But here, as man must cope with man, a struggle went on similar, only on a higher intellectual plane, to that which goes on in the animal world, a veritable struggle for existence.

In this great struggle brute force played a diminishing part, and mind an increasing one. Low cunning and animal sagacity, though very prominent, were more and more supplanted by more refined and subtle manifestations of the same psychic principle. This advance was greatly accelerated by the growth of institutions and the establishment of codes of conduct requisite to life in collectivity. The rude animal methods were intolerable, and by natural selection, if not otherwise, society discarded them. Something less objectionable and more refined must control the relations of men in the social state. But while social regulation grew stronger human acquisitiveness strengthened also. With the legal protection of property its desirability increased and every art was resorted to in the universal effort to obtain it. No combination can be conceived of better calculated to call out, develop, and perfect a mental faculty than the prizes and temptations of the social state.

In Dynamic Sociology (Chap. VII, Vol. I, pp. 497–597) I have discussed somewhat exhaustively the law and the various modes of acquisition that prevail in the social world. At present it is only the peculiar principle involved in all this that it is sought to detect. The faculty of intuitive perception which was seen to prevail in the higher animals has now adapted itself to man, to society, and to regulative institutions. The pursuit of subsistence has become the pursuit of the *means* of subsistence, and of enjoyment in general. Animal activity has become industrial activity, and the general term applied to industrial activity is *business*. The great aim and object of life is success in business. Social regulation renders the animal methods unsuccessful and human methods are the ones chiefly employed. But the psychic principle remains the same.

To mere subsistence, i. e., just so much as is necessary to life, considered as the end of effort, there must now be added a great number of things that are not required for that end. Everyone knows how in legal interpretation the word "necessaries" has expanded, and how it is varied even in the same country according to the social standing of the individual. But while things that were not necessary in one age become so in another, and those not necessary for one class are considered necessary for another, there are innumerable objects which no law will declare necessaries that are nevertheless desired even more strongly than many that are really necessary to life—luxuries, refinements, indulgences. An immense number of new desires unknown in the lower stages were created by social existence and civilized life. These include all those enumerated in Chapters IX and X, and many not mentioned there. Besides the heightened and intensified forms of the love of acquisition growing out of the struggle to preserve life, there had been developed the higher desires to which the reproductive instincts gave rise, including the passion of individual love, and the emotions arising through family relationships. Add to these the esthetic, moral, and intellectual cravings, all vehemently asserting themselves and demanding satisfaction.

The indirect method which best insured success in business is perhaps most frequently expressed by the word *shrewdness.* The relations perceived are more numerous and complicated than those for which cunning is sufficient. They are largely the acts of men and presuppose a knowledge of human nature. It is astonishing to observe how little the majority really know of human nature and how easy it is to take advantage of this general ignorance. The prevailing optimism is the chief element that blinds most persons in these matters, and acts, which to the good observer are obviously done from purely selfish motives, are so done as to produce the general belief in their complete disinterestedness. This explains the surprising gullibility of the general public, so obvious that it is common to speak of an actual "love of humbug." A great part of all that is said and done in society proceeds from this self-interest and requires to be interpreted and corrected by this equation.

Besides the *suppressio veri* and *suggestio falsi*, there are all the other arts of speech which have given rise to the French proverb, that language was given us to conceal our thoughts.[1] There is also the art of silence, the reticent, non-committal mood. It is often true from the standpoint of self-interest that where speech would be silver or some baser metal, silence is golden. Nothing is more common than for mediocre persons to possess the shrewdness of knowing that silence will gain them a reputation for wisdom.[2] The assumption of a dignity they do not possess secures to many what volubility would deprive them of. Such persons, while they may really know very little, know this one thing and put this knowledge to the best use. This suggests the important fact so generally overlooked by the modern philosophers who argue for the fullest play in society of the law of natural survival, that fitness to survive does not, as they maintain, depend upon *intelligence* but upon shrewdness, which may be accompanied with very little intelligence. It is the faculty which we are considering that has at its various stages secured success in life, and it is the same that insures success in business and in all the enterprises of civilized men. It is an entirely different thing from intelligence, and, except in one of its phases, hereafter to be considered, it is the lowest and least really superior attribute of mind.

Among the derivative desires that have grown up in society the most powerful is doubtless ambition. This was especially developed under the influence of government, which was one of the earliest of human institutions. It here takes the form

[1] Ils ne se servent de la pensée que pour autoriser leurs injustices, et n'emploient les paroles que pour déguiser leurs pensées. — Voltaire: Dialogue xiv. Le Chapon et la Poularde. Œuvres Complètes, Vol. XXXVI, p. 100.

[2] Stultus tacebit? pro sapiente habebitur. — Publius Syrus.

(Let a fool hold his tongue and he will pass for a sage. Lyman's Translation, No. 914. The Moral Sayings of Publius Syrus, from the Latin. By D. Lyman, Jun., Cleveland, 1856.)

Taciturnitas stulto homini pro sapientia est. — Publius Syrus.

(Taciturnity is the dunce's wisdom. Lyman's Translation, No. 931.)

of love of power and its various manifestations have played a principal rôle in the history of man. Coarse and simple in despotic governments, therefore making little use of the indirect method, it has been curbed and restricted by its oppressed victims until in modern more or less representative governments it has been compelled to employ this method almost exclusively. It is an excellent illustration of the principle now under consideration on account of the great number and subtle character of the forms it has assumed. There is no better subject upon which to exercise the pure intellect than what is called a people. Unthinking and unorganized they are easily managed and incapable, except in extreme cases, of perceiving the motives of rulers, still less of acting concertedly to thwart their schemes. The astute monarch or politician always seeks to make it believed that he is acting for their good, and enough will usually credit him to prevent the action of the remainder. The politicians and demagogues of any country are simply the persons who combine with an unscrupulous love of power or desire for emolument from the public revenues, the highest development of the animal side of the intellect. They are the ones who, from the strictly biological standpoint, are the fittest to survive in society. Those therefore who teach sociology from the laws of biology should not only treat them as the highest types but should welcome them as the most perfect examples of social development. It is thoroughly inconsistent in this school of philosophers to denounce this class as they do, since if there are any who deserve to be here and to be let alone they are the ones.

Different from, and really higher than the tricky, wire-pulling politician, and more nearly on the level of the ambitious but discreet and prudent ruler or statesman, is the successful diplomat. Diplomacy is a typical form of the original intellectual faculty in one of its highest stages. Whether it take the shape of Machiavellian intrigue and disregard of truth and principle, or be conducted honorably and with patriotic motives, it involves intuitive penetration of a high order and, ably employed, proves one of the greatest elements of national success and safety. It need not be said that diplomacy is also extensively practiced by individuals in all the minor affairs of life.

One other application of this principle may profitably be mentioned. The encroachment of tribe upon tribe, and the desire of the ruling class to extend territorial boundaries, made war one of the first concomitants of the social condition, and it continues to be a leading feature of human history. Although depending chiefly on brute force it soon called in the aid of intellectual direction. The particular form which this here assumed goes by the name of *strategy*. The effect of numbers, bravery, and superior weapons may be greatly increased by judicious selection in the time and method of attack. When an inferior army out-generals and defeats a superior one, it is because mind has been at work, and the quality of mind by which the result has been attained is precisely the one that secures success in business, in politics, or in diplomacy. Shrewdness, tact, policy, demogogy, diplomacy, strategy, are only so many applications of the one principle, only so many varying manifestations of the primary intellectual faculty under correspondingly changed circumstances.

If the name intuitive perception may appropriately be given to those manifestations of this faculty in animals and the lower types of men, that of *intuitive reason* will properly apply to the more involved process which accomplishes the same purposes in the higher types of men when dealing with the complicated conditions that society creates. It is still a perception of relations, chiefly of resistance and direction, but the relations are more remote and obscure, more complex and recondite, and not only must the degree of penetration be much greater but the tortuous avenues through which it is necessary to peer, prolong somewhat the act of intuitive vision and raise it to the grade of a sort of reasoning process which justifies a new name, provided the central truth be not lost from view that the difference is wholly one of degree and not at all of kind.

CHAPTER XXIV.

PRINCIPLE OF DECEPTION.

This law [the principle of deception] arises with the development of the intellectual faculty, and, properly viewed, it constitutes the essential form in which that faculty everywhere manifests itself, although this truth is masked by the great variety existing among the objects toward which intellectual operations are directed. — *Dynamic Sociology*, I, 501.

The normal operations of the intellect, as distinguished from those of the emotions, and whereby it accomplishes so much greater results, are essentially of this character, so that it may be said that ***invention is deception.*** By it the forces of nature are ensnared and circumvented. Language itself enforces this truth. The methods of art are ***artifices***, and its mode of procedure is ***artful.*** Machines are ***machinations.*** Primitive man had early to learn that to live he must deceive, and, although this principle has never found expression in any code of ethics, it has found unceasing application throughout history. — *Dynamic Sociology*, I, 502.

Notwithstanding the fine array of maxims so constantly quoted to encourage honesty in the mutual dealings of individuals, scarcely a transaction is ever consummated without some form of deception having been practiced. What is understood as the ability to "drive a bargain" is nothing more or less than a certain species of cunning, in making the facts appear in some way different from what they are, whereby others are somewhat deceived and beguiled into paying for an article, perhaps not more than it is worth, but more than they otherwise would have done. It may not be too much to say that very few dealers who gain their livelihood in trade can afford to be strictly honest in all things according to the received standards of honesty. It is a fair subject for doubt whether such a course would not in many cases be ruinous to their interests . . . Every one expects every one else to practice a certain amount of what is thought by each in his own case to be justifiable deception, and one who should fail to do so would scarcely be adjudged possessed of the full complement of intellectual powers, or, as it is called, wits. For so insensibly does open falsehood shade off into the mere exercise of the normal degree of intelligence that no absolute line of demarkation can be drawn. — *Dynamic Sociology*, I, 511–512.

Complete truthfulness is one of the rarest of virtues. Even those who regard themselves as absolutely truthful are daily guilty of over-statements and of under-statements. Exaggeration is almost universal. The perpetual use of the word "very," where the occasion does not call for it, shows how widely diffused and confirmed is the habit of misrepresentation. And this habit sometimes goes along with the loudest denunciations of falsehood. — HERBERT SPENCER: *Principles of Ethics*, I, p. 400.

L'hypocrisie est un hommage que le vice rend à la vertu. — LA ROCHEFOUCAULD: *Maxime* 218.

Nos vertus ne sont le plus souvent que des vices déguisés. — LA ROCHEFOUCAULD.

Ce que le monde nomme vertu n'est d'ordinaire qu'un fantôme formé par nos passions, à qui on donne un nom honnête pour faire impunément ce qu'on veut. *Ibid.*

And, after all, what is a lie? 'Tis but
The truth in masquerade; and I defy
Historians, heroes, lawyers, priests, to put
A fact without some leaven of a lie.
BYRON: *Don Juan*, Canto xi, Stanza 37.

It cannot have escaped the intelligent reader that there is involved in all the mental acts discussed in the last two chapters a form of deception, and that this constitutes the kernel of the matter and the true key to their successfulness. The intuitive faculty, so far as it has been hitherto considered, expends itself chiefly upon sentient beings and is directed to securing advantage to the agent at the expense of other feeling creatures. As no feeling creature desires this to happen it is necessary that the act be performed against the inclination of those that are the losers by it. These latter must in some way be prevented from knowing what its effect is to be, otherwise they would resist or escape it. This idea lurks in all such words as cunning, crafty, artful, wily, arch, tricky, sly, astute, designing, intriguing, smart, shrewd, etc. There is often little in the etymology of a word, but sometimes it well illustrates the history of an idea. The word *shrewd* is a good example of the latter case. It is derived from *shrew*, which originally meant a wicked or evil person, sometimes the devil. Its early use was in the sense of evil malignant, or malicious, and its present milder meaning was only gradually acquired. The French word that nearly corresponds to it, shows its origin still more clearly. It is *malin*. The American use of the word *smart*, which is nearly the same as the English *clever*, seems to have arisen from the original sense of sharp, cutting or pungent, qualities which produce the sensation called a smart. In fact the word *sharp* applied to persons is rapidly passing into the same sense, and from it has been formed the derivative noun *sharper* which conveys no other idea.

The cunning of the fox and other animals is chiefly a mode of deceiving the creatures that constitute their prey. In such cases the animals deceived are less sagacious than those that circumvent and capture them, but the mother bird that feigns being wounded furnishes an instance in which deception practiced by a mentally inferior creature is often successful against the cunning of a mentally superior one. In fact so much is deception the essence of the principle that as a rule the greater the deception the greater the success.[1]

[1] Mr. Spencer in the excellent treatment of the subject of "veracity" which he gives in Chapter IX of the first volume of his Principles of Ethics, has greatly strengthened this point of view from the side of primitive peoples. He seems somewhat surprised to find that, though not according to any fixed rule, the simpler minded hill tribes are the most veracious, and the more intelligent coast tribes add untruthfulness to their other vices. He even shows that the higher races, including his own, display this quality to a shameful degree, especially in their dealings with inferior ones. All this is what should be expected if deception is the essential element in intellectual exercise. This is clearly brought out in the case of the people of Uganda among whom "a successful liar is considered a smart, clever fellow"; of the Central Americans who say of a cheat: "what a clever fellow"; of the Philippine Islanders who do not "appear to regard lying as a sin, but rather as a legitimate, though cunning, convenience"; and still more clearly from the opposite point of view by the Sowrahs, who "do not know how to tell a lie. They are not sufficiently civilized to be able to invent"; while "a Mahâr [Parwari] is such a fool that he will tell the truth without any reason at all."

In seeking for the cause which determines the relative veracity of races, he arrives at the conclusion "that it is the presence or absence of despotic rule which

In the various modes of acquisition pursued by men in the social state the principle of deception plays an important rôle. The powerful influence of the optimistic habit of thought, which is the latest form of the primitive illusion of the desires, or assertion of the will, blinds nearly everyone to the great prevalence of deception among civilized men, and makes the unthinking masses easy victims to the smaller class who learn to depend upon this method for improving their condition. The almost universal end pursued by men is riches, wealth, property, competency, or by whatever name it may be called. Poverty has become a disgrace and is so feared and dreaded that any means of avoiding it will be resorted to. Therefore those who have little or nothing exhaust every resource to make it appear that they have all they desire. In fact it may be remarked here, that notwithstanding the carnival of desires that is held inside of every human being, very little of it all comes into view on account of the systematic deception constantly practiced to prevent its observance. No one wants others to know that he is suffering, especially that he has wants that he cannot supply, and therefore those that one meets who seem to be fairly swimming in an *embarras de richesses* may be at the same moment in the very throes of agony which they adroitly conceal. It is not always want, poverty, or impecuniosity. It may be domestic trouble, shame over some act known to be against the accepted social code, fear of detection in something that would be ruin if found out.

leads to prevalent falsehood or prevalent truth," and shows with considerable force that lying is a normal result of intimidation and abuse, as is well illustrated by the East African slaves of whom Livingstone says: "One can scarcely induce a slave to translate anything truly: he is so intent on thinking of what will please." I was struck by the same fact among the freedmen of the South at the close of the civil war which resulted in their emancipation. There is no doubt that liberty inspires truthfulness as it inspires other manly qualities, while slavery and tyranny are generally demoralizing. But this only goes to prove that deception in every form is resorted to as an instrument of protection from danger, and is the normal and legitimate exercise of the primal intellect which was developed for no other purpose.

The general concealment of emotion of every kind belongs to this category. The display of feeling is a mark of weakness and tells against success. The feigning of indifference to everything is found to be policy. One who seems dejected is classed as deficient. It is human nature to lift the strong, and neglect or crush the weak. This seems a strong indictment but it is true. Upon what basis does it rest? Doubtless it is vaguely felt that failure is the result of inferiority. One who cannot gain a livelihood is assumed to lack the requisites of personal character for doing so. No one wishes to expend energy on anything that is unworthy. The possession of a fair share of this world's goods has come to be the general mark and measure of character. Carrying it a step further back, since it is a certain mental quality that succeeds in obtaining and retaining wealth, it is evident that it is this quality that is popularly taken as the criterion of worth. There is an instinctive feeling that the intuitive faculty which insures success is the one great element of value in human character, and it is respected accordingly.

It is this attitude of the mind toward the exercise of these mental qualities that has enabled them to take an even more prominent place in social life than they had in pre-social or subhuman life. Joined with the prevailing credulity, gullibility, and optimistic acquiescence, they grew in civilized man with unprecedented exuberance. The consequence is that the whole fabric of society is honeycombed with deception. Life in separate houses, rendering social contact only possible under circumstances favorable to concealment, favors and fosters this tendency. It has often been observed that where men formerly dwelling in the same community are by force of circumstances compelled to come out of their civilized habits and associate more in a state of nature so that all their acts and thoughts are exposed, their true character thus revealed is found to be entirely different from what it had been supposed to be. I made a study of this when in the army, camping and fighting on a level with my townsmen who occupied very different social stations at home. While some who stood at the bottom of the social ladder were seen to possess unexpected sterling qualities, others who had been rated highest proved poltroons and cowards, while still others of the latter class turned out sniveling grumblers. Under the far more trying circumstances of great hardship, suffering, and danger the golden grains of character are still more searchingly sifted from the dust. In civilized life this cannot be done, and what we see on the surface is no indication of that which really exists. Any word, look, or act is likely to be a feint. Everywhere there is artifice, counterfeit, simulation, disguise, sham, and imposture. This, where special opportunity permits, takes the more open and offensive forms of fraud, trickery, swindling, quackery, charlatanism, humbug, and jugglery. While these practises go on only in a mild form with the great mass of mankind they assume a malignant form with a large and ever present minority. These constitute the parasitic class of society, those who, as it is said, live by their wits. Social institutions favor the existence of such a class, and they are the ones who have most to do in framing and perpetuating such institutions. There is, for example, scarcely a doubt that if nine out of every ten members of the legal profession were eliminated entirely from it and turned into some useful occupation the ends of justice would thereby be immensely the gainer and thousands of laborers would be added to the industrial pursuits. But this is the class whom the masses intrust with the framing of their laws, and as long as they continue to do so they must pay the penalty of their stupidity. It is the same in the whole department of exchange, although here intelligent coöperation would be needed to insure success. The other great department which abounds in parasites is that of finance, including the innumerable clever schemes for gaining wealth by the negotiation of all kinds of paper. But this by no means exhausts the list. Witness the so-called real estate "booms," stock-watering schemes, "rings," trusts, combines, "corners" in grain, railroad "deals," and so on to the end. In fact there would be no stopping until all monopolies were included.

These are all perfectly legitimate modes of acquisition so long as we consider sociology from the biological standpoint and admit no other than biological dynamics into the account. It is the method of nature. In the animal world there is no other. There it is called the survival of the favored races in the struggle for existence. Here it is called the law of competition. Animal cunning is succeded by human ingenuity and intuitive perception becomes intuitive reason. Both belong to the normal and primary intellectual faculty, both involve the principle of deception which is the essence of the process employed. It is due to the biological school of sociologists to say that their position relative to this industrial parasitism, if it may be so called, unlike that relative to political parasitism mentioned in the last chapter, is logical, and they teach that it should be let alone and allowed to take its course. Those who by whatever method can gain most of the world's products are those fittest to survive and those who can obtain none deserve, according to the ethics of biology, to die. The worst are thereby weeded out of society and the best preserved, while the exalted faculty which makes this possible is still more highly developed.

CHAPTER XXV.

INTUITIVE JUDGMENT.

It is very possible for impulses and intuitions to be safer than the most deliberate judgment. . . . Everybody knows how, on many great political and judicial questions, the slow detail and careful technicality of legislators and judges do violence to truth and justice, while the public mind has seen the justice of the case from the first, and suffers sore disappointment at the manner in which truth has been smothered under the forms of logic and of law. — *Dynamic Sociology*, II, 327.

Only a very small proportion of our actions are directed to new conditions; experience has already determined the proper conduct in all the circumstances upon which our preservation and well-being most directly depend; and action in these circumtances does not demand comparison and judgment, while it must usually be so prompt as to forbid deliberation or thought. The power of quick and proper action in the innumerable exigencies of ordinary life, independent of reflection, is at least equally important with the power to extend our field of rational action. — W. K. Brooks: *Popular Science Monthly*, June, 1879 (Vol. XV, pp. 154–155).

Experience of the order of events has shown that under certain circumstances, of frequent occurrence, certain conduct is proper and conducive to welfare, while its opposite is hurtful. This experience being constantly repeated, the tendency to do the proper thing when the circumstances occur gradually takes the shape of an instinct, intuition, habit, or law of duty. Hencefoward, all persons who have the impulse which has thus been formed will act in the same way when the circumstances arise, but two persons who have not the impulse will follow their individual judgments, and may or may not act alike. — W. K. Brooks: *Ibid.*, July, 1879, p. 348.

It is necessary to deal next with a form of intuition which differs in its general aspect and mode of application much more from what has been called intuitive reason than this differs from what was called intuitive perception, although it is, unlike the others, an exclusively human attribute. Nevertheless it will, I trust, be shown to the satisfaction of the reader that this divergence is only one of form and application and not of essence. Intuitive judgment does not differ greatly from what is probably the most commonly accepted sense of the word *intuition*. If primitive animal intuition, intuitive perception, and intuitive reason consist psychologically in a perception of relations, however simple or however involved, intuitive judgment may be said psychologically to consist in a perception of *truth*. Truth itself, it may be said, is a relation, and so it is, but we saw that the relations perceived by the primitive intellect were not those of identity, agreement, disagreement, etc., such as are affirmed by an act of judgment, but relations of resistance, direction, velocity, distance, etc. Intuitive judgment does not deal with relations of this latter class, or with such as it is necessary to take immediate advantage of in guiding present movements. It is much less directly connected with the conative powers, and approaches more closely to the derivative intellectual faculties which have formed the almost exclusive theme of philosophy. And yet it is not the same as any of these. It is in no sense a deliberative, reflective faculty, or one of abstraction or disinterested ideation. It is not, for example, as some have supposed, a form of reasoning. The idea that it consists of the rapid or instantaneous combination of a long train of inferences, is one of the errors which have resulted from the inverted order in which mental phenomena have been studied, from beginning at the roof of the structure instead of at the foundations. The intellectual faculties that have chiefly absorbed attention are all secondary or derivative, and it was natural that when any other came forward for consideration it should be sought to explain it in terms of these, whereas in this case, the new-found attribute is really the primary and original one from which as a main trunk the others have been given off as branches.

As a sample of this mistake of the logicians the following remark of Archbishop Whately may be quoted, which might be paralleled in the writings of many others of his school. He says : "It continually happens that even long trains of reasoning will flash through the mind with such rapidity that the process is performed unconsciously, or at least leaves no trace in the memory, any more than the motions of the muscles of the throat and mouth in speaking, or the judgments by which we decide as to the *distances* of visible objects : so that a conclusion may be supposed to be seized by intuition, which in reality is the result of rapid inference." (Logic, Introduction, § 4.) In the same general line Dr. Carpenter remarks : "I have long recognized as a fact that judgments really grounded on a long succession of small experiences mostly forgotten, or perhaps never brought out into very distinct consciousness, often grow into the likeness of intuitive perceptions. I believe this to be the explanation of the intuitive insight thought to be characteristic of women ; and of that which is often found in experienced practical persons who have not attended much to theory, nor been often called on to explain the grounds of their judgments. I explain in the same manner whatever truth there is in presentiments." (Mental Physiology, p. 486.)

Mr. Herbert Spencer in arguing for the simplicity or psychological unity of intuitional judgments (Principles of Psychology, Vol. II, § 277) carries it perhaps too far in applying it to the involved judgments of an engineer, but he is right in saying (ibid. § 278, foot-note) that the common acceptation of the word intuition is that of "an undecomposable mental act." It will not be denied that the mental antecedents of most intuitions of this class are exceedingly complex, the chief contention is that the mind does not go through with any process of connecting these elements into a train of reasoning or methodical arrangement of separate inferences. It is in no sense a process of deduction. The data for an intuition are combined already in the brain into a psychological unit which is used as an integer and not decomposed by the intuitive act. In more physiological terms, the cerebral preparation for such an act has become constitutional, the appropriate cortical nuclei have been previously built up by the registration of experiences, and the discharge is direct and immediate from these ready-made centers.

While this faculty of intuitive judgment is adapted and is frequently applied to questions that have no direct bearing upon self-preservation, such for example as the truth of axiomatic propositions in geometry or logic, or the more complex relations of strength to strain in engineering, it was not by such exercise that its cerebral fabric was originally built up. These are only derivative applications of an instrument which was constructed for a very different purpose. That purpose, like the purpose for which intuitive perception and intuitive reason were created, was an intensely practical one and had to do directly with the interests of the race and its preservation and safety. The other forms of intuition that have been considered were calculated to direct action in the immediate present; this form was adapted to direct action in the near, or more or less remote future. Besides the necessity of knowing what course to pursue to secure the satisfaction of a present desire, it became important to know what course it would be best to adopt in case a certain combination of circumstances should arise. At first such combinations of circumstances were confined to those that were known from repeated experience to be likely to arise, but later those were provided against which were of less and less frequency and probability, and at length a degree of adjustment was attained which would constitute a preparation for, or, defense against almost any possible combination of circumstances. It is this primary and practical side of the subject that has the greatest significance and importance to both psychology and sociology. And if one can once get out of the rut of the old philosophy, it is easy to see that this is the side which furnishes the best and most numerous examples.

Men do not depend upon their reason in the ordinary affairs of life. They do not employ the syllogism in seeking to decide what will be the best course to adopt to insure success in any enterprise. They use what is popularly called "common sense," and this scarcely differs at all from what is here denominated intuitive judgment. One finds little in the books about common sense. When used, as in Reid's works, it is soon either restricted to some one little known application or diverted wholly from its primary meaning. The most that has been written about this faculty beyond the phase to be considered in the next chapter relates to cases in which, as frequently happens, the labored reasoning out of a problem leads to erroneous conclusions which are seen to be so from the start by pure intuition. Elaborate judicial opinions, as is well known, not only often tend to obscure the subject, but actually befog the judge's mind, divert it from the central notions of justice or right involved, and lead him to decide questions wrongly where the truth is intuitively arrived at by others, perhaps by a whole people in great issues, such as the Dred Scott decision.

CHAPTER XXVI.

FEMALE INTUITION.

It is proverbial that the female mind, unaccustomed as it is, in the present state of society, to reason closely, passes to correct conclusions in many cases where the logical mind of man misses the truth after the most careful consideration. — *Dynamic Sociology*, II, 327.

Looking at women as they are known in experience, it may be said of them, with more truth than belongs to most generalizations on the subject, that the general bent of their talents is toward the practical. — JOHN STUART MILL: *Subjection of Women*, p. 105.

If the female organism is the conservative organism, to which is intrusted the keeping of all that has been gained during the past history of the race, it must follow that the female mind is a storehouse filled with the instincts, habits, intuitions, and laws of conduct which have been gained by past experience. The male organism, on the contrary, being the variable organism, the originating element in the process of evolution, the male mind must have the power of extending experience over new fields, and, by comparison and generalization, of discovering new laws of nature, which are in their turn to become rules of action, and to be added on to the series of past experiences. — W. K. BROOKS: *Popular Science Monthly*, June, 1879 (Vol. XV, p. 154).

I use the expression *female intuition* as the title of this chapter in preference to that of *woman's intuition,* because, while it is of course chiefly displayed by women, I believe it has its roots in the subhuman stage, and that woman's intuitional nature is a direct outgrowth of the earlier and simpler mental characteristics of the females of many animals. It should, however, be admitted that there is scarcely any generic distinction between woman's intuition and the intuitive judgment as set forth in the preceding chapter.

The important thing to be noted about woman's intuition from the modern biological standpoint is that it is a highly specialized development of a faculty of the mind which originally had as its sole purpose the protection of the mother and offspring. It is a part of the maternal instinct, and like all instincts, its acuteness and subtlely are proportioned to the narrowness of its purpose. The power in woman of instantaneous and accurate judgment as to what to do when her safety or that of her children is in jeopardy, was developed during the early history of the human race as it emerged from the animal into the properly human state ; its only use was to protect the mother and the young from such dangers as beset them — dangers which increased with the growth of the intellectual faculty and the dispersion of the race over the globe. And with the origin and progress of civilization this power has increased in complexity, and has ever been the safeguard of the family against all attacks, strifes, and abuses from whatever quarter. In the highest stages of enlightment it still comes daily and hourly into use in guarding the virtue of woman, detecting the infidelity of man, protecting the youth of both sexes from temptations and pitfalls of every kind, evading the wrongs of unjust husbands and cruel fathers, checking dangerous financial extravagance or undue liberality in men, and in a thousand other ways. Upon such questions the judgments of women are already formed in the mind, inherited as organized experiences of an indefinite past, with their appropriate cortical centers of nervous discharge constitutionally developed in the brain ; so that when an occasion arises no time is lost in reflection or deliberation. The dangers that have threatened woman and her helpless charges throughout all history have usually left her no time for these slower mental operations. She must act at once or all is lost ; and natural selection has preserved those who could thus act, so that in modern society it is still true, and in a far wider sense than Addison supposed, that

"The woman that deliberates is lost."

This protective quality has been referred to by some authors. Mr. Spencer says (Study of Sociology, p. 376): "In barbarous times a woman who could from a movement, tone of voice, or expression of face, instantly detect in her savage husband the passion that was rising, would be likely to escape dangers run into by a woman less skilled in interpreting the natural language of feeling. Hence, from perpetual exercise of this power, and the survival of those having most of it, we may infer its establishment as a feminine faculty. Ordinarily, this feminine faculty, showing itself in an aptitude for guessing the state of mind through the external signs, ends simply in intuitions formed without assignable reasons; but when, as happens in rare cases, there is joined with it skill in psychological analysis, there results an extremely remarkable ability to interpret the mental states of others."

We may, however, go much farther back in attempting to understand female intuition. In Chap. XXII it was shown that the intuitive perception acquired by animals in circumventing others, and especially that of the males in coping with others of their own species in their rivalry for the females, reacted to some degree upon the females themselves and thus saved this attribute of mind from becoming an exclusively secondary sexual character. It was also pointed out that in a somewhat modified form it was called out in the female by her constant vigils over her young. This latter I believe to be the real origin of the more fully developed female intuition now under consideration, and as already remarked, it is still around the offspring that it chiefly centers, even in developed woman.

Its essentially feminine character is exhibited in several ways. It is a leading feminine characteristic to be always on the defensive. The great end of female action is protection. With the safety of the future members of the race in her charge the mother has had developed a mental constitution which is ever on the alert to perceive and ward off the least danger. She never takes any risks. Non-seafaring people often notice that old sea captains will always choose the safer of two courses, even where either would seem to be perfectly secure, and at first this apparent timidity does not seem to be in harmony with the known intrepidity of these hardy mariners. But it results from a settled rule of life always to choose when at sea the safest way. Now, the female mind possesses this quality of caution as part of its constitution, and it applies not merely to navigation or to any one particularly hazardous employment, but to everything that is done. No matter how secure a woman may be under any circumstances if there is any difference from this point of view between two courses of action she may be depended upon to select the one that she regards as the safer. I say, that she regards as such, because it is this supposed safety, and not necessarily her real safety, that determines her action. She usually bases her judgment on experience, and hence her course will be that which she has formerly pursued and found to be safe. Every one has observed that women will prefer to go the way they have already been, if safe, although there may be a really far better but untried way, and usually no amount of argument drawn from the experience of others or from the natural circumstances of the case will be satisfactory to them. This mental constitution of the female mind manifests itself in all the affairs of life. Its central characteristic is extreme *conservatism*. All innovation is looked upon as likely to be attended with danger. Life is possible under existing conditions, and although it may be scarcely worth its cost it is better than to risk a change. Thus woman becomes the balance-wheel of society, keeping it in a steady and fixed condition of growth. It is for this work that woman's intuition is adapted.

It might be supposed from this essentially conservative nature of woman that she would never be found figuring in the capacity of a reformer, since all reform implies some change in the existing order. The well known facts, therefore, that many women are reformers, that many reforms are led chiefly by women, that their chief argument for political power is based on the claim that they would inaugurate reforms that men will not undertake, and that in the capacity of reformers they are much more ardent and uncompromising than men, certainly seem inconsistent with the position here assumed. But I think it can be shown that the inconsistency is only apparent, and that these facts are reconcilable with true conservatism. Or rather, that conservatism does not alone describe the female attribute in its entirety. Or more accurately still, perhaps, it may be said that woman's conservatism is not directed toward institutions and surrounding conditions, but is centered on self and offspring. It is self-preservation, rather than the preservation of institutions that is ingrained in her nature, and therefore her conservatism is limited to those institutions which she believes to constitute personal safeguards. It is a fact that she is never found advocating the reform of anything that is held to be good in itself, however much it may be capable of improvement. This men are constantly doing. They are not satisfied that it should be merely good, better than nothing; they insist that it shall be improved if it is capable of improvement, and are never satisfied till it is the best it can be made. This is true reform. On the other hand the so-called reforms in which women engage are properly speaking not reforms at all, they are more nearly revolutions. The only institutions they have any interest in reforming are those that they believe to be bad, and the way they propose to reform them is simply to abolish them. It is self-preservation all the time. The bad is the unsafe, the dangerous, and women's reforms are simply crusades against real or supposed evils that threaten the safety of themselves and their children. Viewed in this light the most radical reform is the most complete conservatism, the conservation of all that they cherish in life.

It will thus be seen that female intuition is in strong contrast with the forms treated in Chapters XXII and XXIII. Those forms are adapted to securing the objects of desire. They are the supports of the psychic forces in seeking enjoyment and thus fulfiling the prime functions of existence. They may, therefore, from this point of view, be called positive or active intuition in contrast with the female quality which may be called negative or passive intuition. The latter does not impel the agent actively to go about any labor or undertaking. It merely prepares for action should it be necessary, or it puts a check upon proposed action if it seems inadvisable. A further contrast lies in the fact that female intuition involves no deception, whereas male intuition, as the other form might also be called, has for its essential characteristic the principle of deception. It is true that both these qualities belong, to a certain extent, to both sexes, that intuitive judgment, as defined in the last chapter and seen to be a general property of mind, does not essentially differ in principle from female intuition, while, on the other hand, intuitive reason is often well developed in women. Still, it is also true that when the mental constitution of the two sexes is broadly contrasted, those qualities comprehended under the term intuitive reason, viz., shrewdness, diplomacy, strategy, and the like, are preëminently male characteristics; they are the active, positive, and progressive elements of society, while the passive, negative, and conservative elements of caution, timidity, and apprehensiveness, constituting intuitive judgment, are especially feminine traits. In the next chapter we shall see this contrast still more strongly drawn in a form of intuition not hitherto considered.

It is not, therefore, perhaps too much to say, when all the qualifications are made, that the intuitive faculty has developed along two distinct lines corresponding closely to those followed by the two sexes, and that there practically exist a male and a female trunk of the primary intellectual faculty, the one adapted to the sustentation and continuation, and the other to the protection and conservation of the race. Or the male trunk may be conceived as devoted to the active increase, development, and advancement, and the female to the passive stability, permanence, and persistence of the type. The dominant characteristic of the male faculty is *courage*, that of the female, ***prudence***. These two antithetical psychologic factors are paralleled by the two biologic factors of male activity, favorable to adaptation and variability, as contrasted with female passivity, favorable to hereditary transmission and permanence of type. They also have their analogues in the two sociologic factors consisting of an ever-present radical party of progress held in check by an ever-present conservative party of order.

A concluding thought on female intuition in general and woman's intuition in particular should not go unexpressed. In Chap. XV occasion was taken to remark that in view of the superior antiquity and general importance of the feelings to the intellect, woman, in whom the former are admitted to predominate, must be accorded at least an equal rank with man in the economy of social life. And now from the point of view of intellectual development itself we find her side by side, and shoulder to shoulder with him furnishing, from the very outset, far back in prehistoric, presocial, and even prehuman times, the necessary complement to his otherwise one-sided, headlong, and wayward career, without which he would soon have warped and distorted the race and rendered it incapable of the very progress which he claims exclusively to inspire. And therefore again, even in the realm of intellect, where he would fain reign supreme, she has proved herself fully his equal and is entitled to her share of whatever credit attaches to human progress thereby achieved.

CHAPTER XXVII.

THE INVENTIVE FACULTY.

The intellectual element, though commonly called a force, is not in reality such. It is not comparable with the other true psychic forces. These latter are obliged to do the real work that is performed, the same in the indirect as in the direct method. The intellect only guides them in such a manner as to secure the maximum results. It also brings other natural forces to their aid, and thus increases the effects. The general process by which all this is done is that of *invention*, the product is *art*, and therefore the faculty may be called the *inventive* faculty, and the phenomena produced *artificial* phenomena. — *Dynamic Sociology*, II, 100.

It will have been observed that in all the active or progressive forms of intuition, involving the principle of deception, that have thus far been considered, the faculty expends itself chiefly upon sentient beings. The relations that are perceived and taken advantage of are mainly those arising from the activities of creatures possessing feeling. The benefits derived from efforts directed by the faculty are secured by the agent at the expense of some other living organism. For every pleasure enjoyed by the former there is a corresponding pain suffered by the latter. Indeed, there is often great disparity between the pains and pleasures, the former in such cases usually being largely in excess of the latter. Schopenhauer, in arguing for the excess of pain over pleasure in the world, instances the case of one animal devouring another. It is difficult to conceive of a sufficient disparity in the organic rank or nervous sensibility of the two to make the mere gustatory pleasure of the one balance the horrible sufferings of the other. But one need not seek this explanation, for the cases are without number in which the victim is by far the superior in point of organization and sensibility; an extreme but common case being where man, a sage it may be, is slowly tortured to death to gratify so low an organism as a tapeworm. But all germ diseases, as cholera, yellow fever, and it may be consumption, really constitute still more extreme cases. I do not, of course, mean that these parasites possess the intuitive faculty. They merely illustrate the utter indifference of nature to animal suffering.

Whatever name may be given to this quality in intuitive perception, i. e., the effect upon the lower animals, it is clear that the higher stage which I have distinguished as intuitive reason, in which it is directed toward human beings, is essentially *immoral.* This would probably be held to be true by most persons, even if it could be shown with certainty that the happiness thereby attained was greater than the suffering caused. It is only in the ethics of Herbert Spencer based on the laws that prevail in the animal world that the opposite could be maintained. This question belongs to a later chapter and concerns us here only in so far as it serves to bring out more clearly the precise nature of the intuitive faculty in general. It is only an accident that its exercise should so largely affect sentient beings. It is by no means restricted to these. It simply happens that a clearer conception of its nature could be gained by considering this application first, and by deferring until now the treatment of those manifestations of it which relate to inanimate objects and physical forces.

There is little doubt, as pointed out in Chap. XXI, that the initial efforts which led to the development of such a faculty were made in attempting to overcome material obstacles to the satisfaction of desire. The earliest relations which it was necessary to perceive in order to be able to pursue any but the direct course toward the object of desire were such as subsist between the various physical barriers of the environment. The straight line on which a body moves according to Newton's first law when acted upon by a single force was only possible to living organisms inhabiting either water or air, and this may be one of the reasons why, as paleontology teaches, the earliest animals were aquatic. Vast periods, perhaps greater than all subsequent time, appear to have elapsed after the appearance of marine life before the introduction of land animals — the entire Cambrian, Silurian, Devonian, and perhaps Carboniferous epochs. The known exceptions consist of insects which probably had the power of flight, and may have passed their larval existence in the water, and most of their imago lives in the air. In these media it was possible, when actuated by the desire to obtain food or mates, or to escape enemies, to move in straight lines toward the former or from the latter. The simple psychic forces unaided by any power of direction were adequate to these ends, and there was no need of any intuitive faculty for the perception of complex relations. But it was otherwise with land animals held to the surface of the earth by the force of gravitation. This was also the case with flying insects that must live among rocks, trees, herbage, and undergrowth. Some slight directive power must exist even in the simplest of these, and such an environment would probably have alone sufficed to lay the foundations for the directive faculty. A certain stage of this faculty was, therefore, necessarily developed very early in the history of terrestrial life. This stage may have remained stable during another very long period, and the next advance was probably brought about chiefly by the slow acquirement of the much higher degree of this faculty which was required to perceive the vastly more complex relations of animal movement. It was at this second stage that intuitive perception as described in Chap. XXII began, and from this time until the advent of man its chief exercise was upon these higher relations, although the strengthening faculty was also thereby rendered more and more capable of dealing with the simpler physical relations.

It has been seen that after the human stage was reached the leading application of the indirect method was still to vital and psychic phenomena, that throughout the social epoch and in the highest civilized state this continued to be the case, and that through this means the intuitive reason has reached its highest development in business shrewdness, political diplomacy, and military strategy.

But very early in the human stage, and more especially in the incipient social stage, the application of the directive faculty to inanimate things began to assume importance. As numbers increased and the conditions of life became more complicated the purely animal methods of pursuing subsistence grew more and more inadequate. Foresight in accumulating stores for future and permanent supply of wants may have been the earliest and simplest form of exercising this faculty, but along with it there went the discovery of means for increasing the ease and rapidity with which this could be done. Whether the primary mode was the chase or some primitive form of agriculture, it called forth in either case a new form of the intuitive faculty, not hitherto considered. None of the terms employed in the preceding chapters will properly apply to this form of its exercise, and a different one must be used. The word which most adequately conveys this idea is ***ingenuity***. It is true that in the chase sagacity and cunning were of the utmost value in circumventing the animals to be captured, but something else was required to make this mode of life a successful means of supplying the wants of a large number of individuals. Some additional material instruments must be employed as aids in the chase. The use of a club or a stone to increase the effect of a blow, or overcome the distance between the pursuer and his prey may seem an exceedingly simple device, and yet it is doubtful whether any ape or monkey (these animals having organs adapted to such acts) has been known to resort to it. All animals rely exclusively upon the organic weapons with which nature has endowed them both for attack and defence. The use, therefore, of any material object not a part of themselves for giving greater force to their effort was a complete innovation and involved a new application of the intuitive faculty, or a higher attribute of mind than belongs to any creature lower in the scale than man. But even should it be satisfactorily shown that any other animal than man ever employs such means, this would only be to remove the point of origin of the inventive faculty so much farther back. There is, of course, no end of cases in which animals employ devices to accomplish definite purposes where more or less use is made of extraneous objects and physical forces. Language permits us to call the many remarkable ways in which birds build nests ingenious, and it is also known that they improve their methods under certain circumstances. The archer fish kills insects that fly over, by shooting them with jets of water from its elongated snout; spiders that spin long gossamers *know how* to take in sail like a mariner or to let themselves down at the proper time and place like an aëronaut; and the list might be indefinitely increased. But if such cases are attributed to any high mental faculty, what shall be said of certain insectivorous plants, such as *Genlisea ornata* of Brazil, which catches its prey in a complicated sort of trap, or of *Dionæa muscipula*, which spontaneously closes upon it by a movement of its own? Most of such cases consist of adaptations which have been slowly brought about through the operation of natural selection, and if we may properly call them *contrivances* it is because we really use a figure of speech which has become so common that the fact is lost sight of that it is really metaphorical. It is, however, doubtless true that the practice of using such figures grew up under the influence of a prevailing teleological habit of thought, due to the old cosmology which regarded everything as constructed by an outside power for its specific purpose, and language has so conformed itself to this philosophy that it is impossible to express one's self so as to be understood without employing its formulas. It may, nevertheless, be admitted that in some of the cases, such as the construction of nests, intuitive perception has coöperated with natural selection and the development of the instinct, and this, so far as it goes, does not in the least differ qualitatively from invention, although, quantitatively considered, it falls infinitely below the simplest forms displayed by primitive man.

Returning to the hunting stage of human development we might trace the progress of invention from the club or stone, through all the stages of spears, darts, bows and arrows, slings, boomerangs, etc., to modern fire arms. Similarly might be traced the artificial means of ensnaring and entrapping animals. Among coast dwellers this latter method was directed to the capture of fish and other creatures that inhabit the water, and all the appliances that have been devised by man for this purpose might be passed in review. In the agricultural or georgic stage the quality of forethought was more specially called out by the necessity of sowing or planting and awaiting the harvest, but success depended fully as much upon artificial means as in the chase. Instruments for turning the soil, however rude at first, had to be devised, presenting all the steps from a sharpened stick to the developed plow. To this were gradually added all other agricultural implements.

The pastoral or bucolic stage called forth in the domestication of animals a form of the faculty closely resembling cunning or shrewdness. It consisted mainly in deceiving the less sagacious creatures, but differed from that displayed in the capture of prey in not immediately killing and devouring them, but in what is called *taming* them. It took advantage of the law that injury is what animals seek to escape, and that when they find that they are not to be injured, they submit. A tamed animal is a sort of a parasite living on man whom it has ceased to fear, but in return for the subsistence furnished, man makes certain uses of it, compelling it to work for him, killing it for food, shearing its fleece, milking the females, etc.

With the increase of population and the dispersion of man over the earth many other wants arose, especially those of clothing and shelter. No other wants were more directly conducive to the development of the inventive faculty. However simple man's dwelling places might be, a large amount of ingenuity was required in constructing them. If his clothing consisted solely of the skins of animals these were improved by sewing them together. And from these beginnings might be followed out two of the leading human industries and their progress might be traced to the stage at which they have arrived in civilized countries. But along with these real needs, and often even earlier, man is found exerting perhaps greater ingenuity in the supply of imaginary needs. Ornamentation, antedated clothing and temples of religion preceded human habitations.

One of the strongest spurs to invention was war. Early man was almost invariably warlike. If he preferred peace he was driven to war as a means of defence. Weapons of war must be devised, and thus while the strategic faculty was being developed the inventive faculty was at the same time stimulated. The weapons of war were of two kinds, offensive and defensive, and tribe vied with tribe, as nation still vies with nation in the production of both. No higher stimulus to invention can be conceived of than is afforded by this state of things. For success depends upon the introduction of a more effective means than previously existed. Such a means puts an enemy or foreign power at the mercy of the most ingenious nation. This state of unstable equilibrium always exists, for the moment one power thus gains the mastery it becomes a necessity that others shall outdo it in the same direction. In this way the instruments of destruction and the artifices of protection against them have alternately overreached each other in an ascending series until we have the modern methods of warfare which are still unchanged in this respect.

This progress in the means of warfare well illustrates the question discussed a few pages back as to the real difference between the methods of man and those of nature. The progress that has taken place among animals in acquiring weapons of offense and characters adapted to defense against these —

tusks, horns, claws, spurs, etc., on the one hand, and shells, bristles, quills (as of the porcupine), etc., on the other — seems to be almost an exact parallel on a lower plane to that of man in war. And yet the former is the undoubted product of natural selection and is seen almost as clearly in plants, especially the defensive side of it. It is these analogies, and there are many of them, which so forcibly struck Hugh Miller,[1] and writers of that class, who thought they saw in them the evidences of design in the universe. But they never seemed to reflect to how little purpose this design would thus be put, since at each higher stage the relative positions of the offensive and defensive combatants is the same, and it appears to the rational observer like a vast waste of energy without any result.

The conditions above enumerated that have specially stimulated the inventive faculty are only the most obvious and fundamental ones. With the general upward tendencies of social life they were indefinitely multiplied. The materials and forces of nature were more and more systematically employed to the advantage of man. The wind was utilized first for winnowing and then as a motor force by means of a true machine, the windmill. Water was utilized by the construction of floating objects which eventually took the form of true boats propelled by paddles or oars, or finally by sails, in which latter case both wind and water were brought into service. Later its power was discovered to do other work, and watermills appeared. Gunpowder and other explosives were the products of the war impulse. Gravitation was utilized in weights for various purposes. Elasticity, perhaps first used in the bow, came to play a leading rôle, and springs came to replace weights in many cases. The power of steam was a late discovery and was succeeded by that of electricity. With the former was ushered in the true era of machinery and locomotion. The latter is still far from having reached its maximum utility. Such is the barest sketch of the achievements of the inventive

[1] Testimony of the Rocks, pp. 240–242.

faculty, not intended as such, but merely as furnishing a few of the leading examples of its operation as an agency of civilization. It is easy to see from even so brief a survey of the field that this is the real civilizing agent. If certain refining influences, largely dependent indirectly upon this, be left out of the account, it is correct to say that civilization consists in the utilization of the materials and forces of nature, and the exclusive means by which this is accomplished is human invention.

CHAPTER XXVIII.

PSYCHOLOGY OF INVENTION.

The inventor of a useful instrument is the best illustration of a final cause. With the end distinctly in view but beyond his reach, he sits down and evolves from his knowledge of physical laws an ***indirect method*** of accomplishing it. Unable to perform an act immediately, he reasons out a plan of performing it mediately. By a train of logical calculation, from premises obtained by experience and observation, he determines a mode of taking advantage of blind mechanical forces and directing them into such channels as will accomplish the end in view. This method may be illustrated by the simplest of the mechanical laws, that made use of in the lever and fulcrum. The advantage which man is able to take over nature by an adjustment of appliances is the principle or ***nexus*** which connects mind with matter, and permits the former to manifest itself through the latter as a force. — *Dynamic Sociology*, I, 551–552.

Ad opera nil aliud potest homo, quam ut corpora naturalia admoveat et amoveat; reliqua Natura intus transigit. — BACON: *Novum Organum*, Aph. IV.

Toutes les fois que nous parvenous à exercer une grande action, c'est seulement parce que la connaissance des lois naturelles nous permet d'introduire, parmi les circonstances déterminées sous l'influence desquelles s'accomplissent les divers phénomènes, quelques éléments modificateurs, qui, quelque faibles qu'ils soient en eux-mêmes, suffisent, dans certains cas, pour faire tourner à notre satisfaction les résultats définitifs de l'ensemble des causes extérieures. — AUGUSTE COMTE: *Philosophie Positive*, I, 51.

When the inventive faculty is carefully compared with the other forms of intuition which have been considered there are found to be certain resemblances and certain differences. The resemblances are far more general and important than the differences, all forms agreeing in the fundemental condition of consisting in the perception of relations, chiefly of the same general classes of relations, viz., those of resistance, direction, rate of motion, and distance. The distinction between invention and that primitive form of intuition which was called intuitive perception, beyond its differentiation into the sole perception of physical relations, is mainly one of degree, but the degree is very great. The distinction between it and the higher form of intuition which was called intuitive reason may be illustrated in several ways. Both are limited mainly if not exclusively to man, but whereas intuitive reason is chiefly exercised on other human beings or on the lower animals, i. e., in perceiving psychic relations, invention is exclusively confined to material objects and physical forces, i. e., to perceiving physical relations. But as business shrewdness may, and constantly does take cognizance of the material surroundings, some more exact points of difference must be found. One of these is that in the latter the attention is strictly confined to the question of personal interest. No physical relations are sought for that are not directly advantageous to the subject. The relations perceived are those which subsist between the subject and whatever material objects may be concerned. They are never such as subsist between two material objects without affecting the subject. From this point of view, this form, and indeed all the other forms of intuition, may be called *subjective*, and invention may be distinguished as *objective*. For here the relations perceived are entirely between external objects or forces and never between these and the subject. The moment the subject enters into the process the form is changed and it becomes subjective.

From another point of view invention or objective intuition may be called *disinterested*, in contradistinction to subjective intuition which is essentially *egoistic*. This latter is the immediate servant of the will. Its sole purpose is to assist the psychic forces in securing the satisfaction of desire. This intensely interested nature of the intuitive reason gives it far greater volume and strength, and it pushes on through obstacles and obstructions and makes itself felt. In contrast with this the objective, disinterested form of intuition has little force or self-assertion, loses sight of self and absorbs itself in nature, thus assimilating itself in this respect to the derivative faculties to be hereafter considered.

All these distinctions are illustrated by the well-known fact that inventors seldom profit by their inventions, while shrewd business men frequently make fortunes out of them under the very eye of the inventor. The faculty exercised by the two classes is here seen to be widely different. The sharp egoism of the one is in strong contrast with the neglect on the part of the other of his personal interests for the sake of unfolding an important physical principle. It is profitable to the sociologist to consider carefully these two classes of character. The inventor always sees the utility of his invention. This is the essence of the process. Invention may be defined as the *perception of relations of utility*. It may be said that all intuition consists in this, and so it does, but in all the other forms the only utility considered is immediate utility to self. The utility that the inventor perceives is perpetual utility to all who use the invention. In this sense the inventor may be called the most practical of all men. The relations which the inventor perceives, although physical, are often exceedingly complex and recondite, much more so than the subjective relations, even though psychic, which the business man perceives.

If now we take the case of an inventor who has devised a mechanism or discovered a principle of vast importance to the future of civilization, and suppose that through absorption in this principle and consequent neglect of his personal interests he has, however carelessly and culpably, allowed a shrewd business man to get possession of his invention, and suppose the latter to have introduced it into general use as fully as is consistent with reserving for himself an ample fortune, while the inventor has remained poor so as to interfere seriously with his success in discovering other principles; this would be only a slight exaggeration and simplification of actual cases known to history. Sociologically considered, which of these two men is of most worth? But for the business man the inventor might not have had the sagacity to introduce his principle. But for the inventor the business man would have been obliged to make his fortune out of some other man's talents. Both have done a service. Which has done the greater service? If it were known that but for the business man the invention would have remained as if it had not been made, the services of the two might be regarded as practically equal, although all would concede to the inventor a higher place from the point of view of personal worth. But as it can never be known whether the inventor would have applied his principle, it is clear to every one that his was the essentially meritorious act. It is felt that he possesses something rare and valuable, something of a far higher order of merit. The business man's talent is rather ordinary, it is a lower, coarser-grained form of ability, and it consists to a greater or less extent in gaining for himself what really belongs to another. Yet under the law of competition, i.e., under the only law that most political economists and sociologists recognize, this man is by far the fitter to survive. From the biological standpoint he should survive and the inventor should go to the wall. This case illustrates, as crucially as any, the distinction between the current philosophy of society and that of meliorism; between biologic and psychologic sociology.

If the inventive faculty be compared with intuitive judgment and female intuition much greater differences will be found than those which distinguish it from intuitive perception and intuitive reason. Besides most of the distinctions pointed out as separating the male or active from the female or passive forms of intuition there are other specific distinctions. Passive or negative intuition is as egoistic as active or positive intuition. Self-protection is no more disinterested than self-aggrandizement. The relations perceived in the one, as in the other, are always relations between object and subject, never, as in invention, between two or more objects. They are also usually psychic relations and only rarely physical relations. The conservatism that characterizes negative intuition in tolerating no innovation fosters no improvements. But all improvement results from invention, hence it stimulates no invention. Extreme forms of this tendency are seen in some cases of religious conservatism which looks upon all newfangled contrivances as diabolical, and if allowed prohibits or distroys them.[1] The habit of thought also reacts upon the constitution of the mind rendering conservative persons uninventive. It is difficult to demonstrate this in men, yet could it be investigated it would probably appear. But society possesses a great conservative class — the female sex — and a comparison of the average mental qualities of men and women is not difficult. While many exceptions of course exist, while there are conservative men and progressive women, and uninventive men and ingenious women, it is nevertheless an obvious fact patent to every observer that the female is the conservative and the male the inventive sex, that women as a rule are conservative, and that as a rule they are not inventive. The foregoing considerations go to show that these qualities stand in the relation of cause and effect, that the habitual exercise of the intuitive judgment is not favorable to the development of the inventive faculty.

This exhausts the sources of comparison, and the question reverts to the psychology of invention, the essential nature of an inventive act. All the mental acts of intuition of whatever form, that is, the flow of nerve-currents constituting psychic activity, are attended with corresponding movements of the appropriate organs or of the entire organism. These movements are adapted to taking advantage of the relations perceived. In the subjective forms of intuition these acts are usually such as

[1] Suivant la logique, barbare mais rigoureuse, des peuples arriérés, toute intervention active de l'homme pour améliorer à son profit l'économie générale de la nature, doit certainement constituer une sorte d'injurieux attentat au gouvernement providentiel. Il n'est pas douteux, en effet, qu'une prépondérance trop absolue de l'esprit religieux tend nécessairement, en elle-même, à engourdir l'essor industriel de l'humanité, par le sentiment exagéré d'un stupide optimisme, comme on peut le vérifier en tant d'occasions décisives. — Auguste Comte: *Philosophie Positive*, IV, 517.

to deceive some other sentient being, and cause such being to do what it otherwise would not have done, or to refrain from doing what it would otherwise have done. That is, it consists in a form of inducement, allurement, or attraction to perform certain acts. Certain forces are perceived regularly to actuate living things, and by cunning, sagacity, shrewdness, diplomacy, or strategy these forces are made to impel in directions that will be advantageous to the intuitive agent. Mechanical ingenuity certainly very closely resembles this. Certain qualities of material bodies and certain physical forces (these in the last analysis being really the same) are perceived to exist. It is also perceived that if these forces acted in a different direction, or with a different degree of intensity from what they do when unobstructed, or acted together instead of separately, or with, instead of against each other, etc., etc., they would of themselves accomplish results advantageous to man, primarily, of course, advantageous to self. It is still further perceived that although the agent himself is unable by his own muscular strength to accomplish these desired results, he is able to make such adjustments in the circumjacent objects as will change the direction, intensity, and dynamic relations of these forces, so as to cause them to act as he perceives to be advantageous. Or, dealing with the qualities of materials, he is able to change their form from the amorphous and useless to the definite and useful, as e. g., to convert clay[1] into pots, or trees into boats. Such complicated readjustments as these last named required a high degree of intellectual development, and could only have been finally reached through an infinite number of partial failures and increasingly successful efforts.

[1] Ἀλλὰ γὴν μὲν οὐδεὶς ὕδατι δεύσας ἀφῆκεν, ὡς ἀπὸ τύχης καὶ αὐτομάτως πλίνθων ἐσομένων. — Plutarch : Περὶ Τύχης.

CHAPTER XXIX.

INVENTIVE GENIUS.

The devices and strategems by which he [man] was enabled to circumvent the less sagacious forms of life, and the foresight and calculation which taught him how to multiply the growth and abundance of nutritive vegetables, were of no avail beyond a certain limit unless supplemented and assisted by a still higher order of mental activity, by a practical comprehension of the inert laws of physics and mechanics, and the skillful elaboration of material objects into forms adapted to aid, accelerate, intensify, and focalize the natural forces which were operating in the direction of producing his means of subsistence. The form of mental exertion, the species of cunning, which he had manifested in the primary modes of production, were superficial and general. To make them permanently successful, they required to be seconded by more profound and more specific forms of psychic power and intellectual energy. — *Dynamic Sociology*, I, 549.

Now, what I maintain, and what the advocates of the new education ought to insist upon in the discussion of this question, is, that this exalted faculty of invention, both in its mental and its physical aspects — both as to mind and body, brain and muscle — is susceptible of cultivation in the same manner and to the same degree as all other human faculties. The mind can be directed by appropriate training into habits of inventive thought. It can be habituated to look for possible utilities in all objects and phenomena that present themselves to the senses, and trained to embody these ideas in concrete forms and mechanisms. This is genuine invention. The process consists in forming a mental conception of a given utility, and then in working out the modifications necessary to realize it. . . . The great mistake lies in supposing that this state of things cannot or should not be increased. It can be increased by education to any desired degree, and such a degree can be conceived of as might relieve mankind of nearly all the drudgery that has now to be performed. — *The Forum*, Vol. V, New York, July, 1888, p. 578.

Primo itaque videtur inventorum nobilium introductio inter actiones humanas longe primas partes tenere : id quod antiqua sæcula judicaverunt. Ea enim rerum inventoribus divinos honores tribuerunt ; iis autem qui in rebus civilibus merebantur (quales erant urbium et imperiorum conditores, legislatores, patriarum a diuturnis malis liberatores, tyrannidum debellatores, et his similes), heroum tantum honores decreverunt. Atque certe si quis ea recte conferat, justum hoc prisci sæculi judicium reperiet. Etenim inventorum beneficia ad universum genus humanum pertinere possunt, civilia ad certas tantummodo hominum sedes: hæc etiam non ultra paucas ætates durant, illa quasi perpetuis temporibus. Atque status emendatio in civilibus non sine vi et perturbatione plerumque procedit: at inventa beant, et beneficium deferunt absque alicujus injuria aut tristitia. — BACON: *Novum Organum*, Aph. cxxix.

The higher acquisitions and achievements of intellect have now become so remote from practical life, that their relations to it are usually lost sight of. But if we remember that in the stick employed to heave up a stone, or the paddle to propel a boat, we have illustrations of the uses of levers; while in the pointing of an arrow so as to allow for its fall during flight, certain dynamical principles are tacitly recognized; and that from these vague early cognitions the progress may be traced step by step to the generalizations of mathematicians and astronomers; we see that science has gradually emerged from the crude knowledge of the savage. And if we remember that as this crude knowledge of the savage served for simple guidance of his life-sustaining actions, so the developed sciences of mathematics and astronomy serve for guidance in the workshop and the counting-house and for steering of vessels, while developed physics and chemistry preside over all manufacturing processes; we see that at the one extreme as at the other, furtherance of men's ability to deal effectually with the surrounding world, and so to satisfy their wants, is that purpose of intellectual culture which precedes all others. — HERBERT SPENCER: *Principles of Ethics*, I, pp. 516–517.

Jene Schärfe des Verstandes im Auffassen der kausalen Beziehungen der mittelbar erkannten Objekte findet ihre Anwendung nicht allein in der Naturwissenschaft (deren sämmtliche Entdeckungen ihr zu verdanken sind); sondern auch im praktischen Leben, wo sie Klugheit heisst; da sie hingegen in der ersteren Anwendung besser Scharfsinn, Penetration, und Sagacität genannt wird: genau genommen bezeichnet Klugheit ausschliesslich den im Dienste des Willens stehenden Verstand. Jedoch sind die Gränzen dieser Begriffe nie scharf zu ziehen, da es immer eine und dieselbe Funktion des nämlichen, schon bei der Anschauung der Objekte im Raum in jedem Thiere thätigen Verstandes ist, die, in ihrer grössten Schärfe, bald in den Erscheinungen der Natur von der gegebenen Wirkung die unbekannte Ursache richtig erforscht und so der Vernunft den Stoff giebt zum Denken allgemeiner Regeln als Naturgesetze; bald, durch Anwendung bekannter Ursachen zu bezweckten Wirkungen, komplicirte sinnreiche Maschinen erfindet; bald, auf Motivation angewendet, entweder feine Intriguen und Machinationen durchschaut und vereitelt, oder aber auch selbst die Motive und die Menschen, welche für jedes derselben empfänglich sind, gehörig stellt, und sie eben nach Belieben, wie Maschinen durch Hebel und Räder, in Bewegung setzt und zu ihren Zwecken leitet.— SCHOPENHAUER: *Welt als Wille*, I, 25-26.

The use of the word *genius* has thus far been avoided because there is usually associated with all its uses the notion of disinterested application to some inspiring conception, a notion directly opposed to the intense egoism characteristic of the class of primary intellectual acts that have been considered. But the inventive faculty alone among all these contains the possibility of developing out of self and of losing itself in nature. Originating like the others in pure egoism under the lash of the will, it still possessed even at the outset, as shown in the last chapter, the special privilege of being directed toward the discernment of relations between external things, and of being only secondarily connected with the willing subject. At first this liberty produced no tendency to cut loose from the will, and these relations were perceived only in order to discover thereby a line, however irregular, of least resistance to the object of desire. But at length the habit of treating these means temporarily as ends resulted in transferring some small part of the satisfaction to the successful discovery of the means. The rare and special quality of mind required for this gave it a peculiar relish and it became a pleasure to discover hitherto unsuspected means for the accomplishment even of the primary ends of being. Up to this point we may consider the intellect simply as an instrument of the will, but henceforth it was destined to form, to a greater and greater extent, a part of the will or soul, to become itself a center of emotional feeling, to have wants of its own and desires to satisfy. This datum point may be set down as the true origin of the sense of enjoyment in intellectual exercise, which ultimately developed into a great psychic and social force.

This circumstance soon carried the inventive faculty above and beyond the other forms of intuition. The act of seeking out and discovering useful relations became in a high degree pleasing, and ultimately, in the case of a few individuals, developed into a passion. Ability to discern utilities and make the requisite adjustments was, and still is, recognized as a form of genius — the inventive genius of man. A small but increasing proportion of the population devoted themselves more or less exclusively to this task. At the outset the work was chiefly constructive and consisted in mentally representing a useful object, its form, and size, its adaptation and purpose, and then in proceeding to fashion it out of the materials most fit and accessible. The simpler the laws involved the greater the labor of construction, so that many of the earlier inventions were what are now regarded as merely the products of unskilled labor. But in the infancy of the race all labor was skilled. Labor itself, if it results in anything, involves the element of skill.[1] In early times labor and skill were undifferentiated. Invention and construction seemed one and the same.

Not to dwell on the details, the important truth is that the development of inventive genius in man ultimately resulted in the introduction of *art*. It caused the raw materials of nature which had previously constituted his only resources to be discarded and replaced more and more, and at length almost exclusively, by artificial products. So nearly is this transformation complete in modern civilized countries that the fact is lost sight of even by political economists. That is, they find it so universal that they come to regard it as the natural condition. This leads them into the greatest absurdities. The biological school, which may still be said to be the predominant one, is fond of treating civilization as the product of natural forces and of inveighing against everything that any one attempts to do to modify or in any way interfere with those forces, forgetting

[1] All labor is mental. To a large and controlling extent the mental element is present in the simplest operations. With the laborer who shovels in the gravel pit the directing and controlling influence of the mind predominates, to an indefinite extent, over the simple foot-pounds of mechanical force which he exerts. — J. B. Clark: *Philosophy of Wealth*, p. 21.

entirely that civilization in all its essential characteristics is an exclusively artificial product, the product of the inventive genius of man in modifying and altering the course of nature. Every adjustment made at the behest of inventive genius is an interference with the course of natural law. Every object of art is such as nature never would have created. When one looks about and realizes how extremely seldom any other class of objects are ever used by man, some idea may be gained of the intensely artificial character of civilization. But this is as it should be, for everywhere the artificial is superior to the natural, and what is called progress consists in making everything more and more artificial, i. e., in putting more art into all products, discovering new and added utilities by calling into play still higher flights of inventive genius.

In Chapter XIV it was shown that the great subjective factor of mind, the soul or will of nature, constitutes a transforming agency, and some of the transformations accomplished by it were recounted. Most of those there enumerated belonged to the subhuman stage of development, those of the human stage being purposely omitted because a new and as yet unexplained factor entered into them. That factor is now under consideration. The great psychic, or as it now becomes, social force was undiminished and constituted the impelling factor, but it could accomplish little without the aid of the intellect in the form of an inventive faculty as a directive factor. With both factors at work the transformation became rapid and permanent. Nothing equal or at all comparable to it had ever before been accomplished. It could not await the slow methods of nature in bringing about after millions of generations the anatomical modifications that were referred to. It worked directly upon the environment radically changing it and rendering structural adaptations unnecessary. This may be why man has really undergone so few of the latter. Structural modifications can only go on under the influence of an environmental pressure in the given direction. But if the moment such a pressure is felt it is immediately relieved by an artificial device, the cause of the change is removed and the tendency to change ceases. This was practically done in the case of man, invention being constantly directed toward the relief of environmental pressure and along the line of free activity in the satisfaction of desire.

It is on these grounds that I have maintained in Dynamic Sociology that material civilization has constituted a true human progress under the rigid definition there given of what progress is, viz., increased happiness. For happiness consists in the continuous satisfaction of the desires as they arise, and its increase results from multiplying the desires that can be thus satisfied. This material civilization accomplishes by improving the quality of everything that man uses in his daily life and introducing new means of satisfying new and higher wants. It is true that the introduction of the arts, the products of inventive genius, has entailed upon mankind the necessity of labor, and in most ages and countries this has been a severe hardship upon the great mass, but there are some extenuating circumstances. The first of these is that it is only by labor that so large a number of human beings can live on the earth. It is the condition to their existence. The choice lies between labor and extinction. Without the arts which render labor necessary the earth would support a much less numerous population. The question, therefore, is narrowed down to whether a life of labor is better than no life. If life, such as it is, is a gain, then is the opportunity to labor, i. e., civilization, a means of progress. But if it be said that this hardship is due to the unjust distribution of the products of labor, then the answer must be that this is not chargeable to inventive genius but to rapacity, which is a form of the egoistic faculty, and that it presents a problem for the sociologist. Finally, the hardship is often caused by the influence of those rapid transitions which characterize intellectual as distinguished from the lower agencies of nature, and which do not leave time enough for the proper adjustments to suit the new conditions. Such a transition has recently taken place by the sudden revolution in modes of production caused by the introduction of machinery, and it will require a long time for the laborer to regain the hold on the profits of his labor which he had before the commencement of this era.

A broad distinction is usually made between mechanical invention and scientific discovery, between the Henrys who discover the laws of electricity and the Morses who invent telegraphic alphabets. The difference is certainly striking in such extreme cases, but there are all gradations between them. In all cases there is a perception of relations existing among physical phenomena, the qualities of substances, and the nature of mechanical movements. The extent to which attention is directed to the adjustments necessary to realize the utilities varies. Where such adjustments are the primary consideration, it is pure invention. Where these are made secondary, and attention is concentrated upon the laws and processes, it is chiefly discovery. The distinction is nearly the same as that between science and empiricism. It is not widely different from that between science and art. There can be no successful empiricism, no true art, without an accurate perception of the relations involved. There may be, however, pure discovery without any application of natural principles. That is, there may be science without art, but there cannot be art without science in the full meaning of that term. And in cases of pure, i. e., unapplied science it is always felt that its purpose has not yet been attained, that its application is still to be made, and that until it is made science is without value. This applies even to those cases in which, at the time of a scientific discovery, it is impossible to conceive any practical use to which it can be put. Those who contend for the free exercise of the scientific powers untrammeled by considerations of practical utility maintain that truth thus brought to light is certainly destined to be useful at some future time, and they point to the labors of Volta and Galvani actuated purely by the love of discovery and without the slightest conception of the infinite possibilities of electricity. Truth is rightly conceived as always possessing at least a potential utility and, therefore, as always worthy of investigation. But a still higher ground is also properly taken. Even could it be known that no mechanical inventions, no practical arts, could ever flow from a given discovery, it is maintained that the truth thus made known is worth pursuing for its own sake. By this is meant that there are other utilities than the purely material ones. Not merely either that the intellectual enjoyment of knowing such truths is itself a utility of the highest order, which is true, but that such knowledge cannot fail to prove of practical value to those possessing it in serving as a guide to conduct. It helps to complete that knowledge of their environment, which, taken together, furnishes the rule of action and the key to success. It has been proved that crime may be prevented by broadening the mind of the criminal with knowledge that he can never make any direct use of, and I have myself maintained, and still believe, that astronomy is a more practical subject than ethics to teach to the criminal class.

To the account of inventive genius, then, in the broadest sense of the term, must be set down the spirit of scientific inquiry and the passion for original research which so largely characterize the modern age, and which have wrought such a momentous change in the character of civilization and the condition of society. The theme is much too common to need illustration or elaboration, and it is sufficient for the present purpose to have fixed its position in the general train of psychic events that have succeeded one another in the upward progress of an evolving race.

One question remains. Is the inventive genius of man susceptible of cultivation? In view of its unquestioned value to the world and its freedom from all the evil tendencies shown to inhere in the lower purely egoistic forms of the primary intellectual faculty, it would seem that the more there were of it the better. Is it as high already as it is possible for it to rise? If not, is it possible to raise it higher by any artificial means? These questions may be answered separately.

The great length to which the inventive spirit has actually been carried, the number of individuals who are devoting themselves to invention, and the multitude of attempts that are yearly made to utilize some new principle or improve upon some mechanism already discovered, as shown by the models submitted for patent in the enlightened nations of the world, give the general impression that the inventive spirit is as active as it need be for the healthy development of the mechanical arts. The fact that the love of invention becomes with many a ruling passion, and that, as with all useful mental qualities, it sometimes runs to extremes, as seen in Keely motors and devices to secure perpetual motion — all this tends to strengthen the common belief that this faculty at least can maintain itself without any effort on the part of society. A little reflection, however, should make it apparent that these facts are really only so many arguments for the systematic training of the inventive faculty. Its great intensity argues for checks, regulation, broadening, and deepening. The number of inoperative mechanisms and preoccupied principles for which patents are sought, proves the need of wider information on the part of the public relative to all such matters. The attempts to apply imaginary principles show that knowledge is as necessary to successful invention as zeal in its prosecution.

Granting that the inventive spirit is as strong as it needs to be, granting that no form of education could act directly to increase the native supply of inventive genius in any individual, and that this is a matter of heredity alone, there still remains the argument that this talent, like every other, is likely to remain forever dormant unless called out by some combination of external circumstances. Education properly understood is little more, at best, than the creation of an artificial environment calculated to call into exercise all the latent talents of those who receive it. The number manifesting this kind of genius may, therefore, be greatly increased through a form of education which should be really adapted to calling it forth.

It may be said that this would simply multiply the number of models and flood the world with machines that could not be used. This objection suggests the main argument for the education of the inventive faculty. Civilization has really advanced in exact proportion to the extent to which society was prepared to employ the arts brought out by the inventive genius of a small proportion of its members. This is no measure of the degree of art that it would have been possible to attain. In other words the advance has been in proportion to the demand which is no measure of the possible supply. The latter, it would seem, will always equal the former no matter how great it may be. The fact that modern civilization employs many thousand times as much art as ancient society employed, and continues to employ more and more, shows that there is no necessary limit to the extent to which inventive genius may benefit mankind. The way to bring this about is to increase the demand, that is, to increase the capacity of society for receiving and appreciating these benefits. It is not the inventor who needs educating but the user of his inventions, i. e., the general public. As a matter of fact, while inventors are indeed rare, those who are really qualified to use inventions are also rare. It is astonishing to note how few persons have any idea of the nature of any mechanism at all complicated. When fountain pens were first invented many of my friends obtained them and endeavored to use them, but I know of none who did not soon discard them because the few directions necessary to keep them in order were too intricate or too troublesome to follow. They gave no thought to the principle involved in the mechanism and could not see why they might not as well be kept one end up as the other.[1]

[1] I am writing this with one of the old-fashioned ones that I have used every day for fifteen years.

Every one knows how difficult it is to make servants attend to any but the simplest utensils, and housewives are as a rule equally ignorant of such matters. Wherever there is a furnace or any other of the modern kinds of heater in a house, it is found necessary for some person of judgment and intelligence to take its management in charge. The female sex, as previously shown, is especially deficient in this form of perspicacity. I have recently seen a lady with a letter in her hand approach a letter box, on the lid of which was plainly stamped in relief letters the words "pull down," and after going several times round it and doing everything but the right one, finally go away and give her letter to a drug store clerk to mail for her.[1]

Not only can there be little progress in the arts of civilization while the mass of mankind has so little power to appreciate or ability to employ them, but the progress that takes place is an awkward and unnatural one. The public is constantly using what it does not understand, involving a vast amount of destruction and waste, and making society dependent upon a few experts. What is not understood cannot be properly used, and condemnation and complaint are followed by rejection, whereby the demand is lowered. Old-fashioned and laborious methods are preferred to modern rapid and labor-saving devices. In these and a thousand other ways society is kept from advancing by popular ignorance of the underlying principles of art. The worst of all perhaps is the ignorance of mechanics themselves. They only know exactly what they are taught while learning their trades and the least thing out of the beaten track confounds them completely. It is, for example, almost impossible for any one who has ideas of his own to have a house built in conformity with his ideas. The workmen will have "never heard of such a thing," will object and prevari-

[1] An unreflected light did never yet
Dazzle the vision feminine.
Sir Henry Taylor : *Philip Van Artevelde*, Part I, Act i, Scene 5.

cate, and cause unlimited trouble rather than swerve a hair from some fixed rule of thumb that makes every house an exact copy of every other. But there would be no end if it were sought to present all the examples that occur to the mind whenever the subject is before it.[1]

Even if it be objected that the mind cannot be trained to invent, it at least cannot be denied that the mechanical principles on which all the most common contrivances, machines, and artificial objects generally, which are in daily use are constructed, may be explained and really taught to every pupil of either sex. It may be that much of it would be transient in the minds of many. This is true of all things. But much would abide and bear fruit in later years, while object lessons of this class would be less likely to be forgotten than almost anything else in education. The recent movement in the direction of manual training is the result of a growing recognition of the need of knowing *how* as well as merely knowing *what*. The pitiful helplessness of city-bred persons when thrown into contact with nature has long been manifest, as well as the fact that the best minds in every department are those that have imbibed from an early rural life, however Arcadian, some knowledge of nature's ways, which later stands them in as an aid to success. It would be an easy and natural adjunct to a system of manual training to make it include full and thorough instruction in the mechanical principles of most great inventions and also of those most familiar to the pupil. But beyond this it must be maintained that the mind can be trained to look for utilities, instructed to be ever on the alert for practical principles and effective adjustments calculated to utilize natural forces, qualities, and objects, to set the inventive faculty to work, and thereby, virtually if not literally, increase, develop, and stimulate the inventive genius of man.

[1] Mr. Herbert Spencer has given a number of other good examples in his Study of Sociology, pp. 304–305.

CHAPTER XXX.

CREATIVE GENIUS.

The love of the beautiful, both in sight and sound, has ever been and ever must be a reliable social force, ready to manifest its power on every occasion, whenever the great vital demands of existence cease to absorb the energies of society. In proportion as man's physical wants are supplied, and his social and sexual relations placed upon a natural and satisfactory footing, the practical arts, the industrial character, and the cold business features of human life will be relieved, subdued, and embellished by the softening and cheering presence of works of art, and by the perpetual charm of music and poetry. — *Dynamic Sociology*, I, 674.

The eye of the intellect sees in all objects what it brought with it the means of seeing. — CARLYLE.

In Part I was considered, from the standpoint of its origin and genesis, the great primary psychic trunk — the feelings — with its roots far down in the bathybian ooze of organic life. Thus far, in Part II, attention has been confined to the principal secondary trunk or dominant branch — the intuitive intellect — which began to diverge from the main trunk coincidently with the appearance of the highest insects and the earliest birds and mammals, near the beginning of Cenozoic or Tertiary time. This great branch, as has been seen, was twofold, though not bifurcate or divergent, and may be figuratively represented as double, or consisting of two approximate or contiguous complementary trunks, an active, positive, and progressive male trunk, representing biological variation and adaptation, and a passive, negative, and conservative female trunk, representing heredity. The active trunk assumed the several forms described as intuitive perception, intuitive reason, and the inventive faculty ; the passive trunk consists of the intuitive judgment typified by female intuition. These forms of intellectual manifestation were developed out of the primary psychic trunk as accessories to, and servants of the will, for the better accomplishment of the object of sentient life, the satisfaction of desire. With all this philosophy has had little or nothing to do.

At this point is reached the domain of philosophy as it has always been understood, which, it is thus seen, only deals with faculties or branches of the intellect which are secondary in rank and derivative in character, having grown out of the main trunk and departed more or less from the original nature of the intellectual process. It is safe to say that none of these could by any possibility have been developed directly from nature. There is nothing upon which any of the primary biological laws could seize to give an initial impulse to such faculties. For this there is required some powerful motive, and in biology that motive always is advantage. There are certain mental qualities which are admitted to be exempt from the biological law of advantage, since their excercise in no way tends to render their possessor any more fit to survive in the struggle for existence. Any faculty of which this is true has in this quality the stamp of derivativeness ; has, as it were, a modern *facies*. When Schopenhauer insisted with so much force and truth that the intellect was a mere accident, a late graft upon the will as the main psychic trunk, he had in mind only the intellect of Kant and the other philosophers who ignored the great intuitive branch out of which these modern disinterested, and therefore dependent branches, have developed. His charge was therefore doubly true as thus restricted. It would be sufficiently true of all intellect, as has been abundantly shown, but intellect proper, and in its essential nature, as a servant of the will and a new means of securing the objects of sentient life, is as much more ancient than the derivative intellect of the philosophers as it is more modern than the will from which it sprang.

Of all these modern, derivative outgrowths of the primary and original intellect, the one which seems to be genetically the most intimately connected with it, is the faculty of rearranging the materials in the possession of the mind into new forms, combinations, and relations. The old philosophers have treated this faculty chiefly in its passive and less important aspect under the head of *imagination.* But its more important aspect is the active one in which it is seen as a so-called creative faculty. Just as in imagination all admit that nothing can be constructed by the mind whose materials were not all there already, so the term *creative* is uniformly understood to refer to the elaboration of ideas already existing, the only thing that is new being the form, combination, or arrangement of these ideas. But creation in this sense differs from imagination in implying that the resultant idea is strong enough to produce a motor discharge to the appropriate muscles, thus causing the bodily activities necessary to realize the ideal. That is to say, the active form of the imagination *makes* something. Here, as in some cases previously referred to, language supplies a link in the evidence of the primary process afterwards lost sight of. For among the first things *made* by the creative faculty were literary productions, and the earliest form of these was the poetic form ; and a poem in its etymological significance is simply something *made.*

The faculty, however, had a much earlier origin. In fact it was simply a development from the inventive faculty, and can be successfully affiliated upon that. It was seen that so soon as that faculty had fairly cut loose from the lower forms of egoistic intuition and began to be independent of the bodily desires it took the character of inventive genius, the first work of which was the fashioning of objects of utility. Pari passu with this intellectual step there was developing a rude esthetic sentiment which began to furnish a new attraction and to become an end to be satisfied. Its earliest form was probably the love of ornamentation, and inventive genius was directed to the production of such objects as ministered to this incipient sense of the beautiful. This form of utility was felt to be generically distinct from the primary form, which related solely to the satisfaction of real wants or needs. Hitherto the useful was that, and that only, which made existence possible or less difficult. It was chiefly limited to supplying the prime necessities of life, food, clothing, shelter, protection, and the successive improvements to these. It was soon extended to the means of increasing the quantity and quality of these supplies, and at length to the means of obtaining any form of property or wealth. Whatever contributes to those ends is recognized as practical, and, as already stated, it is inventive genius which furnishes the practical arts. Creative genius, on the contrary, while it also yields a form of art, ignores the practical and pursues only the esthetic. It results in what are popularly distinguished as the *fine arts*. But the distinction is not always well defined. There are thousands of useful objects of art which are at the same time ornamental, and wherever this is the case, both inventive and creative genius have been at work ; the useful part has resulted from the former and the esthetic part from the latter. One of the great departments of fine art, viz., architecture, occupies an intermediate place between the two. History shows that at the outset domestic architecture belonged exclusively to the practical arts while religious architecture was chiefly a fine art. In many parts of the world this is still largely the case. In the large cities of Mexico the only buildings over two stories in height are the churches and these are almost the only ones that are at all embellished. In such lands it would seem that God alone is thought worthy to dwell in a beautiful house.

It thus appears that creative genius is near akin to inventive genius, and it is this close relationship that makes it necessary when seeking the genesis of the intellectual faculties to place it first in the secondary or derivative series. Inventive genius is itself derivative, since it makes its own operations and products an end instead of a means to the great end of being, but the obvious identity of its modus operandi with that of the inventive faculty in its primary form, where this was not the case, renders it impossible to separate them in a logical arrangement of the intellectual faculties. It is here, within the life history of that form of intuition, that the first divergence from the primordial egoistic type took place. But creative genius, which has cut loose not only from self but from everything practical and is following after the esthetic alone, constitutes a distinct branch of the intellect, leading far away from the original intuitive trunk.

The divergence of creation from invention may be explained in the following manner: In dealing with the actual materials and forces of nature the mind found itself constantly hemmed in by facts. It could only go so far when it would gladly go farther. The brain had registered a thousand perceptions from observation and experience which could not be realized in the inventive product. That could only embody so much as could be made to conform to the actual environment. An invention is therefore a compromise between the ideal of the inventor and the hard facts of nature. To be useful it must respect the latter. Practical art can only rise so high. Above the limit its practical character is lost and it becomes merely ornamental. But the mind itself, untrammeled by material conditions, possesses the power of selecting from among all its airy materials just such as it esteems the best, and of combining these into any desired form, thus mentally realizing its highest ideal. And having thus constructed a mental image the passion for beauty is often strong enough to impel the execution of this ideal with greater or less fidelity and its reproduction in visible or audible form by means of the appropriate material adjustments. This latter part is always the result of skill prompted by vivid mental representative power and usually prolonged labor. In the execution of a statue or a painting, or in the production of a poem or a romance, the mind is set free from the stern realities of the world, unimpeded by the properties of material bodies or the nature of physical forces, and only limited by the mental and muscular powers of representation and execution, and the tools and materials employed in the work. But objects thus created can have no practical value in the popular sense; they can only contribute to esthetic gratification.

Schopenhauer maintained that this pursuit of pure ideals, this contemplation of nature apart from utility, might be carried so far as to constitute a denial of the will to live, and a complete identification of the subject with the object. This is one of the few cases in which his zeal for a favorite theory led him astray from the path of sound logic. For he rightly maintained that pleasure was the satisfaction of desire and that the will was a blind pursuit of pleasure. He also held that the denial of the will was an abnegation of pleasure and if complete would reduce life itself to zero. And yet in his apotheosis of art we actually find him using language which implies the recognition of pleasure derived from the act of denying the will. Such expressions as "esthetic enjoyment" (*ästhetischer Genuss*), "joy in the beautiful" (*Freude am Schönen*), "happiness and mental repose" (*Seligkeit und Geistesruhe*), as well as his stronger statements that the pure willless cognition of the beauty of nature is the only pure happiness, and that moments in which we are freed from the pressure of the will are the happiest that we know, betray a remarkable confusion in his ideas both of pleasure and will.

This point of view is of interest here in illustrating the important fact that with the creative faculty, and to a great degree with the inventive genius, the will itself in Schopenhauer's acceptation took on a considerable extension; that the brain had now become an emotional center and seat of enjoyment, and that henceforth the mind itself was to have desires to satisfy, and to become in so far itself a dynamic factor or psychic force.

CHAPTER XXXI.

SPECULATIVE GENIUS.

The developing intellect was at the outset placed face to face with two classes of phenomena, not indeed generically distinct, but whose extremes present vast differences in many respects. One class embraced the simple mechanical phenomena which lie upon the surface of nature, and which were fortunately of the greatest immediate practical importance to the physical life of the race. The other class embraced all the deeper cosmical phenomena, of vast importance to a developed race, but with which primitive man really need have had little to do. The lower animals do not appear to have any thoughts whatever about this class of natural events, although they manifest considerable acquaintance with the other class which materially improves their ability to provide their own subsistence. But to the uninstructed intellect of primitive man no distinction in point of importance was recognized between these two classes of phenomena, and it immediately began to manufacture beliefs from both classes alike. The impossibility of comprehending those of the deeper and more recondite class led at once to the adoption of all the errors attendant upon the fundamentally erroneous supernatural explanation, and gave rise to religion as an inseparable element in the future culture and progress of the race. —*Dynamic Sociology*, II, 273–274.

So far as the development of brain mass and consequent brain power is concerned, it must be conceded that no "character" could possibly be more directly the subject of natural selection, since the primal quality of brain is cunning, and this is more important in fitting a creature to survive than any other attribute. It is, therefore, only in the cases of certain derivative faculties that have little or nothing to do with the fitness to survive, many of them rendering man unfit and almost helpless in the struggle for existence, that we find the really strong claims of those who advocate the doctrine of the inheritance of acquired mental qualities, or post-natal increments to faculties already existing. What are these qualities? Dr. Wallace believes them to consist chiefly of the mathematical, the esthetic (sculpture, painting, etc.), and the musical; but he also very properly mentions the power of abstract reasoning, the metaphysical faculty, or talent for abstruse speculation, that which gives rise to wit and humor, and the moral or ethical attributes. Others might be enumerated, such as the talent for scientific observation, for laboratory experimentation, for mechanical invention, and for literary research; and, in general, all the powers of mental application, abstraction, and attention, of study, and of investigation, by which knowledge has been increased. — *The Forum*, Vol. XI, New York, May, 1891, pp. 315–316.

The power of Thought, — the magic of the Mind! — BYRON: *The Corsair*, Canto I, Stanza 8.

On earth there is nothing great but man; in man, there is nothing great but mind. — SIR WILLIAM HAMILTON.

In the evolution of the human mind, the instinct of cosmic interrogation follows hard upon the instinct of self-preservation. — J. W. POWELL.

Under the head of speculative genius I shall include all the disinterested or non-egoistic intellectual faculties or attributes not embraced by either inventive genius or creative genius as above defined. As the former was extended to include the faculty of scientific discovery, which might also in a certain sense be called speculative, we are here chiefly limited to what is commonly embraced under the term philosophy as distinguished from science, and have now to inquire what the attributes are that speculative philosophy in its widest sense calls into exercise. We are also concerned with the precise manner in which, and the particular egoistic faculty out of which, these attributes have been developed. Following the genetic method which has been employed from the first it will be necessary to seek an answer to the last of these questions first, in the hope that this may lead to a solution of the others.

The inventive faculty after it threw off its allegiance to the will, or, more properly, after it had created a new conative center in the brain, began, as was shown, to busy itself with the wider relations subsisting between all the observed facts of nature, whereby it was able to discover truth and lead the way to science. Still having as its primary purpose the discernment of utilities, first to self and later to all men, it nevertheless soon encountered relations and began to discover truths whose utility either to self or to mankind was doubtful or even imperceptible — truths which were beyond its power to seize upon and convert through any exercise of ingenuity to human use. The sun, moon, and stars were perceived to have definite relations of direction, motion, and distance from one another, but the mind had no power to modify these relations. The mountains loomed up in the distant horizon against the background of sky, but no effort of will or of muscle could raise or lower them or alter their form. The sea lashed the beach with its incessant roar, but man was powerless to increase or diminish its rhythmic ebb and flow. The rivers swept on in their never-ceasing rush and murmur resistless for the puny arms of man. The clouds sped across the sky or floated in fantastic ever-changing forms far above and beyond the reach of earth-chained mortals. And so it was on all sides. Everywhere he gazed, man beheld objects and phenomena over which he had no control, and which were to him incomprehensible, inscrutable, and unchangeable.

Of all the relations that the intellect most strenuously sought to grasp, that of causation was the most fascinating. The principle of sufficient reason was the one which most strongly asserted itself, for it was only through this that the inventive faculty had been able to direct the simpler and more comprehensible relations within its scope. And it is possible that the still egoistic intellect in striving to master these wider relations may have been, at least at first, largely influenced by a vague sense that could it but once understand them it might bend even these to its selfish uses. When storms and floods and thunderbolts rode and dashed through the abodes of men scattering havoc, destruction, and death in their path, there might, at least, have lurked in the audacious brain of the being who had already grown to be the master of so large a part of nature the irreverent belief that these too would yet be made to feel his power and bow in suppliance to his ambitious will.

Thus began the great and long-protracted quest on the part of the growing intellect of man for the causes of the unexplained and irresistible phenomena of nature. Its own power and its own ways it well knew. The power and the ways of nature it knew not, but what could be more natural than to project itself behind the phenomena of nature and to postulate the same or similar causes and methods with those which it employed? The first explanation which man was led to offer for the phenomena of the universe was the anthropomorphic explanation, and this, it is scarcely too much to say, is still the current explanation of all phenomena for which no natural explanation is known. It would carry me too far afield to undertake to point out in detail how the anthropomorphic theory of the universe became at the same time the theological one, but such appears to have been uniformly the case. Whether the man-power behind nature was contemplated as single and the theology made monotheistic, or whether, as was the far more common case, it was regarded as multiple and the theology made polytheistic, in either and any case the inscrutable and unalterable events of nature were conceived as presided over by intelligence and will in all essential aspects similar to those of man.

Thus arose the mythologies of the world, and mythology is neither more nor less than theological cosmology. But along with the theological there was always manifest a tendency to a rational cosmology. The former was felt by the best minds of every race to be a sort of *ignava ratio*, an attempt to escape the severer intellectual effort really to explain phenomena, and therefore along with it we find associated a great number of partly theological and partly rational cosmologies. This was the case in ancient Greece as well as in most of the early civilizations, and became increasingly so in the two or three centuries which preceded the scientific era. Since the beginning of that era there has been a marked and rapid differentiation of these two kinds of cosmology, so that at the present time in all enlightened countries there exists a purely theological alongside of a purely rational cosmology. With the flood of knowledge which the invention of printing, the circumnavigation of the globe, the extension of the world's commerce, and the great scientific discoveries of Kepler, Galileo, and Newton poured in upon the world during the 16th and 17th centuries the speculative genius of man was furnished with the necessary data for inaugurating a rational philosophy of the universe, which, supplemented by the additional light of the 18th and 19th centuries of scientific investigation, has become, under the guiding principles of gravitation, evolution, and the conservation of energy, so complete as to dispense entirely in the minds of many with the theological hypothesis, except in some highly generalized form.

But the speculative faculty early took another direction and turned itself inward upon itself. It was not enough that it should seek the explanation of the phenomena of the universe, it must also seek an explanation of those of mind. Here, as stated in the introduction, and as frequently intimated in different chapters of this work, it was much less fortunate, in that it confined itself to the higher and more complex of those phenomena. But there can be no doubt that upon these difficult and recondite problems there has been expended the highest degree of intellectual power of which the human mind is capable. The theories set on foot by Plato and his followers relative to the nature of ideas and their relations to the outside world gave an impetus to the study of the most abstruse of all problems, and caused the discussions to be directed chiefly to the question as to whether anything really exists except the thinking subject. Thus cut loose from its realistic base, philosophy floated for ages in the air and fought the battles of the shades. Brought partly back to earth by Locke, Descartes, and Kant, it continued the struggle with one foot on the ground until physiological psychology at length pricked the metaphysical bubble and it collapsed. But it is found that too little is as yet known of the occult causes of mental phenomena to dispense entirely with the great thoughts of the past, and just now there is noticeable a sort of reaction; if not a real *Flucht zurück zu Kant,* at least a tendency to search through the rubbish of metaphysical speculation for certain golden grains that are found buried in it, and to bring these forth and confront them with the facts that science has revealed. Everywhere now-a-days one sees evidence of a sort of catabasis from the high throne of pure reason and pure intellect to the humbler sphere of feeling and will, and from the regions of abstraction, reflection, and speculation to the simpler fields of intuitive intellection, for it is here only that there is hope of finding a true scientific basis for the philosophy of mind.

Two other great fields for the operation of the speculative genius need to be mentioned, those of logic and mathematics. This form of the faculty must be regarded as the most remote from the egoistic base of mind. We have seen the intellect leaving self to revel in the search for universal utilities; we have seen it leave utility to sport with the phantoms of its own creation; we have seen it wrapped up in the objective contemplation of the macrocosm without and the microcosm within. We are now to behold it abandoning everything material and losing itself in the purely hypothetical and the purely abstract. For such is logic and such is geometry, which may be taken as the type of mathematical ideation. Of these two fields, that of logic is the most purely abstract, since geometry may be regarded simply as the application of logic to quantity. Logic deals only with the forms of thought, and therefore requires complete intellectual abstraction. While mathematics is the test or criterion of all science, logic is the test or criterion of all reasoning. Untrammeled by facts or concrete conditions, mathematics reaches the absolutely exact, and all the sciences in the hierarchy seek to approach as closely as possible to its perfect standard. Similarly logic affords the laws or canons by which all the intellectual operations must square themselves.

But it is not the nature of these intellectual domains that specially concern us, except as this helps us to see how the mind must operate under such circumstances. In mathematics everything is divested of all attributes except those of quantity or number. In logic they are divested of all physical attributes whatever, and reduced to pure intellectual relations. Not, of course, that these quantitative and intellectual relations are not capable of being afterward clothed with a material garb and applied to concrete facts and real things. This is the use and purpose of both logic and mathematics. But before this can be done laws must be discovered which are capable of fitting all possible cases, and in order to do this they must be made absolutely abstract and without condition or dependence upon anything in nature. Abstract reasoning, as it is called, may therefore be regarded as the highest stage which has been attained by the human mind, measuring the ascent exclusively by the degree of divergence from the purely concrete, interested, egoistic base of the intuitive reason. This form of development, however, is by no means necessarily a progress in the direction of practical importance. No amount of abstract reasoning could save the race from destruction under the law of competition, and not one of the derivative faculties considered in this chapter and the last have the least value in rendering its possessor capable of survival in the general struggle for existence. This is why it is necessary to exempt them from the law of natural selection, and the fact that they have developed is the strongest proof that has ever been presented that a faculty strengthened by use transmits to posterity the increment acquired during the life in which it has been exercised. There is no other way of explaining the increase. The fortuitous commingling of favorable germs which is offered by Weismann and his disciples as an explanation, is unintelligible and wholly inadequate, and we are forced to conclude that these biologically useless acquired characters are really transmitted.[1]

But it will not do to underrate the value of speculative genius to civilization. Invention and scientific discovery have furnished the material factors of civilization, but generalization and speculation, with all the aids of philosophy and scientific reasoning, have given the world an intellectual civilization, without which material progress would have little value.[2]

[1] It would be out of place to argue this point here. I have done this elsewLere. See Neo-Darwinism and Neo-Lamarckism: Proc. Biol. Soc. Washington, Vol. VI, 1891, pp. 11-71; The Transmission of Culture: The Forum, Vol. XI, New York, May, 1891, pp. 312-319; Weismann's New Essays: Public Opinion, Vol. XIII, Washington and New York, Sept. 10, 1892, p. 559.

[2] Scientific methods bear the same relation to intellectual progress that tools, instruments, machines — mechanical contrivances of all sorts — bear to material progress. They are intellectual contrivances — indirect ways of attaining results too hard for bare, unaided intellectual strength. As the civilized man is little, if at all, superior to the savage in bare-handed strength of muscle, and the enormous superiority of the former in accomplishing material results is wholly due to the use of mechanical contrivances; even so in the higher sphere of intellect, the scientific man boasts no superiority over the uncultured man in bare, unaided intellectual power. The amazing intellectual results achieved by modern science are due wholly to the use of intellectual contrivances or scientific methods. As in the lower sphere of material progress the greatest benefactors of the race are the inventors or perfectors of new mechanical contrivances or machines, so in the higher sphere of intellectual progress, the greatest benefactors of our race are the discoverers or perfectors of new intellectual contrivances or scientific methods. — Joseph Le Conte: Relation of Biology to Sociology. The Berkeleyan, May, 1887, Vol. XXIII, p. 123 (separately paged reprint, pp. 4-5).

CHAPTER XXXII.

THE INTELLECT.

The mind-force, as popularly understood, is no force, but only a *condition*. It does not propel, it only directs. It is not mind, except within the narrow limits of this definition, that achieves the vast results which civilization presents, and which, it must be admitted, could not be achieved without it. It is the great social forces which we have been passing in review that have accomplished all this. Mind simply guides them in their course. The office of mind is to direct society into unobstructed channels, to enable these forces to continue in free play, to prevent them from being neutralized by collision with obstacles in their path. In a word, mind has for its function in civilization to preserve the dynamic and prevent the statical condition of the social forces, to prevent the restoration of equilibrium between the social forces and the natural forces operating outside of them. Just as it is not psychological force which propels the water-wheel or the piston — which could not, nevertheless, be made to operate without it — but merely the forces of gravity and gaseous expansion compelled by mechanical power under the guidance of intelligence to operate for the benefit of man, so it is not mind which moves the civilization of the world, but only the great and never-ceasing forces of society, which but for the guidance of mind would rush blindly on into a thousand entanglements with rival forces, and assume that position of statical equilibrium which represents social stagnation. — *Dynamic Sociology*, I, 698–699.

Alle Physikotheologie ist eine Ausführung des, der Wahrheit entgegenstehenden, Irrthums, dass nämlich die vollkommenste Art der Entstehung der Dinge die durch Vermittelung eines Intellekts sei. Daher eben schiebt diselbe aller tiefern Ergründung der Natur einen Riegel vor. — SCHOPENHAUER: *Welt als Wille*, II, 305.

L'histoire de la civilisation peut se résumer en six mots: plus on sait, plus on peut. — EDMOND ABOUT: *A B C du Travailleur*, p. 39.

The long, dark, and winding path that has been followed in the preceding thirty chapters, beginning with Chap. II, has only brought us to the point from which mental philosophy set out, viz., to the intellect. It was seen to exist, but no one ever attempted to inquire how it came to exist. This has been our special task, and if a way has been opened to a true explanation of the origin and development of the intellect, that task has been performed. But Bacon declares *vere scire esse per causas scire*, and if the logic of this book is sound we may claim truly to know something about the intellect. Much is being said about *psychogenesis*, and laudable attempts are being made to explain the genesis of mind, but in most of this it is only its *ontogenesis* — the history of its development in the individual — that has engaged attention. Far more important is its *phylogenesis* — the history of its development in the race. A bare outline of this field was sketched in the fifth chapter of Dynamic Sociology, but its inadequacy was even then clearly felt, and its only purpose was to place the phenomena of mind in their proper relations to those of life on the one hand, and those of society on the other. While the present work may be looked upon as an expansion of that chapter, still it could not have been written then, because its matter had not been fully thought out, and because several great fields had not as yet been opened up to my mind. Its defectiveness from similar causes is still manifest, and others with the aid of better light will doubtless soon remedy much of this; but it is to be hoped that no backward step will be taken, and that the real origin and nature of mind will yet be made known to men.

Time was, and not long agone, when life was looked upon simply as an observed fact. Now, thanks to Darwin and his predecessors and successors, it is seen as a development, and there is no good reason why mind as a whole, or even the intellect, as the latest expression of the psychic law, should not also be recognized as having had a cause, an origin, and a history. The reason will never be satisfied with any fact until its source is known. All antiquity was doomed to know the river Nile only as a fact, but *Nili caput quærere* became a proverb that then expressed the restless dissatisfaction of the time with such a state of things, and still expresses the ceaseless effort that will ever be put forth to explore the unknown source of every stream of knowledge. The theologian may pronounce it irreverent and the positivist declare it useless, but the search for the beginnings of things will still go on and the hidden secrets of Nature will be laid bare.

The intellect thus seen in perspective across the expanse of time stands out in the foreground in a hitherto unknown clearness. All the past philosophy of mind, centering as it has upon this one faculty, however voluminous, brilliant, or profound, was incapable of thus bringing it out into bold relief. It is seen as a becoming, as a begotten child, as a product, as a reality. Nihilism, idealism, and all the other 'isms of the schools are banished, and psychology as a true natural science succeeds metaphysics as astronomy succeeded astrology, chemistry alchemy, and biology the magic freaks of the mysterious archæus.

Continuing the comparison with biology, primary intuition, as described in Chapters XXI and XXII, may be likened to protoplasm or to the simplest protozoans, such as the Amœba, while the developed intellect would represent the highest types of animals. Intuition, as there stated, is intellect, and embodies the whole of that faculty, just as protoplasm embodies all there is in life. But like protoplasm again, intuition is absolutely simple and undifferentiated. It is a homogeneous property containing within it the germs or potencies of all the intellectual faculties subsequently to be evolved from it. In it are to be found in an undeveloped state the intuitive perception, reason, and judgment, the inventive faculty, and the inventive, creative, and speculative genius, which form the subjects of succeeding chapters.

While the intellect as thus constituted embraces the entire thinking part of the mind, all of mind that is not feeling, it is nevertheless important to distinguish it carefully from several other things with which it is sometimes confounded, at least by those who are not in the habit of analyzing mental operations.

First, it may seem scarcely necessary to say that it is of a purely psychic, and not at all of a physiological nature. Like all psychic phenomena its operations are correlated with actual movements taking place in the brain and higher ganglia, doubtless in the strict relation of effect to cause, but these operations are pure psychoses and must not be confounded with those neuroses which form their physical basis. It may not be out of place to remark here, although the remark applies equally to the subjective phenomena treated in Part I, that this relation of mind to its physical base does not seem to me to embody any such profound mystery as most writers ascribe to it. I think that the habit of imagining an impassable gulf between body and mind has arisen from the time-honored belief in the ontological nature of the mind. If it should ever be possible to escape from that preconception and view mind simply in the light of a property, the mystery would forthwith vanish. It may be truly said that any property involves mystery. Why the peculiar molecular constitution and arrangement of glycerine should render that substance sweet, or of quinine should render that bitter, is as mysterious as that the molecular constitution and arrangement of protoplasm should impart to that substance vital properties, or as that the organization of the brain should give it the capacity to know. Yet no one descants on the wonderful preëstablished harmony which makes salt saline and potash alkaline. These are simply the known properties of these substances, believed by chemists to be due to their chemical constitution, although they could never have been inferred or predicted from a knowledge of that constitution. Viewed in this light, mind in general, and thought in particular, are rescued from the dominion of magic under which the very latest works still persist in holding them, and are placed in the same scientific position that is conceded to all other phenomena that it is proposed to investigate. If I were asked to specify the most serious obstacle which now stands in the way of psychologic progress I should not hesitate to name as such this lingering notion of the necessary entity of mind.

In the second place intellect must not be confounded with consciousness. Few, it is true, are likely to do this, but some are disposed to look upon consciousness as embodying the sum total of the knowing faculty. Under that head Sir William Hamilton grouped all the phenomena treated in his course of lectures on metaphysics. In this, however, he was not wholly wrong, for consciousness is, properly speaking, not a faculty but rather the condition of all mental operations whatever. When consciousness ceases mind ceases. The exceptions that will present themselves to this statement are apparent only. For every ganglionic center must have a consciousness of its own, and one must distinguish in the higher animals and man between the supreme consciousness and the subordinate consciousnesses. Consciousness embraces feeling as well as thinking and knowing, and the common expression "unconscious feeling" is a contradiction of terms. The loose way in which Hartmann employs the term *unconscious* is, to say the least, unscientific, since the Unconscious itself, which he personifies, is shown to be intensely conscious. Even the useful expression "unconscious cerebration" requires to be qualified so as to mean simply that the supreme ego does not take cognizance of such operations. But there must be subordinate centers that are distinctly conscious of them and that guide them along perfectly rational paths, often to the most brilliant results.

Just here it may be well to meet the objection that may be made to the fundamental classification of mental phenomena employed in this work, viz., that into subjective and objective, as defined in Chapters IV and V. It is held by some that all cerebration and ideation are attended with feeling, that to be conscious of thinking, the "stream of thought" as it flows through the brain must produce a sense of its action. Certain writers profess that when performing a mental operation they can detect a distinct sensation in the head, due to the flow of nerve-currents. This is probably more than they can say of either sight or hearing, which, as has been shown, must be attended with feeling, although no one perhaps is able to make this feeling rise into the field of the supreme consciousness. And there seems no good reason to doubt that cerebral neurosis is always and necessarily attended with feeling, as much that form which results in thought, as that which results in emotions. Otherwise there would be motion, molecular at least, without sensation, or an effect without a cause. But this is a very different thing from saying that all thought is feeling, and that no distinction of subjective and objective exists in the phenomena of the mind. Intellection — the acts of perceiving, cognizing, conceiving, judging, reasoning, generalizing, etc., — is an objective fact, a complex psychosis, which is capable of being contemplated apart from molecular change and its accompanying sensations. In and of itself, one may say, it is nothing, but it is known by its effects which manifest themselves in muscular action, in the agent doing something which he would not and could not do without this faculty. The greatest "intellect" in the world, if he had never done anything would have remained unrecognized. It is only by this doing — speaking, writing, constructing, etc., — that an intellect can make its existence known, and this it can only do by means of the bodily organs.

The next distinction may be drawn between intellect and knowledge. It should be premised, however, that the word *knowledge* has two different meanings, being used both in the active and the passive sense. In the sense of knowing or cognizing, knowledge is, indeed, an integral part of intellect, but in this sense it is more rare. In the passive or objective sense, however, the case is quite different. In this sense, although intellect and knowledge are entirely distinct things, still it is impossible for either to exist without the other. They may be separately conceived and treated, but they cannot be separated in fact. It is impossible for a sentient being to move or even for the least important of its organs to act in the most primitive way, at least consciously, without its resulting in knowledge. For every movement is a reaction from some sensation and involves a perception, if it be nothing more than that of its own activity. It is true that intensive sensations as defined in Chap. V, being so strong, cause the perception to be lost sight of and consciousness to be concentrated upon the feeling of pain or pleasure produced, and this gives little or no notion of the qualities of the object, but nevertheless it furnishes an *experience*, and this constitutes an important kind of knowledge. The power of perceiving relations, which is the essence of all forms of intuition, is acquired through innumerable experiences, primarily due to a multitude of trials in exploring the environment, most of which are failures but some successes, and through these repeated efforts the brain and great ganglionic centers slowly learn by comparison to distinguish between fruitless and successful movements.

Experiences of this conative class are supplemented by the regular method of acquiring knowledge through perception accompanying indifferent sensation, yielding conceptions and ideas and resulting in ideation or thought. Thus without any systematic or intentional effort, intellect is constantly and necessarily acquiring knowledge through contact and interaction of the organism with the environment. Fitness to resist the hostile elements of the environment consists in a certain degree of susceptibility on the part of the intellect to the reception of this essential knowledge, and under the law of natural selection only those beings that possess this required degree of susceptibility are able to survive. This results in a true biological development of the intellectual faculty.

But it is well known that developed man possesses a large fund of knowledge which is not acquired in this way. Inventive, creative, and speculative genius is for the most part independent of the law of advantage, and yet it is this that requires for its exercise the largest fund and the highest kind of knowledge. How did it come into possession of it? It has been shown that the real stimulus to the exercise of these derivative intellectual powers is the pleasure which this exercise affords. But such exercise, like that of the intuitive powers, necessarily resulted in the constant acquisition of knowledge, albeit such knowledge was of no practical use to the individual acquiring it except in so far as its acquisition was a pleasure resulting from the satisfaction of a new and elevated desire to acquire knowledge. That such a desire exists in a large proportion of mankind is a well-known fact, and that it was developed through the exercise of the faculties named there can be no doubt. This new desire demanding satisfaction furnished an additional and powerful stimulus to intellectual activity of this class, and it is to the joint effect of these two stimuli — the pleasure derived from intellectual exercise and from the acquisition of knowledge — that must be attributed the amazing heights to which human genius has attained.

Intelligence, though sometimes confounded with intellect, sometimes with genius, sometimes with shrewdness, sagacity, and ingenuity, is none of these, but simply predicates a fair degree of intellectual capacity in possession of an adequate supply of knowledge. The quality of intellect implied in intelligence is of a high order but not so brilliant as to amount to genius. The knowledge implied is a practical acquaintance with those things that everyone should know and does not include purely ornamental accomplishment. This admixture of practical discernment with practical acquirement, constituting intelligence is felt to be the best balance of qualities that one can have to insure success in life. It embraces enough of the egoistic principle to prevent anyone from becoming the victim of that principle in others, enough of the intuitive judgment to hold fast to present good, and enough of the inventive faculty to cope with nature and adversity if required to do so. At the same time it does not preclude the possession of any kind of useful knowledge and recognizes the utility of all refining, elevating, and broadening influences. Neither the capacity nor the aquirement necessary to constitute intelligence is beyond the power of the average individual. It is a condition that is attainable by every adult person of sound mind. The intelligent man or woman is the ideal citizen, and De Tocqueville's saying that representative forms of government necessarily presuppose a certain degree of general intelligence in the people is abundantly sustained by history.

Finally, it is of prime importance to distinguish the intellect from the dynamic agent in the mind. The nature of that agent was fully set forth in Part I, and it might scarcely seem necessary to dwell here upon its fundamental dissimilarity to the thinking faculty whose genesis has been traced. But as one of the principal objects of this work is to show that while the subjective factors of mind furnish the true social forces the objective factors furnish the guide to those forces, this would seem to be the place to justify the latter claim before passing to the social synthesis of the factors. This is important because the idea is so often expressed that mind, by which intellect alone is always meant, is a force. Those who take a theistic or pantheistic view of nature almost unanimously attribute the phenomena of the universe to the action of mind or intelligence conceived as an omnipotent force, and philosophers of this class, if they accept evolution, regard this too as the effect of an intellectual, or as they express it, an intelligent cause. Abundant as are the assertions of this kind they have scarcely ever been answered in the only way that is conclusive. Mr. Herbert Spencer, however, in replying to views of Mr. James Martineau similar to that last referred to, in which the expressions "mental force" and "originating mind" were used, very appropriately says: "In metaphysical controversy, many of the propositions propounded and accepted as quite believable are absolutely inconceivable. There is a perpetual confusing of actual ideas with what are nothing but pseud-ideas. No distinction is made between propositions that contain real thoughts, and propositions that are only the forms of thoughts. A thinkable proposition is one of which the two terms can be brought together in consciousness under the relation said to exist between them. But very often, when the subject of a proposition has been thought of as something known, and when the predicate has been thought of as something known, and when the relation alleged between them has been thought of as a known relation, it is supposed that the proposition itself has been thought. The thinking separately of the elements of a proposition is mistaken for the thinking of them in the combination which the proposition affirms. And hence it continually happens that propositions which cannot in truth be rendered into thought at all are supposed to be not only thought but believed. The proposition that Evolution is caused by Mind is one of this nature. The two terms are separately intelligible; but they can be regarded in the relation of effect and cause only so long as no attempt is made to put them together in the relation." [1]

Besides the wide-spread belief that the phenomena of the universe are either caused by mind or constitute a universal mind-force, it is not infrequently said that the achievements of man are a proof that the intellect is a force. It is clearly perceived that without it these achievements would have been impossible, i. e., that it is in some way a *cause* of them, and the distinction between a *causa sine qua non* and a *causa efficiens* is not drawn. The latter is the essence of a force. It is a *vis a tergo*, impelling whatever is before it. It is in this sense that the will is a true force, but not so the intellect. This, as already remarked, is only a directive agent. A few

[1] Popular Science Monthly, Vol. I, New York, July, 1872, pp. 319–320. Many years earlier, in his Social Statics, Mr. Spencer had used the following language: "Intellect is not a power, but an instrument — not a thing which itself moves and works, but a thing which is moved and worked by forces behind it. To say that men are ruled by reason, is as irrational as to say that men are ruled by their eyes. Reason *is* an eye — the eye through which the desires see their way to gratification." See Social Statics, London, 1851, p. 350.

familiar illustrations of the distinction between propulsion and direction have already been used, such, for example, as that of the wind filling the sail of a ship compared with the helm managed by the practised helmsman ; but the reasons why the intellect when joined to the will is able to produce such enormously increased effects have not been specifically pointed out. In Chapters XVII to XIX, however, the preparation was made for explaining these reasons. This explanation may be introduced by the general proposition that the true secret of the efficacy of intellectual action is that *it makes nature do the work*. This is the fundamental principle underlying all invention. Man has a power within himself — the will — but this is extremely limited. He can accomplish very little of what he desires by the exercise of this power alone. But he finds himself surrounded by the unseen powers of nature over many of which he has no influence, but some of which, through the exercise of his intellect he has learned in a greater or less degree to control. He has learned that whenever he fully understands the nature of these forces it is possible to direct them into channels which will cause them to produce the effects that he desires. The phenomena of nature are uniform and take place according to invariable laws. When those laws are known it is usually possible to utilize them by simple adjustments. Great and irresistible as Nature seems to be, it is found that as a matter of fact she is easily managed. All that is required is to know her thoroughly and to know how to control her. The first is science, the second is art or invention. This is as true of the simplest tools as it is of the most complicated machinery. If it is desired to excavate a tunnel through a mountain the lowest class of labor performed in such an excavation involves this principle. The gang of workmen employed to do the digging could do comparatively nothing without their picks and shovels. These are products of art. Their adaptation to the work required to be done is a result of thought. All *labor* is something more than mere muscular exertion. The lowest class of laborers are *artisans* in a proper sense of the term. Political economists speak of production, but what is production but the work of natural forces directed by intelligence?[1] Not only is the real labor chiefly done by nature but the product is wholly artificial. Man does little but direct. Machinery is simply an extension of the principle that was always employed. It diminishes the agency of muscle and increases the agency of physical force.

Not only is the force that resides in man comparatively feeble, but its effect to secure the ends sought is greatly lessened by friction. By this I mean that when unguided it constantly fails on account of the obstacles in its way. Knowing none but the direct method of going about its work in the great majority of cases it is impeded or wholly prevented from accomplishing its object. The only true psychic force is desire. This in and of itself is unintelligent and blind. The poets have happily represented love, which is the type of pure desire, as blind, and all languages recognize the truth in the expression "blind impulse" (*blinder Drang*). So complicated is the environment of every living creature that it is only through a variety of instincts developed through natural selection, and causing animals to perform acts that so closely resemble rational ones as to be frequently mistaken for them, that any race is able to escape destruction from the barriers to existence which the most simple conditions present. These instincts are fixed and being only adapted to a given environment, the least change in the creature's surroundings, if at all rapid or sudden, results in extinction. Man has instincts too, but his environment is infinitely more complex than that of any species of animals, to meet which something besides instinct is necessary. One of the principal functions of the intellect therefore,

[1] L'outillage du genre humain n'est pas autre chose qu'une collection d'idées. Tous les leviers s'usent à la longue, et toutes les brouettes aussi; les machines à vapeur ne sout pas éternelles, mais l'idée reste et nous permet de remplacer indéfiniment le matérial qui périt. — EDMOND ABOUT: *A B C du Travailleur.* Deuxième Edition, Paris, 1869, pp. 39–40.

is to diminish or remove entirely the friction of his environment, and thus to economize to the fullest extent the true forces that are within him. It is this greater ability to make his acts count by the intelligent avoidance of obstructions and impediments, joined with the faculty of utilizing the forces of nature that more than anything else distinguishes man from the lower animals, and both these qualities belong exclusively to the intellect.

It remains to point out more exactly the nature of what may be called *the psychology of intellectual direction* — the precise process according to which the intellect works in controlling the true psychic, and hence also the social forces. This has already been done in Chapters XXI to XXIII for simple intuition, and again in Chap. XXVIII for the specific process of invention, and the principle is the same for the fully developed intellect, but a more generalized statement of it may now be made. It was seen that the essence of this principle is the erection of the means to desired ends into true objects of desire, and all that intellect does is simply to report to consciousness the fact that a certain act is such a means. It then becomes immediately desired, and action follows this new desire. The simple perception that such indirect action constitutes such a means is the intellectual act, and of itself involves no muscular movement, no desire. It is therefore in no proper sense a force. It may be said that the perception itself implies a change within the brain substance — a neurosis — and that an intellectual act implies action. This cannot be denied. The 'report' to consciousness of the discovery of a means of accomplishing a desired but otherwise unattainable or difficult purpose is certainly a psychosis, and as such involves some form of brain action or nerve metabolism, but it is not the movement which has the effect to contract the appropriate muscles and produce the necessary act, not even the one that is essential to secure the means. That action cannot take place until the desire has been aroused to secure such means, which the intellectual perception has caused to be substituted for the desire to secure the end.

It is also true that all indirect means to ends which intellect perceives, involve some muscular action requiring force, and the popular view seems to be that this force, at least, is exerted by the intellect. With a fulcrum, a long enough lever, and a ποῦ στῶ Archimedes could doubtless move the earth, and in most of the mechanic arts the muscular effort required to be exerted is exceedingly small in comparison with the total force that is brought to bear upon the object to be moved, still, even the application of the lighted fuse made by the little girl that blew up Hell Gate was a slight muscular effort. But the force that produced this effort was not the intellect. It may have been merely a desire to comply with her parents' wishes. Yet all the engineering work and all the labor involved in that enterprise was *directed* by the intellect.

The intellect thus fully fledged is not a rare faculty, latent the greater part of the time, and only occasionally brought into requisition. It is in constant use and ceaseless activity and directs the greater part of the movements of its possessor. That is, the most important actions of human beings at least are performed under its guidance, and the phenomena of civilized life are in the main the results of what was described in the eighth chapter of Dynamic Sociology as "the indirect method of conation." The intellectually directed activities of men may be classed under three general heads ; first, movements of the body and limbs under the guidance of the intellect for the more certain gratification of desire. This class not only includes special and particular acts thus described, but also all the great systematic courses of action. Besides the innumerable efforts to circumvent, deceive, and outwit others, and thus secure unearned gratifications, and besides the devising of the means and instruments for deceiving and outwitting nature in the same way to the same end, it also includes the entire field of human labor of whatever kind, which, as already remarked, always involves more or less exercise of the intellectual powers. The second great class of intellectual activity is that of oral communication or speech. Through this art the intellect finds a fuller expression than through those of mere action. The immense influence which the members of society thus exert upon one another, and indirectly upon their general condition, is too apparent to require illustration. The third class is that of written communication, through which the finest shades of thought and the highest discoveries of truth are not only conveyed to all who can read but are handed on to later ages to form a basis for still higher flights of intellectual achievement.

In all these respects man differs from the highest animals and it is this difference that constitutes him a *rational being*. For reason, as popularly employed, is nothing else than the exercise of the intellect according to the indirect method, and while that faculty is feeble and frequently misleading among the lower types of mankind, and none too strong or reliable among the higher ones, still, all men not only possess it in some degree, but they all exercise it daily and hourly and in all that they do. This fact should be recognized in any system of social science, not merely as a fact but as the prime factor in the treatment of such a science.

PART III.

SOCIAL SYNTHESIS OF THE FACTORS.

This comparison of legislation to invention is not a mere accidental or convenient analogy. So soon as the mind rises to grasp the conception of social forces, possessing all the essential attributes of the physical forces, and differing from them only as these differ from one another, the actual identity of legislation, as it should be conducted, with mechanical invention, as it is alone successfully conducted, becomes at once obvious. The successful inventor, knowing as he first must the nature of the forces and the objects with which he has to deal, so adjusts the latter that the former, though in no way increased or diminished or changed in their essential nature, will, by their natural operation, produce results beneficial to human interests. The true legislator must do precisely this and nothing else. The only difference is, that he is dealing with social forces and objects instead of physical ones. — *Dynamic Sociology*, I, 38.

Throughout the animal kingdom there are found no better examples of energetic industry, than these in which the ends which the activities subserve are altruistic rather than egoistic. And hence we are shown, undeniably, that it is a perfectly possible thing for organisms to become so adjusted to the requirements of their lives, that energy expended for the general welfare may not only be adequate to check energy expended for the individual welfare, but may come to subordinate it so far as to leave individual welfare no greater than is requisite for maintenance of individual life. . . . They show us that it is within the possibilities of organization to produce a nature which shall be just as energetic, and even more energetic, in the pursuit of altruistic ends, as is, in other cases, shown in the pursuit of egoistic ends ; and they show that in such cases these altruistic ends are pursued in pursuing ends which on their other face are egoistic. For the satisfaction of the needs of the organization, these actions conducive to the welfare of others must be carried on. The seeking for the satisfaction which the organization requires, itself entails the performance of those activities which the welfare of the community requires. — HERBERT SPENCER : *Principles of Ethics*, I, pp. 301–302.

For where's the State beneath the Firmament
That doth excell the Bees for Gouernment ?
DU BARTAS : *Diuine Weekes and Workes*, p. 184.

CHAPTER XXXIII.

THE ECONOMY OF NATURE AND THE ECONOMY OF MIND.

The prodigality of nature is now a well-understood truth in biology, and one that every sociologist and every statesman should not only understand but be able to apply to society, which is still under the complete dominion of these same wasteful laws. No true economy is ever attained until intellectual foresight is brought to bear upon social phenomena. Teleological adaptation is the only economical adaptation. — *Dynamic Sociology*, I, 74–75.

The *natural* antidotes to monopoly (i. e., where no attempt is made at social regulation) are counter-monopoly and competition. But these two are essentially the same, counter-monopoly being only competition of monopolies.

There is a constant antithesis between competition and coöperation which applies as well to the non-producer as to the producer. Coöperation always tends to reduce competition, and competition denotes want of coöperation. Whether competition can be trusted to prevent monopoly depends upon the degree of coöperation, and no equitable adjustment of the various relations of industry can be made so long as different industries manifest different powers of coöperation. As society is now constituted, it is the non-producing classes who coöperate most and compete least, while the producing classes coöperate very little and compete strongly. Coöperation is an artificial principle, the result of superior intelligence. Competition is a natural law, and involves no thought. Hence those who coöperate thrive at the expense of those who compete. — *Dynamic Sociology*, I, 594.

Nature is extremely practical, though not what men call economical. Nature's economics differ from man's in being genetic, involving great waste of products. In genetic economy, while no amount of cost is spared to produce the smallest result, nothing is ever done unless it produces some result, however slight. In human, or teleological economy, on the other hand, great parsimony is displayed in the outlay, and frequently much labor is expended without result, owing to erroneous interpretations of phenomena. Nature never errs, but she wastes. Man economizes, but often looses through error. Nature may be called practical, but not economical; man economical, but not always practical. — *Dynamic Sociology*, II, 494.

L'homme n'est ni ange, ni bête : et le malheur veut que qui veut faire l'ange fait la bête. — PASCAL : *Pensées*, I, 185.

C'est ainsi que c'est enfin trouvé provisoirement réalisé, autaut que le comportent les tendances générales de la société moderne, l'étrange type politique propre à la philosophie négative, qui avait si longtemps demandé un système réduisant le pouvoir à de simples fonctions répressives, sans aucune attribution directrice, et abandonnant à une libre concurrence privée toute active poursuite de la régénération intellectuelle et morale. — AUGUSTE COMTE : *Philosophie Positive*, VI, 334.

Nos premières ressources ou, pour parler plus juste, tous les biens de l'humanité sont des conquêtes du travail.

L'homme ne peut ni créer ni détruire un atome de matière, mais il peut rapprocher de sa personne et s'assimiler tout ce qui le menace ; il peut surtout adapter à son usage et tourner à son profit ce qui d'abord était indifférent ou même nuisible. Par le travail, il ajoute à tout ce qu'il touche un caractère d'utilité et s'annexe ainsi toute la terre, petit à petit. — EDMOND ABOUT : *A B C du Travailleur*, p. 29.

I have from time to time shown that there are certain limitations to the application of the doctrines and methods of biology to sociology, and that in every case such limitation is the result of the introduction of some new principle characteristic of *humanity* as distinguished from *animality*, of *reason* as distinguished from *instinct*, of *spirit* as distinguished from *matter*. This is precisely what, even from a purely scientific point of view, we ought to expect, and is in fact necessary. For in the scientific hierarchy each science, in addition to the forces and phenomena of the lower sciences, deals with a new force and a new group of phenomena, and therefore with new doctrines and new methods. — JOSEPH LE CONTE : *Popular Science Monthly*, Vol. XIV, February, 1879, p. 430.

To make a man a machine is to make him anything but productive. That such a result can never be realized in fact is self-evident ; that it should ever be conceived of in thought is an evidence of how little trouble even the greatest writers on political economy have given themselves concerning the real nature of the being with whose actions they deal. If the laborer is an engine, his motive power is fuel ; if he is a man, his motive power is hope. It is psychological rather than physiological forces which keep him in motion. His will, and not merely his muscle, is an economic agent, and he is to be lured, not pushed, in the way of productive effort. — J. B. CLARK : *Philosophy of Wealth*, pp. 53–54.

In this chapter the word *nature* will be used to denote all classes of phenomena, whether physical, vital, or even psychic, into which the intellectual or rational element does not enter, while the word *mind* will, for the sake of brevity, be employed in the somewhat popular or conventional sense of rational or intellectual, the two terms thus mutually excluding each other, and taken together covering all possible phenomena. This broad classification will be seen to be useful and indeed necessary, although the specific object is somewhat narrower, viz., that of emphasizing the distinction between that system of economy which is based upon the actions of the human animal and that which is based upon the actions of the rational man. The former is the system of the Physiocrats,[1] Adam Smith,[2]

[1] "Pas trop gouverner." — LE MARQUIS D'ARGENSON.

"Laissez faire et laissez passer." — DE GOURNAY.

"Qu'on maintienne l'entière liberté de commerce; car la police du commerce intérieur et extérieur la plus sûre, la plus exacte, et la plus profitable à la nation et à l'état, consiste dans la pleine liberté de la concurrence." — QUESNAY: *Maxime* XXV.

"Tous les travaux des hommes peuvent, en quelque sorte, devenir productifs par inhérence, au moyen d'un ordre de dépenses conforme à l'ordre naturel des besoins. Cet ordre s'établit de lui-même. La police ne doit point s'en mêler: En y touchant elle le confondrait, et elle contribuerait à introduire le désordre qui peut rendre tous les travaux stériles." — DUPONT DE NEMOURS: *Abrégé des principes de l'économie politique*, 1772.

[2] The views of Adam Smith relative to competition and the natural laws of trade are perhaps best set forth in Chap. VII of Vol. I of his Wealth of Nations, entitled: Of the Natural and Market Price of Commodities. In Chap. VIII they are applied to the wages of labor. He is, however, chiefly concerned with the freedom of trade, and his strictures upon all attempts on the part of government to regulate it are found in nearly all parts of the work. See especially Chaps. I and V of Vol. II. These strictures, of course, relate largely to transportation, and especially to bounties, duties, subventions, etc. The following passage, however, relates to exchange, and may be taken as indicating the attitude of his mind on the relations of the state to industrial action:

"When the Government, in order to remedy the inconveniences of a dearth, orders all the dealers to sell their corn at what it supposes a reasonable price, it either hinders them from bringing it to market, which may sometimes produce a famine even in the beginning of the season; or, if they bring it thither, it enables the people, and thereby encourages them to consume it so fast, as must necessarily produce a famine before the end of the season. The unlimited, unrestrained freedom of the corn trade, as it is the only effectual preventative of the miseries of a famine, so it is the best palliative of the inconveniences of a dearth; for the inconveniences of a real scarcity cannot be remedied; they can only be palliated." — *Wealth of Nations*, Vol. II, p. 103.

Ricardo,[1] Malthus,[2] Herbert Spencer,[3] and the modern individualists. The latter was foreshadowed by Auguste Comte, but has never taken any systematic shape except in Dynamic Sociology with which the present work naturally connects itself. Although its distorted image is reflected in numerous more or less obnoxious forms from the mirror of modern public opinion, its real character is quite unfamiliar to the greater number even of the best informed persons.

Comte recognized the influence of mind in society and placed psychology in its proper position in his hierarchy of the sciences, but he refused to regard it as a distinct science, and treated it under the name of "transcendental biology." Nevertheless, in his discussions he gave considerable weight to it, and laid stress on the elements of prevision and the control of social phenomena. Spencer, on the contrary, while he treated psy-

[1] "The natural price of labour is that price which is necessary to enable the labourers, one with another, to subsist and to perpetuate their race, without either increase or diminution."—DAVID RICARDO: *Principles of Political Economy and Taxation*, p. 70.

"Like other contracts, wages should be left to the fair and free competition of the market, and should never be controlled by the interference of the legislature." —DAVID RICARDO: *Ibid.*, p. 82.

[2] The now so celebrated Malthusian law or doctrine, as stated in Chap. I of the Essay on the Principle of Population (pp. 4–6,) is as follows:

"Population, when unchecked, goes on doubling itself every twenty-five years, or increases in a geometrical ratio. . . .

"Considering the present average state of the earth, the means of subsistence, under circumstances the most favourable to human industry, could not possibly be made to increase faster than in an arithmetical ratio. . . .

"The power of population being in every period so much superior, the increase of the human species can only be kept down to the level of the means of subsistence by the constant operation of the strong law of necessity, acting as a check upon the greater power."

[3] Social Statics abridged and revised; The Man *versus* the State; Justice; *passim*.

The Malthusian doctrine is quite clearly restated and reaffirmed in his Principles of Ethics, Vol. I, p. 298. Adam Smith's remark relative to speculations in corn is almost exactly repeated in the Social Statics (Abridged ed. p. 104) and in the Sins of Legislators (see same volume, p. 339) the speculator is characterized as "simply one whose function it is to equalize the supply of a commodity by checking unduly rapid consumption."

chology at length and assigned it the same position, viz., between biology and sociology, failed to make it in any proper sense the basis of either his sociology or his ethics, both of which are made to rest squarely upon biology. His psychology, therefore, which indeed, was written before his biology, and largely from the standpoint of metaphysics, stands isolated and useless in his system of synthetic philosophy.

It was early observed that astronomical and physical phenomena were uniform and invariable, and it was also perceived that the actions of animals, though much more complicated, follow fixed laws which could be understood and taken advantage of by man. That the simplest human actions, such as those of children, were equally uniform and determinable was scarcely more than the result of observation. Nothing was more natural than the generalization that the acts of adults do not differ generically from those of children, and the wider generalization that all human activities and all social phenomena are as rigidly subject to natural law as are the activities of children and animals and the movements of terrestrial and celestial bodies, was but an additional short step. The early political economists seized upon this specious bit of reasoning and made it the corner-stone of their science, formulating from it their great laws of trade, industry, population, and wealth.

It is curious that this altogether sound abstract principle, the indispensable foundation of all economic and social science, should have led to the greatest and most fundamental of all economic errors, an error which has found its way into the heart of modern scientific philosophy, widely influencing public opinion, and offering a stubborn resistance to all efforts to dislodge it. This error consists in practically ignoring the existence of a rational faculty in man, which, while it does not render his actions any less subject to natural laws, so enormously complicates them that they can no longer be brought within the simple formulas that suffice in the calculus of mere animal motives. This element creeps stealthily in between the child and the adult, and all unnoticed puts the best laid schemes of economists and philosophers altogether aglee. A great psychic factor has been left out of the account, the intellectual or rational factor, the cause, origin, and nature of which were considered in Part II. From what was there said it must appear that this factor is so stupendous that there is no room for astonishment in contemplating the magnitude of the error which its omission has caused.

Although the question is primarily a psychological one, still, it is, as we now perceive, also an economic one, and it will be profitable to consider it now from this latter point of view. There are two distinct kinds of economics which may be called biological economics and psychological economics, or the economics of life and the economics of mind. The word economics is here used in its narrow or primary sense. The question is one of economy, and it is of the first importance to contrast sharply these two kinds of economy, the economy that prevails in the animal world, in the domain of life, in organic nature generally, with the economy that prevails in the human sphere, in the realm of mind, in the domain of reason.

Every one is now, since Darwin, familiar with the general nature of animal economics. It is the survival of the fittest in the struggle for existence. It is the mere physics of life, the pure unmodified and undirected psychic forces, as defined in Chap. XV, working themselves out in nature. Just as in the physical world and the great clash of mechanical forces the superior prevail and produce the observed results, so in this animal physics it is superior force that counts and might is ever uppermost. The animal forces are their instincts, appetites, wants — in short, their desires. These are ever seeking satisfaction and only lack of strength can prevent them from attaining it.

It was formerly supposed that organic nature was economical of its energies. The facts of adaptation, while they gave rise to the theological error of special creation, gave rise at the same time to the biological error of natural economy. In the first place it was supposed that the adaptation was always perfect. This was repeatedly asserted and much dwelt upon in early ante-evolution days. It is still widely believed with the modification that while a changing environment constantly disturbs the equilibrium, natural selection as constantly tends to restore it. Weismann, in the authorized translation of his Essays, allows the statement to stand that "each existing species shows the purpose of its being in every detail of its structure, and in its perfect adaptation to the conditions under which it lives. But it is only adapted so far as is actually necessary, only so far as to make it fittest to survive, and not a step further."[1] But even this much cannot now be admitted, since, as will be hereafter explained, the struggle for existence consumes the organic energy and dwarfs all beings that engage in it. The notion of perfect economy naturally goes along with that of perfect adaptation. Nature was regarded as the great economist from whom man was to copy. Biologists, of course, now know better than this, and yet it continues to be reaffirmed by popular writers. Even Mr. Spencer has failed to strike out of his revised edition of Social Statics (1892) the remark of the original edition (1850) that "with a perfect economy, Nature turns all forces to account.'[2]

It is indeed true that nature creates nothing that is necessarily useless, that everything produced has a possible utility. This follows from the genetic method of evolution. Everything that exists is pushed into existence by a *vis a tergo*. This is the efficient cause, and nature works only through efficient causes. The universal life force is perpetually creating new forms, and these must be adapted to their environment, otherwise they cannot even be brought into being. But this adaptation need only reach the minimum stage. If it is sufficient to insure continuance the end is attained, though higher degrees are always being aimed at. The means, however,

[1] Essays, Vol. II, Oxford, 1892, p. 29. [2] American edition, 1892, p. 178.

through which this adaptation is accomplished are not the most economical means conceivable. They often seem to be the least economical conceivable. They are just those that all the circumstances of the case combine to produce. Provided the end be accomplished the character of the means is wholly immaterial from a purely biological standpoint.

The extravagance of these means has become a common subject of discussion, and the facts that have accumulated are of a surprising character. A few of these were enumerated in Dynamic Sociology (Vol. II, p. 87,) but any number of other cases might be adduced. Thus in a lecture on the herring by Prof. Huxley, after giving 10,000 as probably an underestimate of the number of ripe eggs shed in spawning by a moderate-sized female herring, he remarks: "Suppose that every mature female herring lays 10,000 eggs, that the fish are not interfered with by man, and that their numbers remain approximately the same year after year, it follows that 9,998 of the progeny of every female must be destroyed before they reach maturity. For if more than two out of the 10,000 escape destruction, the number of herrings will be proportionately increased." [1]

Darwin, as all know, was so struck with the redundant fertility of the organic world and the necessary destruction involved that he made it the starting point of all his investigations. One of his earliest observations is recorded in a foot-note in his Journal of Researches,[2] as follows: "I was surprised to find, on counting the eggs of a large white Doris [kind of sea-slug] how extraordinarily numerous they were. From two to five eggs (each three-thousandths of an inch in diameter) were contained in a spherical little case. These were arranged two deep in transverse rows forming a ribbon. The ribbon adhered by its edge to the rock in an oval spire. One which I found, measured nearly twenty inches in length

[1] A lecture delivered at the National Fisheries Exhibition, Norwich, April 21, 1881. *Nature*, April 28, 1881, Vol. XXIII, p. 612.

[2] New York, 1871, p. 201.

and half in breadth. By counting how many balls were contained in a tenth of an inch in the row, and how many rows in an equal length of the ribbon, on the most moderate computation there were six hundred thousand eggs. Yet this Doris was certainly not very common : although I was often searching under the stones, I saw only seven individuals. *No fallacy is more common with naturalists, than that the numbers of an individual species depend on its powers of propagation.*"

These, of course, are much more moderate cases than many that have been cited. According to M. Quatrefages two successive generations of a single plant-louse [plant-lice are parthenogenetic] would cover eight acres. The vegetable kingdom is equally full of examples. A large chestnut tree in June probably contains as much as a ton of pollen. Considering the size of a pollen-grain the number on such a tree would be next to inconceivable. Certain pines are almost equally prolific of their male spores, and these pine pollen-grains are very light so as to be wafted on the wind to immense distances. The "showers of sulphur" that are sometimes reported to have fallen in the states bordering on the great lakes have proved to consist of such pollen-grains that continuous south winds had borne from the great forests of the long-leaved pine that border the Gulf of Mexico. Many herbs, as orchids, the broom-rape, etc., produce minute seeds in vast quantities, and some of these are rare plants. Burst a puff-ball and there arises from it a cloud that fills the air for some distance around. This cloud consists of an almost infinite number of exceedingly minute spores, each of which, should it by the rarest chance fall upon a favorable spot, is capable of reproducing the fungus to which it belongs.

The defenders of natural economy who are acquainted with such facts excuse them on the ground of their necessity. They say that it is the only way in which organic life can progress. Thus Prof. Grant Allen, in treating the origin of fruits, remarks : "Those plants which merely cast their naked embryos adrift upon the world to shift for themselves in the fierce struggle of stout and hardy competitors must necessarily waste their energies in the production of an immense number of seeds. In fact, calculations have been made which show that a single scarlet corn-poppy produces in one year no less than 50,000 embryos ; and some other species actually exceed this enormous figure."[1] The late Prof. E. L. Youmans, the leading American disciple of Herbert Spencer, and an uncompromising individualist, once used the following language : "Nature seems to have been no more economical of her mental than of her material resources. There is a prodigality in her ways which a narrow philosophy cannot comprehend. Of her profusion of flowers, but few issue in fruit ; of her myriads of eggs, but few are hatched ; of her numerous tribes of life appearing in the remote past, multitudes are extinct ; and, of the achievements of her intellect, the great mass is lost in oblivion. But, through all her seeming waste, Nature has, nevertheless, a grand economy. She gives the widest chances, under a system which favors the best ; the failures are rejected and the fittest survive."[2] Spencer himself hints at an explanation of this wide-spread state of things when he says : "Those complex influences underlying the higher orders of natural phenomena, but more especially those underlying the organic world, work in subordination to the law of probabilities. A plant, for instance, produces thousands of seeds. The greater part of these are destroyed by creatures which live upon them, or fall into places where they cannot germinate. Of the young plants produced by those which do germinate, many are smothered by their neighbors ; others are blighted by insects, or eaten up by animals; and, *in the average of cases*, only one of them produces a perfect specimen of its species which, escaping all dangers, brings to maturity seeds enough to

[1] Cornhill Magazine for August, 1878, Vol. XXXVIII, p. 180.

[2] Popular Science Monthly, Vol. V, New York, August, 1874, p. 494.

continue the race. Thus it is with every kind of creature. And he goes on to show that civilization has developed in substantially the same way, ignoring, however, the psychologic factor.

A few writers have taken a somewhat less optimistic view. Dr. Asa Gray remarks: "The waste of being is enormous, far beyond the common apprehension. Seeds, eggs, and other germs, are designed to be plants and animals, but not one of a thousand or of a million achieves its destiny. Those that fall into fitting places and in fitting numbers find beneficent provision, and, if they were to wake to consciousness, might argue design from the adaptation of their surroundings to their well-being. But what of the vast majority that perish? As of the light of the sun, sent forth in all directions, only a minute portion is intercepted by the earth or other planets where some of it may be utilized for present or future life, so of potential organisms, or organisms begun, no larger proportion attain the presumed end of their creation." And he immediately proceeds to quote to the same effect from the article he has been considering in the Westminster Review; "When we find, as we have seen above, that the sowing is a scattering at random, and that, for one being provided for and living, ten thousand perish unprovided for, we must allow that the existing order would be accounted as the worst disorder in any human sphere of action."[2]

The last sentence quoted from this reviewer is precisely to our present point. No one denies that all this waste in the inorganic world is necessary, because neither man nor mind is responsible for it. No one either will contest that in the long run this method has actually resulted in what we recognize as general organic progress, although it is well established that retrogression may result as easily as progression, and certainly has resulted to a great extent. But the algebraic sum is what

[1] Social Statics abridged and revised, New York, 1892, pp. 237–238.

[2] Darwiniana, by Asa Gray, New York, 1877, pp. 372–373.

we have, and if there was a beginning in some primordial form, as most biologists suppose, that sum is quite a plus. Nor will any one object to having nature's method fully explained and exposed, and thoroughly taught as a great truth of science. It is only when it is held up as a model to be followed by man and all are forbidden to "meddle" with its operations that it becomes necessary to protest. I shall endeavor still further to show that it is wholly at variance with anything that a rational being would ever conceive of, and that if a being supposed to be rational were to adopt it he would be looked upon as insane.

Amid all this literature, only a small part of which can be noticed here, there has not been, so far as I am aware, any attempt to formulate the true law of biologic economics. Much has been said of the law of parsimony, which is a very subordinate one sometimes called into exercise. But of the great law of prodigality, which is universal, no adequate definition has yet been offered. We have seen that from its genetic character the organic force is incapable of producing any necessarily useless form. Its products, while they only rarely possess an actual value, nevertheless must all possess a potential value. This part of the law may therefore be expressed by the formula that *every creation of organic nature has within it the possibility of success*. Thus far the biologic law is economical. But, as we have seen, only the minutest fraction of that which is created becomes an *actual* success. The definition must therefore have another member to cover this part. Mr. Spencer, as quoted above, suggested that it involved the doctrine of probabilities. This does not seem precisely to express it. It is more correct to call it a process of trial and error. The fundamental principle may be called *the necessity for certainty*, or *the paramount importance of certainty*, while the process consists in *the multiplication of chances*. There seems to be no limit in nature to the degree of energy that may be put forth in the direction of securing certainty. The chances of survival, though they may seem to be abundant, will be multiplied a thousand fold in order that certainty may be made a thousand times certain. The complete law of biologic economics may therefore be expressed in the following form :

1. All organic energy results in potential utility.

2. Actual utility is secured through the indefinite multiplication of efforts.

It thus appears that in biology, while nothing takes place which does not secure some advantage, however slight, the amount of energy expended in gaining this advantage bears no fixed proportion to the value of the result. Nature acts on the assumption that her resources are inexhaustible, and while she never buys a wholly useless article she usually pays an extravagant price for it. The expressions ***natural selection*** and ***survival of the fittest*** both contain the significant implication that the bulk of things are not selected, and that only the select few who prove fit survive, while all else perishes. The first member of the biologic law of economy may be characterized by the term ***practical.*** The second member may in like manner be characterized by the term ***prodigal.*** Nature is therefore at once the most practical and the most prodigal of all economists ; practical in that she never makes anything which has not the elements of utility, prodigal in that she spares no expense in accomplishing even the smallest result.

Nature may be said to be engaged in creating every conceivable form. Every one is familiar with the wonderful variety in the actual forms of vegetable and animal life. But these, innumerable as they are, only represent nature's successes. Intermediate between them there must be imagined an infinite number of failures — conceivable forms in the production of which the organic energy has expended itself in vain, and which really represent a much greater expenditure than that which has been required to create all that exists. Again, among the successful forms there are all degrees of success. There are the vigorous and robust, rejoicing in a full measure of vitality and marching forward toward the possession of the earth ; and there are the weak and languishing, which the former class is gradually crowding out of existence. Between these there are all the intermediate grades. But even the successful are only temporarily so. Like human empires they have their rise and fall, and the path of natural history, like that of human history, is strewn with the remains of fallen dynasties and the ruins of extinct races.

This law may be illustrated in physics as well as in biotics. If the expenditure of energy be designated as the *cost* of any given result, then it may be said in general that *nature tends to exaggerate the cost of whatever is produced.* Thus, it may be assumed that the most economical way in which a river can flow would be in a straight line from its source to its mouth. But even if it were to begin in this way it would soon become irregular, sinuous, and crooked, and then more and more crooked, until at length the distance traversed by every drop of water would be at least doubled. This physical law which has been called "the rythm of motion" and rests on the "instability of the homogeneous," prevails also in the organic world. The tendency is everywhere to exaggerate the irregularities of normal development. This is often carried so far as to result in the production of abnormalities that cause their own extinction. Such were doubtless the strange dragons of Mesozoic time, the perhaps stranger mammals of early Tertiary time, the still more recent mastodon and mammoth, the moa and apteryx, and other wingless birds, while the living elephant and other overgrown creatures must also doubtless soon disappear. In the vegetable kingdom the coal flora is full of examples, as is also the less known flora of the Trias and Jura, and we still have many waning types, such as the maidenhair tree and the mammoth and redwood trees, whose paleontological record shows that they are just passing off the stage. Many other living plants, either through parasitism, as the Rafflesia, or through extreme specialization, as many orchids and yuccas, further exemplify this law. Such monstrosities inevitably perish with the slightest alteration in their material surroundings. The progress of organic development has thus been to a large extent the successive creation of types that have contained within themselves the elements of their own destruction — that have, as it were, broken down with their own weight. New ones of course have succeeded them, adapted for the time being to their environment, but destined in turn to outgrow their conditions and perish from the same cause. This rhythmical character of organic progress is therefore essentially self-defeating, the only progress taking place, if any, being the marginal increment resulting from the excess of the pluses over the minuses. This is the characteristic of all genetic progress. Teleological progress takes place according to an entirely different law, involving a true economy of energy.

In this sketch of natural or biologic economics I have not gone into the physical explanation of the reason for the difference between it and what I shall now distinguish as human or rational economics, as set forth in Dynamic Sociology (Vol. I, p. 73; Vol. II, p. 99ff.,) viz., that in the former effects are only just equal to causes. The organic force is applied directly to the object to be transformed, and the forms to be created are molded into the required shape by an infinite number of minute impacts, the sum of which is represented by the transformation effected. No advantage is taken of any mechanical principle whereby the effect is made to exceed the energy expended, as was shown in the last chapter to be the normal characteristic of all intellectual action. There is, it is true, a certain class of facts in which natural selection imitates rational design so closely in its ultimate products that it was formerly supposed, and is still supposed by many, that they must be the result of intelligent direction. Sharp teeth and claws, for example, are similar to edged and pointed tools or weapons, and take advantage of the principle of the inclined plane in the form represented by the wedge, and this may in some cases be carried so far as to involve the principle of the screw, as in certain spirally arranged seed-vessels that bore into the ground to plant their seeds. Other cases were mentioned in Chap. XXVII. It is also a fact that in the arrangement of muscles and the passage of tendons through their cartilaginous sheaths the principle of the lever and fulcrum is utilized to a greater or less extent. All such cases, however, constitute exceptions to the law of biologic economy, and only serve to show how instinctively all men recognize the distinction, from the surprise and interest felt at seeing nature do anything that seems to involve rational economy. That distinction is, that the latter is teleological and deals with final causes, while the former is genetic and deals with efficient causes. This means that while organic forms are merely pushed into existence by the pelting of atoms from behind, and are fortuitous, or literally chance products, human creations are conceived in advance by the mind, designed with skill for definite purposes, and wrought by the aid of a variety of mechanical principles, such as those mentioned above, by which means the energy expended is small, usually trifling, in proportion to the result accomplished. The inventive faculty of man is the primary application of reason. No other animal possesses it, not even to the extent of wielding a weapon that is not a part of its organic structure.[1] The beaver, indeed, builds dams by felling trees, but its tools are its teeth, and no

[1] See p. 184, *supra*. This statement, made in my address as vice-president of the Section of Economic Science and Statistics of the American Association for the Advancement of Science, at the Rochester Meeting in August, 1892 (Proceedings, Vol. XLI, p. 307), of which this chapter is an expansion, has been called in question as contradicted in accounts given by certain African travelers, especially Du Chaillu and Büttikofer, of the gorilla and chimpanzee. I have, therefore, taken the trouble to investigate the matter and I find that no modification of the text is required. The impression, indeed, prevails that these animals, at least the chimpanzees, sometimes employ clubs in self-defense; but no writer has, I think, stated that he has seen them do so, or even himself believes that such is the case, although there is a common report in Western Africa to this effect, and the natives have fanciful notions as to the intelligence of these creatures. They usually confound the two animals, and from their observed resemblance to man attribute to them certain human actions. The following passage in Büttikofer's

further advantage is taken than that which results from the way the muscles are attached to its jaws. The warfare of animals is waged literally with tooth and nail, with horn and hoof, with claw and spur, with tusk and trunk, with fang and sting — always with organic, never with mechanical weapons. And whatever work is done by animals is always done with

Reisebilder aus Liberia (Vol. I, pp. 229–230) probably contains all there is in these reports: —

"Der *baboon* — so wird in ganz Liberia der Chimpanse genannt — wird allgemein für ein über den andern Thieren stehendes Wesen gehalten. . . . Man erzählt unter anderm vom *baboon*, dass er auf zwei Beinen gehe, wie der Mensch, dass alte Exemplare nicht klettern, sich aber mit einem Prügel in der Hand gegen Angriffe zur Wehre setzen, mit geballten Fäusten auf der breiten Brust trommeln und brüllen, dass man es meilenweit in der Runde hören könne (also ganz das nämliche, was uns über den Gorilla berichtet wird)."

The belief of some that the chimpanzee possesses the art of making fire rests on still more slender evidence. The same author gives (ibid., p. 230) the following account, made to him by an old African hunter who had spent his best years in the pursuit of these and other wild animals in that region, which doubtless furnishes the foundation for this and other prevalent notions: —

"Du hast gewiss auf deinen Jagden schon jene auffallenden, reingehaltenen, freien Stellen im Walde angetroffen, über die man sich gewöhnlich keine Rechenschaft geben kann. Das sind des *baboons* Feuerstätten. Die *baboons* haben nämlich die Gewohnheit, in allen möglichen Dingen den Menschen nachzuahmen. Auf diesen Plätzen nun tragen sie trockenes Holz zusammen und schichten es zu einem grossen Stosse auf. Hierauf thut einer der Bande, als ob er das Holz in Brand steckte, worauf dann alle zusammen das vermeintliche Feuer erst vorsichtig, nach und nach immer stärker anblasen, bis ihnen zuletzt fast die Zunge aus der Kehle hängt. Hierauf kauern sie rund um den Holzstoss nieder, setzen die Ellenbogen auf die Kniee und breiten, gleichsam um sich zu wärmen, die Hände aus. So kann man sie bei nassem Wetter halbe Tage lang geduldig neben dem eingebildeten Feuer sitzen sehen."

There can be no doubt that these animals, like all those of the ape family, have great powers of mimicry, and this might readily lead the natives into extravagant ideas of their sagacity. That nothing can be relied upon that is not carefully observed and verified by scientific men is clear from the following further remark of Büttikofer in the same work (Vol. II, p. 350): —

"Nach den Aussagen der Eingebornen zu urtheilen, würde ein ausgewachsener Chimpanse dem Gorilla so wohl an Grösse als auch an Körperkraft gleichkommen, und spielt derselbe überhaupt in ihren Sagen als Sinnbild von Kraft und Klugheit eine bedeutende Rolle. Einige ganz alte Exemplare beiderlei Geschlechts, die in unsern Besitz gelangten, haben jedoch den unumstösslichen Beweis geliefert, das die Erzählungen der Eingebornen, wenigstens was die Grösse betrifft, in hohem Maasse übertrieben sind."

tools that nature has provided through a long course of development, none of which takes advantage of any principle of physics further than as already stated.

It is in rational man, therefore, that the first application of anything worthy of the name of economy is made. Nature has no economy. Only through foresight and design can anything be done economically. Rivers thus constructed (canals, mill-races, irrigating ditches, etc.,) are straight, or as nearly so as true economy requires, and Prof. Schiaparelli's inference, from the supposed existence upon the planet Mars of extensive water ways stretching across its disk in right lines, that it is inhabited by rational beings, is generally felt to be a legitimate one, if the facts are as alleged. Everything that is done under the direction of the intellect is as economical as the degree of intelligence will permit. All failures to attain this maximum economy are due to ignorance — to lack of acquaintance with the conditions of the problem. The degree of economy therefore for the same degree of intellectual penetration will be exactly proportioned to the amount of knowledge possessed.

Nature's way of sowing seed is to leave it to the wind, the water, the birds and animals. The greater part falls in a mass close to the parent plant and is shaded out or choked to death by its own abundance. Only the few seeds that chance to be transported by one agency or another to some favorable spot and further happen to be covered up, can grow. The most of those that germinate never attain maturity on account of hostile surroundings, and only the rarest accidents of fortune live long enough to continue the race. To meet this enormous waste correspondingly enormous quantities of seed are produced. Such is nature's economy. How different the economy of a rational being! He prepares the ground, clearing it of its vegetable competitors, then he carefully plants the seeds at the proper intervals so that they shall not crowd one another, and after they have sprouted he keeps off their enemies, whether vegetable or animal, supplies water if needed, even supplies the lacking chemical constituents of the soil, if he knows what they are, and thus secures, as nearly as possible, the vigorous growth and fruition of every seed planted. This is the economy of mind.

A closer analysis shows that the fundamental distinction between the animal and the human method is that *the environment transforms the animal, while man transforms the environment.* This proposition holds literally from whatever standpoint it be contemplated. It is, indeed, the full expression of the fact above stated, that the tools of animals are organic, while those of man are mechanical. But if we contrast these two methods from the present standpoint, which is that of economics, we see at once the immense superiority of the human, or psychological, over the animal or biological method. The economy is of two kinds, economy of time and economy of energy. It has taken much longer to develop any one of the organic appliances of animals, whether for supplying its wants or fighting its enemies, than the entire period during which man has possessed any arts, even the simplest. And yet such appliances, however complete or effective, have not sufficed to enable any species possessing them greatly to expand its territorial range, or to migrate far from the region to which it was originally adapted. Man, on the other hand, without acquiring any new organic adaptations, by the manufacture of tools, weapons, clothing, habitations, etc., by subjecting the animal and vegetable kingdoms to his service, and by the power of "looking before and after"— in short, by the aid of reason — has taken possession of the whole earth, and is the only animal whose habitat is not circumscribed. This, as just remarked, he has accomplished in a comparatively brief period, i. e., wholly since Tertiary time, and chiefly since the glacial epoch.

The economy of energy is fully as great as that of time, and may be regarded as the cause of the latter. It is the result of *art.* It has been seen that the mechanical products of rational design necessarily utilize some economic principle through which the muscular force necessary to be exerted is less for any given result accomplished than it would otherwise be. In the great majority of cases the result could not be produced at all without the aid of the proper implement or mechanism for producing it, and this becomes more and more the case as machinery gains upon hand labor. The sum total of all such devices forms the basis of the mechanic arts. Few realize how completely civilization depends upon art in this sense. The utter helplessness of man without the arts is well illustrated in De Foe's Robinson Crusoe, but the author saw clearly that in order to enable his hero to survive at all, even in a tropical climate where nature's productions were exuberant, he must provide himself from stores of the wrecked vessel with a considerable supply of tools and other artificial appliances. What was true of Robinson Crusoe, thus circumstanced, is much more true of the great majority of mankind who inhabit what we call temperate climates, i. e., climates in which the temperature sometimes falls ten or twenty degrees below the freezing point, and where for several months each year all vegetative functions cease. One winter without art would suffice to sweep the entire population north or south of the thirtieth parallel off the face of the earth.

We are so much accustomed to the terms *labor* and *production* that we rarely stop to think what they really mean. Neither of these terms has any place in animal economics. All labor consists in an artificial transformation of man's environment. Nature *produces* nothing in the politico-economic sense of the word. Production consists in artificially altering the form of natural objects. The clothes we wear are derived chiefly from the sheep, the ox, the silk-worm, and a few other animals, the cotton plant, flax, hemp, and a few other plants; but between the latest stage at which nature leaves these latter and the final form in which they are ready for use there are many transformations requiring much art and great labor.

The houses that man inhabits once consisted chiefly of trees, clay, and beds of solid rock. These, too, have been transformed by labor performed with tools and machinery. In like manner the entire cycle of human achievement might be gone through. It would be found everywhere the same.

The arts taken in their ensemble constitute material civilization, and it is this that chiefly distinguishes man from the rest of nature. It is due exclusively to his mind, to the rational or intellectual faculty. That is, it is an exclusively psychological distinction. Civilization, which is human development beyond the animal stage, goes forward under the economics of mind, while animal development takes place under the economics of life. The difference between these two kinds of economics is fundamental. They are not merely dissimilar, they are the direct opposites of each other. The psychologic law tends to reverse the biologic law. This latter law may be briefly defined as *the survival of the best adapted structures*. Those structures which yield most readily to changes in the environment persist. It has therefore been aptly called "survival of the plastic."[1] The environment, though ever changing, does not change to conform to the structures but in the contrary direction, always rendering the partly adapted structures less adapted, and the only organic progress possible is that which accrues through changes of structure that tend to enable organic beings to cope with sterner and ever harder conditions. In any and every case it is the environment that works the changes and the organism that undergoes them.

But the most important factor in the environment of any species is its organic environment. The hardest pressure that is brought to bear upon it comes from the living things in the

[1] Address of Mr. Clarence King on Catastrophism in Geology, delivered at the Yale Scientific School in 1877. The principle is not as different from that of natural selection and the survival of the fittest as Mr. King seems to suppose.

midst of which it lives, and though paradoxical, it is those beings which most resemble it that crowd it most severely. The least advantage gained by one species from a favorable change of structure tends to make it spread and infringe upon others, and soon to acquire, if not strenuously resisted, a complete monopoly of all things that are required for its support. Any other species that consumes the same elements must, unless equally vigorous, be crowded out. This is the true meaning of the survival of the fittest. It is essentially a process of *competition*, but it is competition in its purest form, wholly unmixed with either moral or intellectual elements, which is never the case with competition in human society.

The prevailing idea is wholly false which claims that it is the fittest possible that survive in this struggle. The effect of competition is to prevent any form from attaining its maximum development, and to maintain a certain comparatively low level of development for all forms that succeed in surviving. This is a normal result of the rhythmic character of all purely natural, i.e., not rational or teleological, phenomena, as explained a few pages back. The greater part of what is gained in the flood tide is lost in the ebb. Wherever competition is wholly removed, as through the agency of man in the interest of any one form, great strides are immediately made by the form thus protected, and it soon outstrips all those that depend upon competition for their motive to advancement. Such has been the case with the cereals and fruit trees, and with domestic animals, in fact, with all the forms of life that man has excepted from the biologic law and subjected to the law of mind. The supposed tendency of such forms to revert to their original wild state, about which so much has been said, is simply their inability when remanded to their pristine competitive struggle to maintain the high position which they had acquired during their halcyon days of exemption from that struggle, which they can no more do than they can attain that position while subjected to it.[1] Competition, therefore, not only involves the enormous waste which has been described, but it prevents the maximum development, since the best that can be attained under its influence is far inferior to that which is easily attained by the artificial, i.e., the rational and intelligent, removal of that influence.

Hard as it seems to be for modern philosophers to understand this, it was one of the first truths that dawned upon the human intellect. Consciously or unconsciously it was felt from the very outset that the mission of mind was to grapple with the law of competition and as far as possible to resist and defeat it. This iron law of nature, as it may be appropriately called (Ricardo's "iron law of wages" is only one manifestation of it), was everywhere found to lie athwart the path of human progress, and the whole upward struggle of rational man, whether physical, social or moral, has been with this tyrant of nature — the law of competition. And in so far as he has progressed at all beyond the purely animal stage he has done so through triumphing little by little over this law and gaining somewhat the mastery in this struggle. In the physical world he has accomplished this so far as he has been able through invention, from which have resulted the arts and material civilization. Every implement or utensil, every mechanical device, every object of design, skill, and labor, every artificial thing that serves a human purpose, is a triumph of mind over the physical forces of nature in ceaseless and aimless competition. The cultivation and improvement of economic plants and the domestication of useful animals involve the direct control of biologic forces and the exemption of these forms of life from the operation of the

[1] I have long regarded this as one of the most important truths in biology, and am disposed to emphasize it the more because it seems to have been wholly overlooked and an erroneous view maintained by leading biologists. I first gave distinct expression to it in an article on the Local Distribution of Plants in the Popular Science Monthly for October, 1876 (Vol. IX, pp. 676–684), and have illustrated it on numerous subsequent occasions (see especially the Forum, December, 1886, Vol. II, pp. 347–349).

great organic law which dwarfs their native powers of development. All human institutions — religion, government, law, marriage, custom — together with innumerable other modes of regulating social, industrial, and commercial life, are, broadly viewed, only so many ways of meeting and checkmating the principle of competition as it manifests itself in society. And finally, the ethical code and the moral law of enlightened man are nothing else than the means adopted by reason, intelligence, and refined sensibility for suppressing and crushing out the animal nature of man — for chaining the competitive egoism that all men have inherited from their animal ancestors.

One important fact has thus far been left out of view. Man, it is true, is a rational being, but he is also still an animal. He has struggled manfully against the iron law of nature, but he is far from having overcome it. He has met with wonderful success in this direction in his dealings with it in the physical world ; he has laid a firm hand upon it in the domain of organic life ; by the aid of well ordained institutions he has dealt it heavy blows in its social aspects ; and the suicidal tendency which it exhibits when operating upon dense masses of people has enlisted against it with telling effect the counter-law of ethics. But all this has fallen far short of completely eradicating the deep-seated principle that lies at the foundation of animal economics. Aside from these few directions in which he has succeeded in partially supplanting the competitive economics of life by the coöperative economics of mind, he is still as completely under the dominion of the former as is any other organic being.

The fact thus far omitted in this chapter is the principal one that it was sought to enforce in the early chapters of Part II, viz., that the intellect itself was developed under the influence of the purely egoistic law. That extraordinary brain development which so exclusively characterizes man was acquired through the primary principle of advantage. Brain does not differ in this respect from horns or teeth or claws. In the great struggle which the human animal went through to gain his supremacy it was brain that finally enabled him to succeed, and under the biologic law of selection, where superior sagacity meant fitness to survive, the human brain was gradually built up, cell upon cell, until the fully developed hemispheres were literally laid over the primary ganglia and the cranial walls enlarged to receive them. The brain of man was thus itself originally an engine of competition. Intellect was a mere servant of the will. It was only by virtue of its peculiar character through which it was capable of perceiving that the direct animal method was not the most successful one, even in the bare struggle for existence, that it so early began, in the interest of pure egoism, to antagonize that method and to adopt the opposite and indirect method of design, calculation, and coöperation.

The competition which we see in the social and industrial world, competition aided and modified by reason and intelligence, while it does not differ in either its principle or its purpose from the competition among animals and plants, differs widely in its methods and its effects. We see in it the same soulless struggle, the same intense egoism, the same rhythm by which existing inequalities are increased, the same sacrifice of the weaker to the stronger, and the same frenzy of the latter to possess and monopolize the earth. But along with this the antagonistic principle is also in active operation. This is the law of mind making for a true economy of energy. It is mind alone that perceives that competition is wasteful of energy, and therefore in the interest of the very success that competition seeks, it proceeds to antagonize competition and to substitute for it art, science, and coöperation. By the aid of these the success of those who use them is increased many hundred fold. In society, therefore, competition tends to defeat itself by inciting against it the power of thought. It cannot endure. It is at best only a temporary condition or transition state. On the one hand the competition between men resolves itself into a competition between machines, and instead of the fittest organism it is the fittest mechanism that survives. On the other hand the competition between individuals becomes a competition between associations of individuals. Such associations are the result of coöperation which is the opposite of competition. Economists talk of free competition, but in society this is scarcely possible. Only the simplest operations, those conducted with the least intelligence, can continue for any length of time to compete. The least skilled forms of labor approach this condition most closely, but freedom is here limited by the relations that labor sustains to capital. The chief difference between employers and employed until recently has been that the former have used the rational method while the latter have used the natural method. Capital has always combined and coöperated while labor has only competed. But such is the power of the former method and its superiority over the latter that competing labor has had no chance in the struggle with combining capital. Latterly, however, labor has begun in a small way to call to its aid the psychological economy of coöperation. So strange and unexpected did this seem that it was at first looked upon as a crime against society, and many still so regard it. Indeed, all the laws of modern nations are framed on the assumption that capital naturally combines while labor naturally competes, and attempts on the part of labor to combine against capital are usually suppressed by the armed force of the state, while capitalists are protected by the civil and military authority of the state against such assumed unlawful attempts. This enormous odds against which labor struggles in its effort to adopt and apply the economics of mind will greatly retard the progress of industrial reform which aims to place labor on an equal footing with capital in this respect.

Competition between industrial associations, or corporations, follows the law of competition among rational beings in general, and is only a brief transition stage, to be quickly followed by further combination. Just as competition among individuals soon resulted in that combination by which corporations were formed, so competition between corporations soon results in the amalgamation of all in any one industry into one great compound corporation, now commonly under the form of a "trust." This process of compound coöperation does not stop until the whole product of the given industry is controlled by a single body of men. Such a body thus acquires absolute power over the price of the commodity produced, the only limit being that of the maximum profit that it can be made to yield. Thus, for example, all the petroleum a country produces may be under the control of a single trust, and in order to secure for the members of that association of capitalists the maximum return for the petroleum, its price will be placed at the highest figure that consumers of petroleum will pay, rather than, in whole or in part, return to candles or resort to gas or electricity. There is no necessary relation that this price shall bear to the cost of production. It may be twenty or it may be a hundred times that cost, and the profits accruing to the trust will be proportional. The same may be true of coal or iron or sugar or cotton, and even in the case of breadstuffs something analogous can occur through the device which is known as "cornering." All monopolies rest on the same principle, and they are as common in the industries of transportation and exchange as in that of production. Not only do the railroad[1] and telegraph systems furnish illustrations, but

[1] "It soon became evident also that the competition on which the community had counted with so much certainty as a means of regulating the railway system failed utterly to be a satisfactory means of securing the reformation of abuses and the lowering of the fares. . . . Now and then a struggle would occur between competing lines, but it did not last long and was generally followed by a relapse into the old way of doing things. Either some sort of agreement was arrived at by which both companies agreed to divide traffic or earnings, or to maintain rates, or some other device was adopted to abolish competition and put combination in its place. Ultimately one road would be bought up by the other, and the semblance even of competition would disappear. . . . The outcome would be an enormous loss of money, respectively capital, not merely to the men

they may be found in the mercantile business of every country, in all of which competition is short, heated and fitful, ending in the swallowing up of the small industries by the great ones in ever widening cycles.

Bad as all this appears to be, it is by no means an unmixed evil. This purely egoistic application of the law of mind to business interests still bears the marks of its economic superiority to the purely natural method by preventing the normal and necessary waste of competition. Although this immense saving nearly all goes into the coffers of the lucky few who chance to control these great currents of wealth, nevertheless the maximum cost to the consumers of all classes of commodities thus monopolized is usually less than it was when they were left entirely to the influence of competition. This may seem strange to those economists who look upon competition as the only antidote to monopoly, and who have been taught that its normal effect is to keep down prices. But the facts are against this view, and it may be worth our while to glance at a few of them. I cannot do this more effectively than by a few quotations from a remarkable paper by one of our leading representative political economists :[1]

"I use the term 'waste' in a broad way to indicate all those causes which keep the price of goods higher than they might be if the sellers made no effort to attract customers. In former times the sellers of goods remained quiet in their places of business and awaited the arrival of buyers. If one store sold cloth at a lower price than its competitors, the buyers of themselves sought out the place and made their purchases.

who had put their money into the concern, but to the country as a whole. It happened at times, indeed, that a road was built merely for the purpose of making some other competing road buy it out, which was nearly sure to be done in the long run." The Railway Question. Report of the Committee on Transportation of the American Economic Association. Publications of the Association, Vol. II, No. 3, July, 1887, pp. 28–29.

[1] The Principles of Rational Taxation, by Prof. Simon N. Patten. Published by the Philadelphia Social Science Association before which it was read Nov. 21, 1889. 25 pp. 8°.

But those good old days are gone. A seller must now be ever on the alert to attract trade or his rivals will soon displace him. His store must be upon a good street. He must pay large sums for advertising. Agents on large salaries must be sent out to induce customers to buy his goods. These and many other expenses must be met by any one who expects to be successful in trade at the present time. But what is the result upon prices? Are not prices in our stores much higher than they would be if the buyers sought the sellers instead of the sellers the buyers? Would not sewing machines and organs be cheaper if the persons who desired to purchase them should look up the dealer instead of the latter searching carefully all over the city for them? The number of dealers in any article is but a small fraction of the number of buyers, and they can find the proper store much more easily than the dealers could hunt up their customers. . . . If a given merchant does not use all the familiar means to advance his interests some more pushing rival will steal away his trade; yet is the trade of the city as a whole increased by all these efforts to displace rivals? Is any more soap, coal, or shoes sold in this city because they are advertised in the street cars? Do all the circulars our grocery men leave at our doors, increase the quantity of coffee and sugar consumed in the city? Do the high rents paid for good localities increase the whole local trade, or does the rent merely indicate the advantage which one rival for the same trade has over another?

A little thought, I think, will show that a large part of these expenses do not add to the general welfare of the city. If they are incurred by one of a number of rivals he can gain trade at the expense of the others. But if they are incurred by all of the dealers alike no one gets more trade than he would have had without them. The merchants must all charge a higher price for their wares to make good this expense and the public have a burden without a corresponding benefit.

Another form of waste arises from a great increase of retail stores. Each new store has attractions by which it secures a share of the trade. Take the shoe stores of the city as a sample. Think how thick they are, sometimes several in a single block. As they must duplicate the stock of goods, employ many extra hands and pay rent on many unnecessary buildings, is it any wonder that the price of shoes is so high? Notice also the increase of milk and baker's wagons. The continuous rattle of their wheels on our streets every morning tells only too well the miles of useless journeying they necessitate. These causes are at work in nearly every line of retail trade. A recent investigation shows that the number of retail dealers in this country has increased four times as fast as population.

Keeping these facts in mind it is easy to see where a large part of the increase of productive power has gone. In proportion to their product our factories employ fewer men, but these displaced men have been to a large extent absorbed by the retail trade. . . . The same tendencies show themselves in the wholesale trade. Each manufacturer or dealer must resort to many costly means of preserving his trade, which are of no advantage to the ultimate consumer. Each one must do what his rivals do to keep himself afloat, but the public must foot the bills. Do farmers get any advantage from the intense rivalry of the firms who resort to so many costly expedients to sell them their machinery? How much do the whole body of commercial travelers, who are said to cost the wholesale trade $200,000,000 a year, increase the quantity of goods which are annually sold to the American people?

This enormous waste is a leading cause of the present tendency to form trusts or similar combinations. As soon as a trade becomes united in some organized way the whole body of these useless expenses can be lopped off, and the resulting economy is the main source of the increase of dividends. A legitimate trust is an organization to save waste and it is not likely to continue long in existence if it tries to raise prices higher than they would have gone if a reckless competition had continued. Of course the results of the saving pass largely into the possession of the trust, yet saving is better than wasting, whoever may get the benefit. . . .

The effect on prices of the modern system of competition encouraging waste is the same as that of a monopoly or combination. Prices are forced to the upper limit, above which they could not go without discouraging trade. When the conditions of a business are such that a large expenditure of money in attracting customers, will give a merchant an advantage unless his rivals follow his example, the general use of extensive advertising, traveling salesmen, expensive stores in fashionable localities, raise prices far above the cost of production. The small dealer who has not the capital to increase his trade by such expensive means moves his store nearer to the homes of the customers, so that the advantage of locality may in a measure counteract advantages possessed by richer rivals. A multitude of small stores spring up to profit by the advantage of locality, and prices are separated still farther from the cost of production to allow the dealer to pay his rent and secure his living from the small stock of goods demanded by the locality. When all these causes get in full operation, and each rival resorts to new expedients to draw the trade of others to himself, there is no limit to the rise of prices except at the point beyond which the people will cease to purchase in large quantities. So we have practically the same limit to the rise of prices for a system of wasteful competition as for monopolies. If they follow their own interest monopolies cannot force prices higher than a system of waste can. To the public as buyers, the effect on retail prices is the same under both systems. All is gotten from the buyer it is possible to do without preventing a sale.

In the leading professions the same influences are at work by which the price of services is forced to the upper limit.

The tendency of lawyers' fees is not towards the real cost to the lawyer in time and energy, but towards the point beyond which people would cease to employ them. And with the doctors the same tendencies are even more easily seen. A young doctor could not rely upon cheapness to attract business. He must in some way get into the good graces of a part of the public, take an active part in some church, or society, and in other ways get himself into notice. But all these means of securing trade cost money, and he must make his bills large enough to get it all back and leave enough for a good living.

The old formula about competition reducing prices has yet so strong a hold on the public that they do not appreciate the changes in the business methods which are now in common use. They think that a multitude of competitors in any trade is a safeguard to low prices. Yet these rivals find that passive cheapness brings little trade. Costly agressiveness brings ten customers where cheap passivity secures one. Doubtless the public desire cheapness, but they are willing to pay dearly to those who aid them in the search. When dealers recognize these facts and organize their business on an aggressive basis, real cheapness becomes a thing of the past, and prices, in such a business, approximate what they would if they were controlled by a trust or an intelligent monopoly.

There are, then, good reasons why we should think of the tendencies of wasteful competition towards higher prices as having the same results upon prices, and following the same laws that monopolies do. When we wish to ascertain the effects of present economic conditions we will arrive much more nearly the truth if we think of a multitude of our industries and trades as monopolies than if we adhere to the old hypothesis that an intense competition in them brings cheapness. The law of monopoly governs the price of drugs just as much as it does of sugar. The retail price has no more tendency to conform to the lowest cost of their production than the price of sugar does under the present trust. The difference is merely that in the latter case the increased price passes into the hands of the refiners, while in the former it is wasted by the large number of persons who get a living by handling and distributing them.

The public think that aggressive competition brings them cheap goods, because they assume that the reduction of price is a necessary result of the action of self interest in the sellers. But the action of self interest may lead a dealer to attract trade by expensive means as well as by mere cheapness. In which way his self-interest will prompt him to act is determined not by himself but by the social condition of the people with which he deals. If the people are easily misled and their standard of living does not require all their productive power, aggressive action on the part of the dealer counts for more than mere cheapness. The real limit of the upward movement of prices is fixed by the action of buyers and not of sellers. Prices cease to rise at that point above which the demand of the public would rapidly fall off. For this reason the upper limit of prices is the same for aggressive competition as for intelligent monopoly, The increased net revenue is the controlling motive of both competing sellers and monopolies. The price is fixed by that buyer who, if he ceased to buy, would reduce the net revenue of the seller."

I have quoted thus at length from this extraordinary document because it presents such an array of cogent facts in such a lucid manner. Although the authority for the statements made is as high and as sound as any that could be desired, still they are to so large an extent statements of facts of common observation that no authority is required in support of them. And still their statement is required, since, as is seen, notwithstanding their clearness, the error which they are calculated to overthrow is wide-spread and deep-seated. The author's purpose in presenting them is, however, widely different from the use which it is here proposed to make of them, and need not be discussed. Their value in the present connection is primary and fundamental, and fully justifies the space they occupy in this work. Better than any other class of facts they show the fundamental difference between competition under the influence of the rational faculty and mere animal or biological competition. And if there has been the change to which Prof. Patten alludes in the business methods of the present and the past, it is a change which has been wrought by the greater introduction of the mind element into business affairs. Increasing density of population, as all know, by the friction it produces of mind with mind, tends of itself to sharpen the wits and increase that practical form of intelligence which counts in the struggle for existence. But along with this there has gone an immense increase in the educational facilities offered in cities. Not to mention the improved public school system and lengthened terms of general study with the high schools added on, some of which fit their pupils for entering college, there are the multiplied business and commercial colleges specially adapted to teach young people how to transact business, conduct enterprises, and in general to "make money."

Notwithstanding all the hollow cant about the "dignity of labor," to work with one's hands in any productive occupation is looked upon by all as degrading, and those who do so are denied all social position. To avoid this worst of all conditions and live by his wits or by some of the more genteel and less debasing occupations is the supreme effort of every "intelligent" person. The effect is to throng the "learned professions" with aspirants to this honor; multiply the town lawyers, attorneys, constables, notaries, justices, and "officers"; breed swarms of real estate agents, insurance agents, bankers, brokers, and shavers; overdo all newspaper and literary enterprises; develop a vast army of reporters, stenographers, typewriters, and copyists; and make everyone fit himself to be at least a clerk, or something besides a mere laborer, mechanic, or artisan.

Immensely overdone as all these departments are, they still manage to exist and flourish, and they do this by increasing the cost of the products to the maximum limit at which the public will use them. How competition of this class can be kept up under such influences is well shown by the number of "first class restaurants" in all large cities, feeding only a few accidental stragglers or wealthy persons, and where one seems to be paying almost exclusively for the costly silverware and mostly idle retinue of attendants.

This "aggressive competition" also clearly reveals its origin in the mind element as described in Chapters XXIII and XXIV. As the embodiment of business shrewdness it involves in a high degree the principle of deception. All forms of solicitation are conducted with a view to deceiving the customer. The essence of an advertisement is a falsehood. It is an intentional effort to make the public believe that the particular article advertised is either better or cheaper than the same article sold by rivals, which the dealer knows is not the case. Every sale thus secured is therefore really "obtaining money under false pretenses," which is nominally a punishable offence, but which is winked at except in the most flagrant cases. In fact, society is based on the normal occurrence of this form of lying, and its legal recognition is embodied in the maxim of common law, *caveat emptor*.

Such is the legitimate effect of competition among rational beings. The law of nature quickly succumbs to the law of mind, and whether it continues for a time, or whether, as it sooner or later must, it defeats itself and results in monopoly, the general effect on society is the same. If it be regarded as a sad commentary upon the operations of a rational being that there is no escape from the necessity of paying the highest price for everything that will be paid rather than do without, and irrespective of the cost of production, it must be remembered that it is only the individual that is as yet in any proper sense rational. If society itself were rational this would indeed seem absurd, and if it shall ever become so no such absurdity will be tolerated for a moment. Those who compare society to an organism have failed to observe that in this respect it resembles only some of the very lowest Metazoa, such as the hydra, which possesses no proper presiding and coördinating nerve ganglia, or still more closely some of those lower colonies of cells, each of which, like the individual members of society, is practically independent of the general mass except that by the simple fact of coherence a certain degree of protection is secured to both the individual cells and the aggregated mass. And yet many advocate a still greater independence of the individual, and deprecate all steps in the direction of integration, which they know to be the only way in which organic beings can make any progress in organization. So little have the principles of biology impressed themselves upon the students of sociology, even those who profess a synthetic grasp of both fields !

The reader cannot have failed to perceive the fundamental difference between the social phenomena above reviewed and those that take place everywhere in nature below the level of man's rational faculty, and hence, even when dealing with the universal law of competition, an entirely different set of principles must be applied to man from those which can be applied to irrational life. There competition is free, or rather it is pure. It continues as long as the weaker can survive it, and when these at last go to the wall and the better adapted structures survive and triumph, it is the triumph of a real superiority, and the strong and robust alone are left to recruit the earth. But when mind enters into the contest the character of competition is at first completely changed, and later competition itself is altogether crushed out, and while it is still the strong that survive it is a strength which comes from indirection, from deception, artfulness, cunning, and shrewdness, necessarily coupled with stunted moral qualities, and largely aided by the accident of position. In no proper sense is it true that the fittest survive. If this were their only function it is evident that brains would be a positive detriment to society. Pure animal competition would be far better. It is probably the contemplation of the hopelessness of this state of things which has given the gloomy cast to Oriental philosophy, and it is no wonder that those moderns who consider the present order unalterable should maintain that we live in the worst possible universe. Those who can see a surplus of good in things as they are, or can hope for their improvement under the laws of evolution unaided by social intelligence must be set down as hopelessly blinded by the great optimistic illusion of all life.

While competition is not to be looked upon as a social desideratum, even in its pure animal form, much less in its aggressive human form, free individual activity under the full play of all natural motives is of the utmost importance. Among these motives those of friendly rivalry and honest emulation are legitimate, harmless, and powerful. These competition suppresses; it tends to choke individual freedom and clog the wheels of social progress. How can this true individualism be secured and complete freedom of individual action be vouchsafed? Herein lies a social paradox. It is clear from what has been said that this will never bring itself about. The tendencies are strongly in the opposite direction. Competition is growing more and more aggressive, heated, and ephemeral. Combination is growing more and more universal, powerful and permanent. This is the result of the most complete *laissez faire* policy. The paradox therefore is that *individual freedom can only come through social regulation.* The coöperative effects of the rule of mind which annihilate competition can only be overcome by that still higher form of coöperation which shall stay the lower form and set free the normal faculties of man. Free competition that shall be both innocent and beneficial may be secured to a limited extent in this way and in no other way.

As a single illustration of this, let us suppose a railroad to be constructed alongside of an existing canal. Negotiations will be at once set on foot on the part of the railroad company to purchase the canal, not because it is wanted, but merely to remove it from competition. Such negotiations would be sure to succeed and leave the railroad master of the field. Competition would be removed, rates of transportation increased, and a valuable water way would be abandoned. But suppose society in its collective capacity, however constituted, seeing the situation and the danger, were to step in and itself purchase the canal, and to continue in spite of the railroad to conduct it in the interest of traffic ; here would be a case in which the law of mind would be directed to maintaining instead of destroying competition.

A new and revised political economy will doubtless be largely devoted to showing, not so much the glories of competition, which society does not enjoy, as how society may conduct itself in order to secure whatever benefits competition can offer, and also how the competition that cannot be prevented can be shorn of its wasteful and aggressive features. Neither should the higher attributes of reason and intelligence be discouraged. They represent the true elements of civilization and progress. But these, too, should be deprived of their fangs. The way to counteract the evil effects of mind operating in the individual is to infuse a larger share of the same mind element into the controlling power of society. Such a powerful weapon as reason is unsafe in the hands of one individual when wielded against another. It is still more dangerous in the hands of corporations, which proverbially have no souls.[1] It is most baneful of all in the hands of compound corporations which seek to control the wealth of the world. It is only safe when employed by the social ego, emanating from the collective brain of society, and directed toward securing the common interests of the social organism.

[1] "They cannot commit treason, nor be outlawed, nor excommunicate for they have no souls." — Sir Edward Coke: Reports, Vol. V, Part X, 32 b, London, 1826, p. 303 (Case of Sutton's Hospital).

But the object of this chapter was not to point out remedies for social evils. It was, as stated at the outset, to show that any system of economics which is to deal with rational man must rest upon a psychologic and not upon a biologic basis. In full view of all the facts that have been set forth, facts that are for the most part obtrusive and have always been available to all, it is certainly remarkable that there should be any necessity for calling attention to this truth; but the only system of social economics that we possess, and the only social philosophy, other than the one referred to early in this chapter, that has been promulgated, completely ignore it and treat the human animal only as an animal. Not the economic writers alone, but the great philosophers as well, persistently cling to the law of nature and disregard the law of mind. A system of so-called "political economy," in which the *political* aspect, i. e., the relation of the state to society, is for the most part ignored, has grown up and been reduced to a series of dogmatic canons which until recently it was considered next thing to sacrilege to question or criticise. But partly with the increase of general intelligence, whereby the mind element is more clearly seen in industrial and social phenomena, and partly with the increase of critical independence on the part of economic students, the truth has at last begun to emerge that the greater part of these supposed economic axioms are not only open to criticism but positively untrue. So thoroughly current had most of them become that any fact established in opposition to them might appropriately be called a paradox, like some phenomenon that seemed to counteract the law of gravitation. On this ground was justified the title of a paper which I presented to the American Economic Association at Philadelphia in 1888,[1] in which a considerable number of these economic maxims were analyzed and shown to be true only when all their terms were reversed. A further examination of such maxims, in which

[1] Some Social and Economic Paradoxes. The American Anthropologist, Vol. II, Washington, April, 1889, pp. 119–132.

I have been greatly helped by Dr. E. A. Ross,[1] professor of political economy in Cornell University and secretary of the above-named association, has shown that this process of destructive criticism may be carried much further, and can scarcely stop until the entire fabric of which they constitute the timbers has crumbled and fallen. To substantiate these statements I will introduce here quite a list of the more important cases, preserving the form previously adopted and presenting the propositions which the industrial history of the world has established, although for the most part in direct opposition to the hitherto accepted tenets of political economy. They may therefore continue to go by the name of Economic Paradoxes.

1. Subsistence increases instead of diminishing with population (reversal of the Malthusian dictum).

2. The interest of the individual is rarely the same as that of society.

3. Owing to ignorance of the remote effects of actions men do not always do what is for their own interests.

4. Cheapness is a stronger inducement than quality, and the consumer cannot be depended upon to encourage the better producer.

5. Competition raises prices and rates.

6. Combination often lowers prices and rates.

7. Free competition is only possible under social regulation.

8. Private monopoly can only be prevented by public monopoly.

9. The hope of gain is not always the best motive to industry.

10. Public service will secure better talent than private enterprise for the same outlay.

11. Market values and social values are not identical.

12. The prosperity of a community depends as much upon the mode of consumption as upon the quantity produced.

[1] It is not intended hereby to commit Dr. Ross to all or any of these propositions.

13. Private enterprise taxes the people more heavily than government does.

14. The social effects of taxation are more important than its fiscal effects.

15. The producer cannot always shift the burden of taxation upon the consumer, e.g., under monopoly and aggressive competition.

16. Protection may reduce the price of the commodity protected, not only in the protecting but even in the importing country.

17. Capital, as embodied in machinery, contributes more than labor to the production of wealth.

18. Wages are drawn from products and not from capital, and the "wage-fund" is a myth.

19. Increase of wages is attended with increase of profits.

20. Prices fall as wages rise.

21. Diminished hours of labor bring increased production.

22. Reduction of the time worked enhances the wages received.

23. A man working alone earns the same as when his wife and children also work.

24. Lowering the rate of interest may lead to increased savings.

This enumeration falls far short of exhausting the list, but must suffice for the present purpose. One may imagine a modern economist trained in the Ricardian, Malthusian, and Manchesterian schools which still prevail even in American universities, looking with an unbiased mind into such an array of facts and convincing himself of their substantial correctness. His situation would be naturally bewildering, and he might at first cast vaguely about for an explanation. If he should prosecute this search thoughtfully and fearlessly, intent only upon the truth, he must at length find the full and only explanation to be that the whole farrago which has so long passed for political economy is true only of irrational animals and is altogether inapplicable to rational man.

Darwin modestly confesses that he derived his original conception of natural selection from the reading of Malthus on Population.[1] But he did not perhaps himself perceive that in applying the law of Malthus to the animal world he was introducing it into the only field in which it holds true. Yet such is the case, and for the same reason that has been already given, viz., that the advent with man of the thinking, knowing, foreseeing, calculating, designing, inventing, and constructing faculty, which is wanting in lower creatures, repealed to this extent the biologic law, or law of nature, and enacted in its stead the psychologic law, or law of mind.

[1] Autobiography. Life and Letters, Vol. I, p. 68.

CHAPTER XXXIV.

MELIORISM.

From mere impulse to true sentiment, and from sentiment to reason, are the psychic steps corresponding to the series of benevolent acts which lead from promiscuous alms-giving, through the expanding systems of charity, to the broadest forms of philanthropy and deep-laid schemes of humanitarianism. But from humanitarianism it is but one more step in the same direction to ***meliorism***, which may be defined as humanitarianism ***minus*** all sentiment. Now, meliorism, instead of an ethical, is a dynamic principle. It implies the improvement of the social condition through cold calculation, through the adoption of indirect means. It is not content merely to alleviate present suffering, it aims to create conditions under which no suffering can exist. — *Dynamic Sociology*, II, 468.

I don't know that I ever heard anybody use the word "meliorist" except myself. But I begin to think that there is no good invention or discovery that has not been made by more than one person.

The only good reason for referring to the "source" would be, that you found it useful for the doctrine of meliorism to cite one unfashionable confessor of it in the face of the fashionable extremes. — GEORGE ELIOT.

In her general attitude towards life, George Eliot was neither optimist nor pessimist. She held to the middle term, which she invented for herself, of "meliorist." She was cheered by the hope and by the belief in gradual improvement of the mass; for in her view each individual must find the better part of happiness in helping another. — J. W. CROSS: *George Eliot's Life*, III, 377.

Our line of reasoning provides us, then, with a practical conception which lies midway between the extremes of optimism and pessimism, and which, to use a term for which I am indebted to our first living woman-writer and thinker, George Eliot, may be appropriately styled meliorism. By this I would understand the faith which affirms not merely our power of lessening evil — this nobody questions — but also our ability to increase the amount of positive good. It is, indeed, only this latter idea which can really stimulate and sustain human endeavor. — JAMES SULLY: ***Pessimism. A History and a Criticism***, London, 1877, p. 399.

Priestley was the first (unless it was Beccaria) who taught my lips to pronounce this sacred truth: That the greatest happiness of the greatest number is the foundation of morals and legislation.—JEREMY BENTHAM: *Works*, Vol. X, p. 142.

In equal degrees of happiness, expected to proceed from the action, the virtue is in proportion to the number of persons to whom the happiness shall extend . . . so that That action is best, which procures the greatest happiness for the greatest numbers.—FRANCIS HUTCHESON: *An Inquiry concerning Moral Good and Evil*, II, pp. 184, 185.

La massima felicità divisa nel maggior numero.—CESARE BECCARIA: *Opere*, I, p. 10.

He never would believe that Providence had sent a few men into the world, ready booted and spurred to ride, and millions ready saddled and bridled to be ridden.—MACAULAY (said of Richard Rumbold when about to be executed): *History of England*, *Works*, I, 441.

In Parts I and II, I have attempted to set forth the leading psychic factors of civilization. Although when viewed in detail they may seem to be somewhat numerous, still, a general glance over the field will show that they may all be reduced to two distinct classes, the subjective and the objective factors. It is also possible to reduce the psychic faculties that contribute to human progress to two generalized ones and call them respectively the *conative* and *intuitive* faculties. Using the term *will* in Schopenhauer's sense it may be said that will and intellect constitute the progressive mind-elements of man. The subjective, conative faculty, or will, furnishes the propelling agent, while the objective, intuitive faculty, or intellect, furnishes the directing agent. Will is the force, intellect is the guide, and it is through the coöperation of these prime factors that civilization has advanced.

As compared to mere biologic progress that of man has indeed been rapid and brilliant, and it might be supposed that any one who is competent to make this comparison, and a fortiori one who has been to the pains of working out the steps by which the transition has taken place, would be not only content to contemplate so remarkable a result, but even exultant over it. As a matter of fact this is the attitude of most writers on the general subject. They see that nature has proved capable of doing all this, and they really do not consider it altogether sane to talk about any other way. For them it is simply a step in the great scheme of evolution. It was to be and it is, like the condensation of nebulæ into worlds, the development of oaks from sea-tang or of mammals from worms. Although none of them have shown, as has been attempted here, how the intellect of man came into existence under the laws of evolution, it is assumed that it did so, and although no one has pointed out, as has been done in this work, how the human intellect has proceeded to make civilization possible, it is also assumed that it has done this according to the normal laws of evolution. The acts of man and the laws of society are regarded as natural in the same sense that the movements of the solar system and the instincts of animals are natural.

The dissatisfaction that is manifested in certain quarters at the state of things that nature has thus brought about is looked upon as growing chiefly out of ignorance of these wide truths, as the result of narrow views of the world, unscientific habits of thought, and foolish exaggeration of human power to influence such stupendous movements. It is not denied that attempts of this kind are sometimes made, but it is asserted that they have all been failures, usually that they have made matters worse. If any one examines the cases that are adduced in support of this assertion he will find that they are confined to a single class, viz., attempts at governmental reform. It is not perceived that there exists any other class. If a *laissez faire* philosopher were asked whether government itself, such as it has been and now is, should be considered a failure the reply would probably be in the negative, at least he would not admit that the particular government under which he happens to live was worse than no government at all would be, although it might be regarded as exceedingly bad, and although the governments of other countries of which less was known might perhaps be thought worse than pure anarchy. But, it would probably be said, government is a part of civilization, it has developed like the other institutions, it is a product of mind, and belongs to human progress in general.

At this point a few questions may profitably be asked. Is not our supposed philosopher's own government better than any other? He would probably admit that it was. Is it not better now than it formerly was? On this point there would probably be no hesitation in giving an affirmative answer. Then it is not impossible to reform government. The existing governments of the world are not the very best they can be or can ever be made. Other governments at least stand a chance of being brought up to the standard of our philosopher's present government, and as that is admitted to be very bad, there may, at least if his teachings are heeded, be some hope of improving even that. But how does the improvement of an existing government differ in this respect from the origination of a government where none existed? At what point in the progress of governments did it become preposterous to attempt to reform them? If that point is the one at which our philosopher happened to live and write, how is it that it might not have fallen at some other time? It would probably be urged that all real reform in government has consisted in restricting its action. This carried to its logical results would take us back to anarchy, and this we may assume would not be advised. Then there must be such a thing as governmental reform somewhat short of the complete abolition of government. What such reform would consist in need not now be considered; the fact of its possibility is all that is contended for.

No one will deny that government is a part of evolution, a product of human intelligence operating in a normal manner, but it is only one of the many human institutions that have been developed in the same way. The attempts to reform or in any way change it belong to the same class as the attempts to establish it, and are also normal. Intelligence has operated on government in the same way that it operates on all other things. Why then should government be singled out as the only product of intelligence that furnishes illustrations of the failure of all attempts to counteract the law of evolution? Civilization consists of something else besides government. That institution has indeed played an important rôle, but this has been thus far chiefly that of enabling the more direct civilizing influences to operate. Its function has been principally that of protection, that of affording security to other normal processes. It has done this with a certain degree of efficiency, a very variable and imperfect degree, it is allowed, but it has done it. Few will probably insist that it has wholly failed, and nearly all believe that without it there could have been very little or no social progress. Let any one reflect how jealously vested rights are guarded by law, how commerce and industry are permitted to go on unmolested, how personal liberty is guaranteed and crimes against person and property are punished, and figure to himself what the state of things would be in the total absence of governmental supervision. The quasi reign of terror so familiar to those who have ever sought to live a little out on the borders of civilization beyond the reach of the law will help to complete this latter picture.[1]

[1] Mr. Herbert Spencer, who certainly will not be suspected of any partiality to government, bears witness to the truth here stated in the following language: —

"Defective as is the administration of law, yet men's properties as well as their lives are far safer than they were in early times; by which there is implied an increase of those feelings which embody themselves in equitable laws. If we again look at the growth of govermental forms, which have gone on from period to period decreasing the unchecked powers of ruling classes, and extending to lower and lower grades shares of political power, we see both that the institutions so established are more altruistic in the sense that they recognize better the claims of all, and in the sense that they are advocated and carried on grounds of equity and by appeal to men's sense of justice — that is, to the most abstract and latest developed of the altruistic sentiments." Principles of Ethics, Vol. I, p. 294.

If the organization and improvement of government and of all other human institutions as well as the operation of the various civilizing agencies of mankind are normal products of evolution, and have taken place under the operation of natural laws, made possible only through the existence of the intellectual faculty of man, as all will probably admit, what is there in the world that can be called artificial? Or if any part of all this is entitled to be so called why is it not all so entitled? We are told to let things alone and allow nature to take its course. But has intelligent man ever done this? Is not civilization itself with all that it has accomplished the result of man's not letting things alone, and of his not letting nature take its course? If not, then, even the foolish attempts of modern social reformers to make impossible changes in the assumed unimprovable condition of existing government and society are the legitimate effect of natural laws, and those who inveigh against them are indulging in *bruta fulmina.* They, too, are of course products of natural law, but the injunction *laissez faire* can be as legitimately served on them as on those on whom they would have it served.

The simple truth is that everything that is done at the behest of the intellectual faculty is per se and of necessity purely artificial in the only sense that the word has. The whole difference between civilization and other forms of natural progress is that it is a product of art. As was shown in Chapters XXVII to XXIX, art is the natural product of the inventive faculty which is only a form of intuitive perception or intuitive reason, and belongs to the main trunk of the intellect. It is the prime and initial factor in everything distinctively human, everything truly progressive, the sole cause of all social progress and of civilization itself. The artificial is infinitely superior to the natural, and civilized man is satisfied with nothing that has not been wrought and finished by the skill and handiwork of the artisan or the artist. The constant tendency is to render everything more and more artificial, which means more and more perfect. Human institutions are not exempt from this all-pervading spirit of improvement. They, too, are artificial, conceived in the ingenious brain and wrought with mental skill born of inventive genius. The passion for their improvement is of a piece with the impulse to improve the plow or the steam engine. Government is one of these artificial products of man's devising, and his right to change it is the same as his right to create it. That he has greatly improved it there is no doubt ; that he will still further perfect it there is every promise.

The words civilization and social progress are not strictly synonymous. There may be a high state of civilization which produces little or no true progress. So loose a term as progress requires rigid definition. As the only final end of human effort is human happiness, so there can be no true progress except toward that end. Progress is therefore increase of human happiness, or, negatively considered, reduction of human suffering. Civilization does not essentially consist in securing this end. If it does so this is only an incidental effect. That upon the whole it does secure it there can be no doubt, but there may be and doubtless are instances in which this is not the case. Civilization is the product of many men at work with their inventive brains, each seeking to compel the forces of nature to do something for himself. But the number who really contribute to it is exceedingly small compared with the aggregate of population, and although what one man wants is usually also that which many others want, still this individualism necessarily results in a very unequal distribution of the product. There are those who, admitting this inequality, maintain that an equal distribution would be unjust in not rewarding intelligence and industry. This should be readily conceded. But, as was shown in Chap. XXVIII, it rarely happens that the discoverer of a fertile principle secures a just share of its returns. This goes not to genius but to the comparatively low quality of cunning or business shrewdness.

Almost any other distribution would be more just than the actual one. Moreover, it would be unjust were the inventor to secure all the returns. He would soon have many thousand times as much as he could make any good use of. And so in whatever way we look at the subject it presents a problem. This problem fully generalized is that of identifying civilization with progress, of making society at large the beneficiary of the products of art, skill, industry, and labor. It is clear that in order to solve this problem, material civilization cannot be wholly left to individual preferences. Aside from the unequal and inequitable distribution of the products of industry and thought there will always be immense waste. The individual will never make social progress an end of his action. He will always pursue a narrow destructive policy, exhausting prematurely the resources of the earth, caring neither for the good of others now living nor for posterity, but sweeping into the vortex of his own avarice all that he can obtain irrespective of his real needs. If this is ever to be prevented it must be by society putting itself in the place of the individual and seeking its interests as the individual seeks his, and caring for the welfare and comfort of all its members as the individual cares for the health and soundness of all the organs of his body.

The chief defects of the social system as it is now, and always has been constituted, are due to social friction as defined in Chap. XVII. The problem is therefore reduced to that of lessening social friction. Social friction is mainly the result of the biologic law of natural selection and the struggle for existence, which in economic parlance is called competition. This is pursued by man under the powerful influence of the intuitive reason taking the various forms described in Chapters XXIII and XXIV. The biological sociologists, seeing the identity of this with what goes on in the animal world, suppose it must be a healthy state of things, and the best state possible. They imagine that it results in real social progress. They of course forget that, as shown in the last chapter, with the advent of the intellectual faculty an entirely new dispensation was inaugurated, that the old and slow biologic method of organic or structural development was superseded by the new and rapid anthropic method of transforming the environment and adapting it to man, so that this holding over of the principle of animal rapacity becomes an anachronism, loses all its former developmental value, and stands as the one great obstacle in the path of human progress. Much has been done even by individual effort to break it down. The social state of mutual dependence and coöperation was a heavy blow against it. The division of labor in art and industry, by which every one is working for every one else, has further hedged it about. The spread of intelligence through the diffusion of education and knowledge has served to hold it up to general reprobation. Commerce, travel, and the intercourse of people with people and race with race have liberalized thought and tended to make it unpopular. The growth of sympathy with the growth of intelligence has proved a powerful antagonist to its advance, and the influence of eleemosynary efforts in softening its worst effects cannot be ignored. But still it lives, and it is probably beyond the power of all these influences wholly to dislodge it. If it is ever completely overthrown it will be by a conscious social effort wisely directed to the removal of all inducements to the indulgence of selfish greed. Schemes with this end in view have been proposed, upon the wisdom or success of which it would be needless to enlarge here. It is only essential to deny the antecedent impossibility of one day freeing society of this the worst enemy of its peace and progress.

It will be said that this presupposes a change in human nature. The answer is that the intuitive reason does not crave the injury of others. If its egoistic ends can be attained without this it will not be resorted to. The only essential difference between it and the inventive intuition is that the latter is directed upon non-sentient things and loses its moral, or rather immoral quality. The principle by which a physical force is directed into a channel of human advantage does not differ in any respect from that by which an animal is decoyed into a snare, or a human victim fleeced by a confidence man. The subject cares only for the end — his personal advantage. He ignores the means and its consequences to others. The inventor is a deceiver as well as the sharper, only what he deceives has no feelings to injure. The application of all this is that if all inducement to satisfy self at the expense of another can be removed, the principle of rapacity will have lost its sting. Its immoral quality will be gone. It may then exert itself as powerfully as ever and be doing no harm, nay, it may be made an agent of good. There is then no antecedent impossibility in the removal of the principal cause of social friction, and it becomes simply a question of its practical possibility. Let the light of intelligence, and especially of inventive genius, fully in upon it as a great and burning question for solution and there can be no predicting what the result may be.

These problems have nothing to do with ethics. They are not moral questions, although upon their solution more than upon anything else depends the moral progress of the world. They are purely social problems and can only be properly considered in the dry light of science. The proper name for this science is *meliorism*, the science of the improvement or amelioration of the human or social state.

CHAPTER XXXV.

SOCIAL CONSCIOUSNESS.

Intellectually considered, social differentiation has always been far in advance of social integration. As in the solar system, the outlying members — the planets — have vastly exceeded the central mass — the sun — in the progress which they have made toward the dissipation of their inherent motion and the integration of their constituent matter, so, in society, while individual men have, at different times and in varying degrees, arrived at full consciousness both of themselves and of the universe, the social mass, the supreme psychic center of the social organism, still consists of a chaos of undifferentiated elements in the crude, homogeneous state. So great is this lack of integration in the social consciousness that society as a whole is still broken up into a large number of more or less remote and independent sub-societies, joined together more or less feebly by ties which differ in strength, from those of language and national characteristics in politically dependent states, to those of commerce, more or less irregular, between wide-separated peoples speaking in different tongues. — *Dynamic Sociology*, II, 397.

Society, possessed for the first time of a completely integrated consciousness, could at last proceed to map out a field of independent operation for the systematic realization of its own interests, in the same manner that an intelligent and keen-sighted individual pursues his life-purposes. — *Dynamic Sociology*, II, 249.

A time arrives in the progress of social development when societies of men become conscious of a corporate existence, and when the improvement of the conditions of this existence becomes for them an object of conscious and deliberate effort. At what particular stage in human history this new social force comes into play, we have no need here to inquire. What I am concerned to point out is that *it is a new social force*, wholly different in character from any which had hitherto helped to shape human destiny — wholly different also from those influences which have guided the unfolding either of the individual animal or of the species. We cannot, by taking thought, add a cubit to our stature. The species, in undergoing the process of improvement, is wholly unconscious of the influences that are determining its career. It is not so with human evolution. Civilized mankind are aware of the changes taking place in their social condition, and do consciously and deliberately take measures for its improvement. — PROF. J. E. CAIRNES : *Fortnightly Review*, Vol. XXIII, January, 1875, p. 71

But I pass these by with bare mention to fix attention on only one, viz., the modern social doctrine of ***human progress***. Observe, however, I mean not mere natural evolution, or unconscious progress according to necessary law, but ***conscious voluntary progress*** according to a free law, a conscious striving after a higher goal, for the individual and for the race. — JOSEPH LE CONTE : *Relation of Biology to Sociology*, p. 7.

If the resemblance between the body physiological and the body politic is any indication, not only of what the latter is, and how it has become what it is, but of what it ought to be, and what it is tending to become, I cannot but think that the real force of the analogy is totally opposed to the negative view of State function. Suppose that, in accordance with this view, each muscle were to maintain that the nervous system had no right to interfere with its contraction, except to prevent it from hindering the contraction of another muscle ; or each gland, that it had a right to secrete, so long as its secretion interfered with no other ; suppose every separate cell left free to follow its own "interests," and *laissez faire*, Lord of all, what would become of the body physiological ?

The fact is, that the sovereign power of the body thinks for the physiological organism, acts for it, and rules the individual components with a rod of iron. Even the blood corpuscles can't hold a public meeting without being accused of "congestion" — and the brain, like other despots whom we have known, calls out at once for the use of sharp steel against them. . . . Hence, if the analogy of the body politic with the body physiological counts for anything, it seems to me to be in favor of a much larger amount of governmental interference than exists at present, or than I, for one, at all desire to see. — PROF. T. H. HUXLEY : *Administrative Nihilism*.

The term consciousness has been used in three different senses : first as applicable to all feeling whatever ; second, as applicable to such feelings only as are referred to the brain and become known to the integrated organism ; and third, as applicable only to feelings that are sanctioned by the intellect and under its control. This last sense is that of Schopenhauer and Hartmann, difficult precisely to define, but clearly exemplified by the case of the will as that function is understood by them, which they always regard as unconscious. Hartmann's

Philosophy of the Unconscious is little more than a philosophy of the Will, in this sense. But according to the more accurate definition of consciousness accepted by physiologists and most philosophers it is the essential part of feeling or sentiency itself, to the extent that feeling without consciousness would be a contradiction of terms. But as animal motion implies feeling it is necessary to assume the consciousness of the lower ganglionic centers, although the ego is not aware of it, just as we ascribe feeling and consciousness to animals that cannot tell us of their mental states. In like manner we must extend the term consciousness as far down in the scale of being as feeling is conceived to exist. Whether this is coextensive with life is a disputed question, no feeling being commonly ascribed to plants. Still it may coexist with motility in the protoplasm of vegetable cells, and may be a property of all protoplasm. But as the purpose of feeling is the protection of such organisms as are not otherwise protected, it may be that it arose along with the development of such organisms. Schopenhauer projected the will much farther, and made it include chemical affinities and all physical forces. But having denied consciousness even to the human will he was not obliged to search for the point where it finally disappeared.

The principal objection that has been offered to the doctrine that society is an organism is that it possesses no organ of consciousness. But as the whole theory is merely an analogy it would not perhaps be more difficult to find the analogue of the brain than any of the other analogues that have been so carefully searched for. If we look into the constitution of society we find that besides the discrete units called individuals there are a great many other units of somewhat higher orders, each consisting of groups of individuals. These are of very different kinds, formed for widely unlike purposes, varying indefinitely in size, constitution, and composition. These groups of individuals may be divided into two general classes, which differ fundamentally from each other. Those belonging to one of these classes are variously denominated organizations, societies, corporations, companies, associations, sects, churches, etc., etc. All such groups are further seen to agree in one particular, however much they may differ in all others. None of them embraces all the individuals within any given territorial area. Many of them are not restricted to any one area or country. They may have members in various parts of the country in which they usually meet, and some in other countries, or they may be "international." Again, even when they are "local," e. g., have no members outside of some particular city, they never, any more than the more general ones, include all the inhabitants of that city. Many of the members of one such society or association are at the same time members of one or more of the others, and membership and allegiance thus crosses, and may even conflict and interfere. The various groups of this general class may be collectively called ***partial*** or ***incomplete*** social aggregates.

The other of these two general classes of social aggregates or units, may, for the sake of distinction be called, ***universal*** or ***complete***. The difference consists in the fact that these latter always include all the inhabitants of some definite territorial area. Moreover, if two such organizations are coördinate they cannot both occupy any part of that area, and no one individual can be a member of any two such associations. But a number of subordinate organizations of this class may be under one superior one, the territory of which is then coextensive with that of all the subordinate ones that fall within it, and all the members of the subordinate organizations are also members of the superior one. All the members of all partial or incomplete organizations are also members of one, and only one, universal or complete organization, and in addition to these also all individuals who are not members of any partial organization.

All organizations, whether partial or universal, have some rules governing their members, those of the former class being formed for a great variety of more or less limited and definite objects. All organizations of the latter class, however, are formed for a single purpose or group of purposes, so that while partial associations are extremely heterogeneous in their aims, universal associations are absolutely homogeneous in this respect throughout the world. This single purpose or group of purposes which constitutes the sole function of all universal organizations is *the general good of its members.* Partial associations are also often formed for the good of their members, but it is always some special good, usually some one restricted object; they may, however, be formed for purposes quite apart from the interests of the members, as in the case of benevolent associations which seek only the good of others who are not members.

Another peculiarity of universal organizations is that the rules governing their members are not only much more severe and rigid but are capable of being enforced. This is only to a limited extent the case with partial organizations. The church formerly, and the catholic church still, inflicts penalties, but the penalties of other churches at the present day are feeble, and, to outsiders, ludicrous. But the complete organization of any territorial area has full power over its members, even to the taking of their lives where their crimes justify this according to their rules of government.

The reader has not failed to perceive that by universal or complete organizations in the above paragraphs the existing governments of the world have been described, and I have often thought that if we could only get rid altogether of the word government, except in the sense of a body of rules, better results might be reached in attempting to discuss social questions. It is useless to inquire how government originated, or by what right it operates. Unless we propose to play the part of avowed anarchists and wage a general crusade against it, it is as well to accept what actually exists and make the best of it. As a matter of fact, in nearly every part of the world society is under some form of organization which embraces all its members and exercises plenary powers over them, ostensibly at least for their own good.

Some might object that the only real members of a governmental organization are the officers of the government. Such is the position taken by the school of *misarchists* who are habitually denouncing government as a mere band of politicians who at any time happen to hold office. They would probably deny that they were themselves members of the government of the country in which they live. But they are certainly members of the society which constitutes the nation which is under that government. Moreover, certainly in representative countries, those who vote or may vote must be regarded as forming part of the government which their votes create. But it would seem a strange place to draw the line, viz., so as to make the officers and voters constitute the government and to exclude all others. Many who are not voters contribute to the support of the government. Why should not these be included? But if the government consist of officers, voters, and tax-payers, this will include a very large proportion of the people. Moreover, it is sometimes very difficult to tell just what constitutes a tax-payer. The mere names under which property is assessed come very far from revealing this. But if an attempt is made to find the real tax-payers, not only is it impossible to stop short of including all property owners, but it is equally impossible not to include all consumers. For are not half the national revenues raised on imports which those who possess no property must consume and thus pay taxes? And the same holds for internal revenues, so called. Besides these there are various other ways in which every member of society contributes to the support of the government under which he lives. Then, there are other ways besides voting and holding office in which individuals take part in government. Indeed, everyone who exerts any influence in political affairs may be said to take part in government, and it is well known that many women who cannot themselves vote determine the votes of others. This fact has even been urged as a reason for not extending suffrage to women, as it is said that their influence is stronger without it than it would be with it. I do not mean to endorse this statement. I only mention it to show how clearly the influence in governmental affairs of those who neither vote nor hold office is popularly recognized.

It would seem, therefore, that there is no line that can be drawn which will satisfactorily exclude any person from membership in a government organization, and a government may, therefore, be regarded as consisting of all the individuals within its jurisdiction. If any one, however, objects to this use of the word government, there is no reason why the word *nation* or *state* may not be substituted. The name is not essential, only the fact that there exist such universally inclusive organizations as have been described.

The question to which all this is preliminary is: Why may not this universal or complete organization of any given country be taken as the analogue of the organ of consciousness in the animal, and thus complete the analogy of the social to the animal organism? By consciousness, as here used, is meant both the feeling and knowing faculties as attributes of the nervous system including the brain. The analogy is then made complete by looking upon the brain of developed animals as represented in society by the complete independent national autonomy, as, e. g., in this country, the federal government; and the hierarchy of subordinate ganglionic centers by the corresponding subordinate governments, such as state, county, municipal, etc., each of which latter has functions to perform which are not sufficiently important to be referred to the supreme central authority, the same as in any animal organism. From this point of view the independent political autonomies or *nations* of the world constitute each a social *ego*, while the subordinate governments are the several ganglionic centres of society that regulate its minor activities.

Symmetrical as this scheme appears to be, it would not be worth proposing if it did not help in understanding the real character of society. Does it do this? Perhaps as good a definition as can be given of consciousness would be: ***a knowledge of a feeling.*** If the individuals composing the social organism be compared to the *parts* of an animal organism (which may be restricted to those parts that are supplied with sensory nerves) both are alike composed of a great number of sensitive points or *loci* of feeling. In the animal it is the reports from these various loci of feeling, both external and internal, that determine and regulate its action, insure its nourishment, and preserve it from danger. This only applies to individuals. It does not extend to the species or any higher groups. It is, therefore, only possible to compare any one fully integrated and independent political autonomy with an individual organism. The feelings of individual men are cognized by the national consciousness in much the same way that the feelings of the parts of the animal organism are cognized by the animal consciousness. The chief point of resemblance is the purpose for which it takes place. In the animal it is always for its good that consciousness works, and we have seen that the sole purpose for which government exists is the good of individuals. There are other agencies, such as newspapers, popular rumor, etc., that acquaint individuals of the feelings of other individuals, but these are purposeless sources of knowledge. The reports that are registered in the seat of political consciousness are so referred only in order that some action may be taken for the good of those experiencing the feelings reported. This is closely analogous to the sensory and consequent motor action of the nervous system under like circumstances. In the animal the feelings are all of the conative class and result in desires to satisfy, and the motor discharges tend to contract those muscles which are intended to satisfy those desires. In society the feelings belong to the same class and the responsive action of government is always in the same direction. Some want is to be supplied, some right enforced, some evil remedied. Government, therefore, whether in its legislative, executive, or judicial function, in so far as it acts at all, is the servant of the will of its members in the same way that the brain is the servant of the animal will. In the next two chapters the analogy will be pushed a step further, but it will suffice here to remark that it is only in its psychological aspects that it is properly applicable. Just as the biological theory of society was seen to be everywhere unsound from ignoring the interjacent science of psychology, so the organism theory of society holds good even analogically only in so far as the comparison is confined to its psychic aspects.

CHAPTER XXXVI.

THE SOCIAL WILL.

Whatever be the objects of government, it is clear that it can have no other just origin than the *will* (not the "consent," which is merely negative and permissive, but the positive, declared will) of society. — *Dynamic Sociology*, II, 230.

It [the executive branch of government] alone knows what the real demands of the state are. It is constantly subjected to pressure from various quarters arising out of the normal operations of trade, manufactures, and industry in general. These pulsations it cannot help instantly feeling, and it is ever stepping to the verge of its statutory authority to meet these demands. — *Dynamic Sociology*, II, 575.

The individual will, in the only proper and intelligible sense of the word, is the conative faculty — the faculty through which a being strives to satisfy its desires. It is the means by which it exists, leading to the supply of its wants and the safety of its life. All feelings, internal and external, that reach the seat of consciousness react as motor discharges determining the appropriate actions. In society the wants of individuals struggle to reach the seat of social consciousness, the organized state, and produce like reactions, tending to their relief. In highly developed governments this analogy is very clear, and a degree of responsiveness is attained corresponding somewhat closely to that of the individual will. But even in the lower and cruder forms there is some degree of responsiveness. Every government, even the most despotic, is to a certain extent representative of the state of society over which it acts, and all government is much more nearly the best that can exist under the circumstances than is generally supposed. For example, it is common to regard the present government of Russia as greatly out of harmony with the people of that empire, but this is probably a mistake. It arises from two causes. First, those living under a more liberal government are apt to judge other societies by their own. They forget that the very reason why their government is so much more liberal is because their society is so much more intelligent, and that it is society which determines the character of government. The second mistake in this case is that the people of Russia are so heterogeneous in this respect. There exists there a large intelligent class for whom the government is undoubtedly ill-adapted, and who necessarily chafe under it. But this class is numerically small and the government does not well represent it. It represents rather the great mass for whom a better government would not be adapted. Government must always adapt itself to its worst class and even a small class of unintelligent citizens lowers its standard out of proportion to the importance of that class. This makes the intelligent class appear to be the dangerous and turbulent one, and leads some to regard intelligence as a curse rather than a blessing. The greatest of all desiderata in society is a degree of uniformity of intelligence, or intellectual and moral homogeneity.

The important fact to be noted in connection with the manifestations of the social will is that in all existing governments they are so frequently abortive or unsuccessful. Government is perpetually trying to satisfy the demands of individuals and a large proportion of its efforts prove to be failures. In the main they are successful, otherwise society itself would fail, but the successes do not attract attention, while the failures are seized upon as proofs of the entire futility of all governmental action. Laws are enacted which do not accomplish their purpose, some of them have effects which are the opposite of those which were intended. Numbers of them have to be repealed because they are found injurious, etc., etc. This is not the place to answer the superficial arguments that are based upon such facts. What concerns us here is to inquire into the causes of these failures. And first, it is nothing more than what takes place in the acts of will on the part of individuals. When undirected by intelligence the will is constantly prompting acts that fail to secure desired ends, acts that produce effects which are the opposite of those intended, and acts which prove injurious to those who commit them.

It is obvious that in both cases the failures are chiefly due to what is commonly called ignorance. But it is a special kind of ignorance, viz., lack of acquaintance with the principles involved. In individuals it is often ignorance of physical laws, but most commonly ignorance of human nature. By this is meant the motives to human action. Social or governmental failures are almost exclusively due to ignorance of social laws. And by this again is meant the principles of human action in collectivity. In other words, those who enact unsuccessful or obnoxious laws have no knowledge of the nature of social forces. As a rule they are influenced by a blind zeal to secure some perceived end and it is the nature of the will to proceed in the most direct way to the accomplishment of any purpose. The social will acts like the individual will, directly toward the object of desire. This can be a successful method only in the simplest cases. I have somewhat fully discussed this subject in Chap. VIII of Dynamic Sociology under the head of the "Direct Method of Conation" and need not, therefore, enter into it here. It need only be pointed out that for all governments thus far this has been the prevailing method, or if the indirect method has been applied it has been with such a feeble grasp of the complex laws of social phenomena as to amount to nearly the same thing. Only the simpler functions of government can be thus successfully carried on, and these have been satisfactorily performed. All attempts to exceed these have met with varying success, and it has required many failures and renewed trials to make the little progress that has actually taken place in the higher duties of the state.

It is, therefore, in the highest degree illogical to argue that the state can never extend its powers. It is the organ of social consciousness and must ever seek to obey the will of society.

Whatever society demands it must and always will endeavor to supply. If it fails at first it will continue to try until success at last crowns its efforts. If it is ignorant it will educate itself, if in no other way by the method of trial and error. Higher and higher types of statesmanship will follow the advancing intelligence of mankind, until one by one the difficult social problems will be solved. It is useless to maintain that the functions of government are necessarily limited to the few that have thus far been undertaken. The only limit is that of the good of society, and as long as there is any additional way in which that object can be secured through governmental action such action will be taken.

It seems scarcely worth while to notice the exceedingly narrow attitude of a certain class of persons who habitually speak of government as if it were something foreign to the people and hostile to the true interests of society. If there have been cases in which the ruling class wholly mistook their relations to society and seemed for brief periods and in certain countries to justify such a view, events have soon taught them better ; and even where a king has imagined that he was the state he was at that moment only a servant of the social will, refusal to obey which would cost him and his descendants their title to power or their lives. But such views are especially meaningless in modern times when governments have become so extremely sensitive to the social will that a single adverse vote will overthrow a cabinet, and where appeals are every year taken to the suffrage of the people. The fact is that, so far from any modern government daring to inaugurate any scheme of oppression, they are all so intensely deferent to the public will that every new step is tardily taken and only after it has become certain that it will be gladly welcomed and generally approved. This country is to-day fully ripe for a series of important national reforms which cannot be made because a comparatively small number of influential citizens oppose them. Conservatism, fear of disapproval, and general timidity before the people, who are recognized as the real government, characterize the legislation of all modern nations. In order to the introduction and adoption of any reform measure it is necessary that the public will shall have been positively and emphatically made known. But when this is done in an unmistakable manner, such measures are often pushed through with much too great alacrity. Government is becoming more and more the organ of social consciousness, and more and more the servant of the social will. Our declaration of independence which recites that government derives its just powers from the "consent" of the governed has already been outgrown. It is no longer the consent but the positively known will of the governed from which government now derives its powers.

CHAPTER XXXVII.

THE SOCIAL INTELLECT.

The social forces only need to be investigated as the rest have been, in order to discover ways in which their utility can be demonstrated. Here is a vast field of true scientific exploitation as yet untracked, and which to the legislators of this age is not known to exist. . . . If the domain of social phenomena is as completely one of law as that of physical phenomena . . . then may we logically expect the same measure of success, in proportion as these laws are known, which marks the progress of human supremacy in the material world. — *Dynamic Sociology*, I, 43.

Il ne faut pas que l'homme croie qu'il est égal aux bêtes, ni qu'il croie qu'il est égal aux anges, ni qu'il ignore l'un et l'autre ; mais qu'il sache l'un et l'autre. — PASCAL : *Pensées*, II, 85.

The important truth, set forth in Part I, that feeling was developed as a means of preserving life where other means were wanting, is scarcely more momentous than the other great truth, established in Part II, that the intellect was developed as a means of securing ends of being which the unguided will could not secure. The several forms which that faculty assumed in the performance of this function were described and their success and progress traced. It was seen that the purely biological ends of being were successfully pursued through the egoistic forms of intellection, but that the form which led to social progress and civilization was the inventive faculty rising into inventive genius and bringing all the material and dynamic resources of nature into the service of man. In Chap. XXVIII the precise nature of this faculty was described, and the secret of its success was pointed out.

The perpetual failures which in the animal world attended direct efforts of will to secure the higher ends of being and arrested organic development until the intellectual faculty came into existence and gave it such a new and astonishing impetus, also characterized the efforts of the social will to reach forward to better things, and they will continue to characterize them until the social intellect shall be developed and shall begin to organize the forces of human nature and enlist them in the service of society.

Considerable progress has actually been made in this direction, but, as in the animal world, it was the egoistic forms that were first employed. This took place and still takes place chiefly in the relations of tribes with tribes or nations with nations. As self-preservation is for the individual the first law of nature, so is it with tribes and nations, and accordingly it is in obedience to this primary law that the most intense efforts of collective man have been put forth to make the dictates of will successful. Here, therefore, the intellectual auxiliary has been most clearly manifest. The two principal directions in which this has made itself felt were considered in Chap. XXIII, viz., strategy in war and diplomacy in peace. To these may, however, be added retaliatory laws, discriminating duties, and a variety of other efforts to checkmate rival nations and insure national safety and industrial prosperity. But the exercise by nations of the inventive faculty even in dealing with other nations has been rare. It is still rarer in dealing with their own citizens. It is here that the great opportunity is open, and this may now be briefly considered.

In Dynamic Sociology the principle was distinctly formulated under the name of "attractive legislation" (see the several passages referred to in the index of that work) and a few illustrations were given of applications that have actually been made of it. Probably the most important examples are those that relate to subventions of various kinds, including tariffs, bounties, and other subsidies. The introduction of stamps in the collection of revenues, whether as postage or excise, was a truly ingenious device of the law-maker, and there are many others. But there is room for the indefinite extension of the principle. There is no doubt that it will one day be carried into nearly every department of legislation. There is nothing that would go so far to remove the odium that seems to attach to the acts of government, however necessary. Not only might all revenues probably be collected in a way that would be far less irritating than present methods, as well as in ways that would be more just, but nearly every other function of government might, if statesmen were sufficiently ingenious, be performed with such smoothness and ease that society would scarcely feel the weight of law upon it.

The principle itself is absolutely identical with that of mechanical invention, the only difference being that it deals with social instead of physical forces, with men instead of with things. The ingenuity which has been displayed in dealing with animals by which wild beasts have become man's most useful servants and through which man has gained the complete mastery over the lower kingdoms of nature, shows that the inventive faculty may successfully cope with vital and psychic forces. It only requires a somewhat higher type of this same quality of mind to tame the human animal and make him as harmless and as useful to society as domestic animals are to man. First of all the idea must be got rid of that there are any essentially evil propensities. Those with which men are endowed have been developed for a useful purpose. They must be recognized as natural and the effort made to direct them into useful channels just as the elements of nature — fire, wind, water, electricity, etc. — are directed by mechanical invention. Instead of the brusque command: "Thou shalt not," there must be devised such measures that when man acts according to nature his act will be at least harmless; if possible, useful. Instead of waiting till the natural result of an action has wrought injury to others and then punishing the agent, the desire to do that which will injure others might in most cases, by the exercise of ingenuity in the modification of his environment, be completely removed. The moralists have undertaken the impossible task of removing the so-called evil propensities of man. Meliorism teaches that there are no such, but that the evil consequences of actions dictated by natural impulses may be rendered impossible. Desires there will be, for so is man constituted, but these seek only their own satisfaction. The injury of others is only incidental, and the problem is to get others out of the way.

It is true that the desires of men can be changed in their nature. The same individual will have entirely different desires if reared under one environment from what he would have if reared under an entirely different one. And this constitutes the overwhelming argument for the creation of a proper social environment. The desires and consequent conduct of men depend upon their ideas, that is, their opinions and beliefs, and these depend in turn upon their education, using the term in its broad sense. It is, therefore, this education that requires first to be attended to, and, as I have shown in Dynamic Sociology, the highest duty of society is to see to it that every member receives a sound education. This should not be like the education which interested individuals furnish, the inculcation of a particular set of beliefs without any reasons therefor, but it should consist exclusively in furnishing the largest possible amount of the most important knowledge, letting the beliefs take care of themselves. This alone would extract the fangs from nearly all human propensities and reduce the problem of attractive legislation to its lowest terms.

But should this great initial step be taken, and all the practical knowledge of the world be given to every member of society for his guidance, there would still remain, especially during the transition period before such a measure could bear its full fruit, a wide field for the exercise of the collective ingenuity. As happiness is the great object of man the problem before the social intellect is nothing less than that of the organization of happiness. The existing evils of society are so great and so universal that the first steps would necessarily be taken rather in the direction of mitigating or removing these than in that of increasing or extending the positive enjoyment of life. So long as there is pain to be relieved, the attempt to heighten pleasure seems a sacrilege. The social intellect should, therefore, first and foremost, grapple with the whole problem of reducing the social friction. Every wheel in the entire social machinery should be carefully scrutinized with the practiced eye of the skilled artisan, with a view to discovering the true nature of the friction and of removing all that is not required by a perfect system.

With regard to the method by which all this may be made practicable a final word may be indulged in. Before any such sweeping social regeneration as that which is here hinted at can be inaugurated a great change must be wrought in the whole theory of legislation. It must be recognized that the legislator is essentially an inventor and a scientific discoverer. His duty is to be thoroughly versed in the whole theory and practice of social physics. He is called upon to devise "ways and means" for securing the true interests and improvement of the people for whom he is to legislate. This obviously cannot be done by existing methods. A public assembly governed by parliamentary rules is as inadequate a method as could well be conceived of for anything like scientific legislation. Imagine all the inventors in the country assembled in a hall acting under the gavel of a presiding officer to devise the machines of the future and adopt the best by a majority vote! Or think of trying to advance scientific discovery by a general convention! Scientific associations there are, usually for the reading of papers setting forth the discoveries made by the members in their laboratories, and there would be no objection to this class of legislative assemblies. But in the latter case as in the former, the real work, the thought, research, observation, experimentation, and discovery of laws and principles of nature must be done elsewhere, under appropriate conditions, in the great field or in the private cabinet.

It may at first glance seem absurd to propose that legislation be done in any such way, but a little reflection will show that it is not only not absurd, but that there is at this moment a strong tendency in all enlightened countries toward its adoption. It is a well known fact that at the present time the greater part of the real legislation is done by committees. The members of legislative committees are carefully chosen with reference to their known fitness for the different subjects intrusted to them. These committees really *deliberate*. They investigate the questions before them, hear testimony and petitions, and weigh evidence for and against every proposed measure. This is truly scientific and leads to the discovery of the principles involved. Unless biased by partisan leanings they are very likely to reach the truth and report practical and useful measures. The body to which these committees belong respect their decisions and usually adopt their recommendations. The other members usually know very little about the merits of the questions, or at least, not having studied them, they defer to the superior judgment of those who have. Committee work is, therefore, the nearest approach we have to the scientific investigation of social questions. It is on the increase, and is destined to play an ever increasing rôle in national legislation.

There is one other important way in which the social intellect is being applied to human affairs. The theory is that the executive branch of government merely administers national affairs. This is a great mistake. A very large part of the real legislation of a country is done by the executive branch. The various bureaus of government are in position to feel the popular pulse more sensitively than the legislature. The officers charged with their administration become identified with certain industries and are appealed to by the public to adopt needed reforms. After stepping to the verge of their legal authority in response to such demands, whereby much real legislation is done not contemplated by those who framed the laws under which these bureaus were established, they finish by making recommendations of the rest to the law-making power. This latter usually recognizes the wisdom of such recommendations and enacts them into laws, thus ever enlarging the administrative jurisdiction of government. Such legislation is in a true sense scientific. It is based on a knowledge both of the needs of the public and of the best means of supplying them. It has been subjected to thoughtful consideration and mature judgment. It is a method that is being every year more and more employed, and its results are usually successful and permanent.

History furnishes the statesman an additional basis for legislation. It is now possible to acquire a knowledge of the industrial history of nations, not complete, it is true, because so much was lost during the period when history was supposed to relate exclusively to the operations of the state and those who stood at its head, but sufficiently full to serve as a valuable guide to the legislator. No man should consider himself qualified to legislate for a people who is not conversant with the history of modern nations at least, with their various systems of finance, revenue, taxation, public works, education, land surveying, patent and copyright law, military and naval equipment, general jurisprudence and constitutional, statute, and unwritten law. It will, of course, be said that very few legislators are thus informed, and this is true, but these few will be the ones who will do most to shape the action of the state and will furnish examples to all who aspire to play a leading part in the political drama.

Again there is the statistical method. No one will deny that this is rapidly becoming a leading factor in legislation. Statistics are simply the facts that underlie the science of government. They are to the legislator what the results of observation and experiment are to the man of science. They are in fact the inductions of political science, and the inductive method in that science is of the same value that it is to science in general, its only true foundation. There is no great state at this day that does not make an effort to collect statistics ; in most of the leading nations of the world this is now done on an extensive scale. A census, which a short time ago was merely an enumeration of the population of a state, now means an exhaustive inquiry into its entire vital, industrial, and commercial condition. In this and many other ways governments furnish to their legislators the most important facts required to guide them in the adoption of the measures needful for the prosperity of the people.

There are many other ways in which the tendency toward scientific legislation is steadily growing, and, without indulging in any undue optimism on the subject, the fact may be considered established that no revolution is necessary in the character of society in order to bring about the gradual transformation required to realize all that has been foreshadowed in this chapter. The machinery already exists for the needed reformation and all that is necessary is that it be under the control of the developed social intellect. The quality of statesmanship is increasing. More thought is being devoted to the deeper questions of state and of society than ever before, and the signs of healthy progress are unmistakable. A modern Solon, paraphrasing the oft-quoted saying[1] of the ancient one, has defined a statesman as "a successful politician who is dead." He doubtless intended to rebuke the tendency of every age to vilify public men while they are living and canonize them after they are dead. And it would be well if, not only those who stand at the helm of the ship of state at any given period, but also the achievements of this directive social intellect in guiding that ship into smoother waters, were looked at from the standpoint of some remote future date and estimated in the light of the history which is being made.

[1] Εἰ δὲ πρὸς τούτοισι ἔτι τελευτήσει τὸν βίον εὖ, οὗτος ἐκεῖνος τὸν σὺ ζητεῖς ὄλβιος κεκλῆσθαι ἀξιός ἐστι· πρὶν δ' ἂν τελευτήσῃ, ἐπισχέειν, μηδὲ καλέειν κω ὄλβιον ἀλλ' εὐτυχέα. — SOLON : *Herodotus*, I, 32, p. 15.

Λόγος μέν ἐστ' ἀρχαῖος ἀνθρώπων φανεὶς,
ὡς οὐκ ἂν αἰῶν' ἐκμάθοις βροτῶν πρὶν ἂν
θάνοι τις, οὔτ' εἰ χρηστὸς, οὔτ' εἴ τῳ κακός.

SOPHOCLES : *Trachiniæ*, I

CHAPTER XXXVIII.

SOCIOCRACY.

To distinguish this general movement in the direction of regulating social phenomena from all other facts in human history, and at the same time to avoid all objectionable terms and express the conception in its widest sense, it may be appropriately denominated *Sociocracy*. It is too late now to object to this new term on the ground of its hybrid Græco-Latin etymology, since the Greek language is known to be deficient in a proper root for its first component, and several kindred terms are already in common use by the best authorities. It means something quite distinct from Democracy, which points, as this term does not, decisively towards a definite form of organization. The term Socialism, too, which might seem akin to it, aside from its unpopularity, has by far too great definiteness, and looks too much to fundamental change in the existing status of political institutions. All of these forms of social organization stand opposed to other existing forms, while Sociocracy stands opposed only to the absence of a regulative system, and is the symbol of positive social action as against the negativism of the dominant *lassez faire* school of politico-economic *doctrinaires*. It recognizes all forms of government as legitimate, and, ignoring form, goes to the substance, and denotes that, in whatever manner organized, it is the duty of society to act consciously and intelligently, as becomes an enlightened age, in the direction of guarding its own interests and working out its own destiny.—*Penn Monthly*, Vol. XII, Philadelphia, May, 1881, p. 336.

But the other branch of social dynamics, that which embraces the influence of those active or positive forces heretofore described, necessarily connects the study of these forces with the *art* of applying them, which is a distinctly human process, and depends wholly on the action of man himself. This art may be very appropriately named *Sociocracy*, although it is the same that has been sometimes called *politics*, giving to that term a much wider range than that now usually assigned to it. We have, therefore, besides social statics, negative and positive social dynamics, all of which classes are necessary to constitute sociology a true science.—*Dynamic Sociology*, I, 60.

We know that by precisely these means man has artificially modified the results of the operation of law in all other sciences, even down to biology, and there can be no longer a doubt of the same power over sociological phenomena. This is the department of active social dynamics, or *sociocracy*, which Comte dimly saw, but which his successors have thus far failed to recognize. — *Dynamic Sociology*, I, 137.

If I might be permitted to hint at the precise direction from which Mr. Spencer's great labors most strongly appeal to my mind, I should do so by intimating the possibility that he himself may fail to appreciate their full scope and influence. Emerson, one of whose wise sayings Mr. Spencer has embodied in his own remarks, has said of the world's greatest artist that —

"He builded better than he knew."

May it not be that the world's greatest philosopher has also "builded better than he knew"? May it not be that in telling us what society is, and how it became such, he has unconsciously pointed out the way in which it may be made better? In laying down the principles according to which social phenomena take place in nature, may he not have rendered possible, in the near future, some practical applications of those principles to higher social needs? I venture to predict that, in thus building the *science* of *Sociology*, Mr. Spencer has prepared the way for the introduction, on the basis of that science, of the corresponding *art* of *Sociocracy*. — *Herbert Spencer on the Americans and the Americans on Herbert Spencer*, p. 79.

So also that highest art, the art of government and social organization, may reach, unassisted by science, a high degree of perfection; but if it be simply an art it quickly culminates and declines, or else becomes petrified and immutable, as we see in the Chinese and Japanese. . . . But if the scientific principles of sociology be once understood, if science or self-conscious reason guide the social development, there can no longer be any limit to its progress. But observe: this indefinite progress is due wholly to the introduction of other principles than those derived from purely animal nature; it violates the perfect analogy to material organisms. — JOSEPH LE CONTE: *Popular Science Monthly*, February, 1879 (Vol. XIV, p. 429).

What iustice is this, that a ryche goldesmythe, or an vsurer, or to bee shorte anye of them, which either doo nothing at all, or els that whyche they doo is such, that it is not very necessary to the common wealth, should have a pleasaunte and a welthie lyuinge, either by Idlenes, or by vnnecessarye busines: When in the meane tyme poore labourers, carters, yronsmythes, carpenters, and plowmen, by so greate and continual toyle, as drawing and bearinge beastes be skant hable to susteine, and againe so necessary toyle, that without it no common wealth were hable to continewe and endure one yere, should yet get so harde and poore a lyuing, and lyue so wretched and miserable a lyfe, that the state and condition of the labouringe beastes maye seme muche better and welthier? . . . And yet besides this the riche men not only by priuate fraud, but also by commen lawes do euery day pluck and snatche awaye from the poore some parte of their daily liuing. So where as it semed before vniuste to recompense with vnkindnes their paynes that haue bene beneficiall to the publique weale, nowe they haue to this their wrong and vniuste dealinge (which is yet a muche worse pointe) geuen the name of iustice, yea and that by force of a law. Therefore when I consider and way in my mind all these commen wealthes, which now a dayes any where do florish, so good helpe me, I can perceaue nothing but a certein conspiracy of riche men procuringe theire owne commodities vnder the name and title of the commen wealth. They inuent and deuise all meanes and craftes, first how to kepe safely, without feare of lesing, that they haue vniustly gathered together, and next how to hire and abuse the worke and laboure of the poore for as little money as may be. These deuises, when the riche men haue decreed to be kept and obserued vnder coloure of the comminaltie, that is to saye, also of the pore people, then they be made lawes.—THOMAS MORE: *Utopia*, pp. 158–160.

Thus far attention has been chiefly confined to the science of society contemplated from the psychologic standpoint. But every applied science has its corresponding art. And although the social art is none other than this same government of which it has already been necessary to say so much, still, our social synthesis would be incomplete without some more special inquiry into the essential character of that art as a product of the combined consciousness, will, and intellect of society. Existing governments, it must be confessed, after all that can be said in their favor, realize this only to a very feeble extent. The social consciousness is as yet exceedingly faint, corresponding more nearly to that of a *cœnobium*, as in the *Flagellata* and *Ciliata*, than to any of the developed animal forms. The social will is, therefore, merely a mass of conflicting desires which largely neutralize one another and result in little advance movement in one settled direction. The social intellect proves a poor guide, not because it is not sufficiently vigorous, but because knowledge of those matters which principally concern society is so limited, while that which exists is chiefly lodged in the minds of those individuals who are allowed no voice in the affairs of state.

In Dynamic Sociology I have pointed out what I regard as the one certain correction possible to apply to this state of things, and have entered into a logically arranged demonstration of this point. "The universal diffusion of the maximum amount of the most important knowledge" was the formula reached for the expression of the result, and it was shown that its attainment is not only practicable but easy and simple whenever the social intelligence shall reach the stage at which its importance is distinctly recognized. It is only after the mind of society, as embodied in its consciousness, will, and intellect, shall, through the application of this formula for a sufficiently prolonged period to produce the required result, come to stand to the social organism in somewhat the relation that the individual mind stands to the individual organism, that any fully developed art of government can be expected to appear. Such an art will partake of the nature of all other arts, as explained in Part II. It will be the product of the inventive faculty perfected through the inventive genius, and systematized by scientific discovery under the influence of the scientific method and spirit.

Contrasted with this the governments of the past and present may be regarded as empirical. Useful, as is all empirical art, necessary, and adapted in a manner to their age and country, they have served and are serving a purpose in social development and civilization. They have taken on a number of different forms, of which the principal ones are called either monarchies or democracies. These terms, however, never very precise, have now become in most cases wholly misleading. The monarchies of Europe, with perhaps two exceptions, are now all democracies, if there are any such, and some of those that still prefer to be called monarchies are more democratic than some that call themselves republics. And in America, where none of the governments have the monarchical form, some of them are decidedly autocratic and elections are either a signal for revolution or else a mere farce. So that the names by which governments are known are wholly inadequate indexes to their true character. A more exact classification would be into *autocracies*, *aristocracies*, and *democracies*. By aristocracy would then be meant a ruling class, not necessarily superior, but held to be so. Most monarchies belong to this class. The aristocracy consists not merely of the royal family or dynasty, but of the nobles, clergy, and other privileged persons, for all such really belong to the ruling class. Most European countries have passed through the first two of these stages into the third. Some may be considered as still in the second, while most half-civilized, barbarous, or savage nations have not emerged from the first.

It was shown in Part II that the intellect was developed as an aid to the will in furthering the personal ends of the individual, and in Dynamic Sociology (Chap. VII) it was pointed out that among the many modes of acquisition government played a leading part. This is more especially the case in the stages of autocracy and aristocracy. It becomes less so in that of democracy, where it is confined to the professional politician and the "legal fraternity." Most of the attacks upon government that it is now so fashionable to make are based upon the vivid manner in which history portrays the doings of the ruling class during the stages of autocracy and aristocracy, and those who make them seem to forget that in all fully enlightened nations this stage has been passed and that of democracy has been fairly reached. But the fear and dread of government still lingers, and its ghost still perpetually rises and will not down. Although modern governments, chiefly on account of the known odium in which they are held, scarcely dare carry out the emphatically declared will of those who create them, and hesitate to take a step forward for fear of being forthwith overthrown by a sweeping plebiscite, still they are the objects of the most jealous vigilance and violent denunciation. Their power for usefulness is thus greatly weakened, and social progress and reform are slow.

It must not, however, be inferred that human nature has been changed by the transition from autocracy and aristocracy to democracy. The spirit of self-aggrandizement is undiminished, but the methods of accomplishing it have been changed. Just as society by the establishment of the institution of government put an end to the internecine strifes that threatened its existence, so also by the overthrow of autocracy and aristocracy it wrested from the autocrat and the aristocrat his power to subsist upon the masses. But the keen egoism of the astute individual immediately sought other means to better his condition at the expense of those less gifted with this irrepressible mental power or less favorably circumstanced for its exercise. What could not be secured through statecraft must be gained through some other species of craft. And soon was found in the very weakness of government the means of accomplishing far more than could ever be accomplished by the aid of the strongest form of government. What could no longer be attained through the universal or complete social organization has become easy of attainment through some one or other of the many kinds of partial or incomplete social organizations, as these terms were defined in Chap. XXXIV. With the rigid system which has grown up for the protection of the individual in his legal vested rights there is nothing in the way of advancing to almost any length in this direction.

The reaction in the direction of democracy, obeying the rhythmic law of social progress, aimed at, and to a large extent attained, a fourth stage which may be appropriately called *physiocracy*. Indeed, it may be said to consist of little else than that which was demanded by the French school of political economists who styled themselves Physiocrats. Neglecting some of their special tenets arising out of local conditions in France, this movement was not essentially different from that which was soon after introduced into England and made such rapid progress that it took complete possession of the public mind and has furnished the foundation of the political philosophy of that country and of the social and economic science taught from the high chairs of learning wherever the English language is spoken. This physiocracy, as a habit of thought rather than a form of government, now goes by the name of individualism, and is carried so far by many as to amount to a practical anarchism,[1] reducing all government to the action of so-called natural laws.

The general result is that the world, having passed through the stages of autocracy and aristocracy into the stage of democracy, has, by a natural reaction against personal power, so far minimized the governmental influence that the same spirit which formerly used government to advance self is now ushering in a fifth stage, viz., that of *plutocracy*, which thrives well in connection with a weak democracy or physiocracy, and aims to supersede it entirely. Its strongest hold is the widespread distrust of all government, and it leaves no stone unturned to fan the flame of misarchy. Instead of demanding more and stronger government it demands less and feebler. Shrewdly clamoring for individual liberty, it perpetually holds up the outrages committed by governments in their autocratic and aristocratic stages, and falsely insists that there is imminent danger of their reënactment. *Laissez faire* and the most extreme individualism, bordering on practical anarchy in all except the enforcement of existing proprietary rights, are loudly advocated, and the public mind is thus blinded to the real condition of things. The system of political economy that sprang up in France and England at the close of the aristocratic stage in those countries is still taught in the higher institutions of learning. It is highly favorable to the spread of plutocracy, and is pointed to by those who are to profit by that system of government as the invincible scientific foundation upon which it rests. Many honest political economists are still lured by the

[1] *Acracy* would be the word necessary to harmonize the terminology.

specious claims of this system and continue to uphold it, and at least one important treatise on social science, that of Herbert Spencer, defends it to the most extreme length. Thus firmly intrenched, it will require a titanic effort on the part of society to dislodge this baseless prejudice, and rescue itself once more from the rapacious jaws of human egoism under the crafty leadership of a developed and instructed rational faculty.

Under the system as it now exists the wealth of the world, however created, and irrespective of the claims of the producer, is made to flow toward certain centers of accumulation, to be enjoyed by those holding the keys to such situations. The world appears to be approaching a stage at which those who labor, no matter how skilled, how industrious, or how frugal, will receive, according to the "iron law" formulated by Ricardo, only so much for their services as will enable them "to subsist and to perpetuate their race." The rest finds its way into the hands of a comparatively few, usually non-producing, individuals, whom the usages and laws of all countries permit to claim that they own the very sources of all wealth and the right to allow or forbid its production.

These are great and serious evils, compared with which all the crimes, recognized as such, that would be committed if no government existed, would be as trifles. The underpaid labor, the prolonged and groveling drudgery, the wasted strength, the misery and squalor, the diseases resulting, and the premature deaths that would be prevented by a just distribution of the products of labor, would in a single year outweigh all the so-called crime of a century, for the prevention of which, it is said, government alone exists. This vast theater of woe is regarded as wholly outside the jurisdiction of government, while the most strenuous efforts are put forth to detect and punish the perpetrators of the least of the ordinary recognized crimes. This ignoring of great evils while so violently striking at small ones is the mark of an effete civilization, and warns us of the approaching dotage of the race.

Against the legitimate action of government in the protection of society from these worst of its evils, the instinctive hostility to government, or misarchy, above described, powerfully militates. In the face of it the government hesitates to take action, however clear the right or the method. But, as already remarked, this groundless over-caution against an impossible occurrence would not, in and of itself, have sufficed to prevent government from redressing such palpable wrongs. It has been nursed and kept alive for a specific purpose. It has formed the chief argument of those whose interests require the maintenance of the existing social order in relation to the distribution of wealth. Indeed, it is doubtful whether, without the incessant reiteration given to it by this class, it could have persisted to the present time. This inequitable economic system has itself been the product of centuries of astute management on the part of the shrewdest heads, with a view to securing by legal devices that undue share of the world's products which was formerly the reward of superior physical strength. It is clear to this class that their interests require a policy of strict non-interference on the part of government in what they call the natural laws of political economy, and they are quick to see that the old odium that still lingers among the people can be made a bulwark of strength for their position. They therefore never lose an opportunity to appeal to it in the most effective manner. Through the constant use of this *argumentum ad populum* the anti-government sentiment, which would naturally have smoldered and died out after its cause ceased to exist, is kept perpetually alive.

The great evils under which society now labors have grown up during the progress of intellectual supremacy. They have crept in stealthily during the gradual encroachment of organized cunning upon the domain of brute force. Over that vanishing domain, government retains its power, but it is still powerless in the expanding and now all-embracing field of psychic influence. No one ever claimed that in the trial of physical strength the booty should fall to the strongest. In all such cases the arm of government is stretched out and justice is enforced. But in those manifold, and far more unequal struggles now going on between mind and mind, or rather between the individual and an organized system, the product of ages of thought, it is customary to say that such matters must be left to regulate themselves, and that the fittest must be allowed to survive. Yet, to anyone who will candidly consider the matter, it must be clear that the first and principal acts of government openly and avowedly prevented, through forcible interference, the natural results of all trials of physical strength. These much-talked-of laws of nature are violated every time the highway robber is arrested and sent to jail.

Primitive government, when only brute force was employed, was strong enough to secure the just and equitable distribution of wealth. To-day, when mental force is everything, and physical force is nothing, it is powerless to accomplish this. This alone proves that government needs to be strengthened in its primary quality — the protection of society. There is no reasoning that applies to one kind of protection that does not apply equally to the other. It is utterly illogical to say that aggrandizement by physical force should be forbidden while aggrandizement by mental force or legal fiction should be permitted. It is absurd to claim that injustice committed by muscle should be regulated, while that committed by brain should be unrestrained.

While the modern plutocracy is not a form of government in the same sense that the other forms mentioned are, it is, nevertheless, easy to see that its power is as great as any government has ever wielded. The test of governmental power is usually the manner in which it taxes the people, and the strongest indictments ever drawn up against the worst forms of tyranny have been those which recited their oppressive methods of extorting tribute. But tithes are regarded as oppressive, and a fourth part of the yield of any industry would justify a revolt. Yet to-day there are many commodities for which the people pay two and three times as much as would cover the cost of production, transportation, and exchange at fair wages and fair profits. The monopolies in many lines actually tax the consumer from 25 to 75 per cent of the real value of the goods. Imagine an excise tax that should approach these figures! It was shown in Chap. XXXIII that under the operation of either monopoly or aggressive competition the price of everything is pushed up to the maximum limit that will be paid for the commodity in profitable quantities, and this wholly irrespective of the cost of production. No government in the world has now, or ever had, the power to enforce such an extortion as this. It is a governing power in the interest of favored individuals, which exceeds that of the most powerful monarch or despot that ever wielded a scepter.

What then is the remedy? How can society escape this last conquest of power by the egoistic intellect? It has overthrown the rule of brute force by the establishment of government. It has supplanted autocracy by aristocracy and this by democracy, and now it finds itself in the coils of plutocracy. Can it escape? Must it go back to autocracy for a power sufficient to cope with plutocracy? No autocrat ever had a tithe of that power. Shall it then let itself be crushed? It need not. There is one power and only one that is greater than that which now chiefly rules society. That power is society itself. There is one form of government that is stronger than autocracy or aristocracy or democracy, or even plutocracy, and that is *sociocracy*.

The individual has reigned long enough. The day has come for society to take its affairs into its own hands and shape its own destinies. The individual has acted as best he could. He has acted in the only way he could. With a consciousness, will, and intellect of his own he could do nothing else than pursue his natural ends. He should not be denounced nor called any names. He should not even be blamed. Nay, he should be praised, and even *imitated*. Society should learn its great lesson from him, should follow the path he has so clearly laid out that leads to success. It should imagine itself an individual, with all the interests of an individual, and becoming fully *conscious* of these interests it should pursue them with the same indomitable *will* with which the individual pursues his interests. Not only this, it must be guided, as he is guided, by the social *intellect*, armed with all the knowledge that all individuals combined, with so great labor, zeal, and talent have placed in its possession, constituting the social intelligence.

Sociocracy will differ from all other forms of government that have been devised, and yet that difference will not be so radical as to require a revolution. Just as absolute monarchy passed imperceptibly into limited monarchy, and this, in many states without even a change of name has passed into more or less pure democracy, so democracy is capable of passing as smoothly into sociocracy, and without taking on this unfamiliar name or changing that by which it is now known. For, though paradoxical, democracy, which is now the weakest of all forms of government, at least in the control of its own internal elements, is capable of becoming the strongest. Indeed, none of the other forms of government would be capable of passing directly into a government by society. Democracy is a phase through which they must first pass on any route that leads to the ultimate social stage which all governments must eventually attain if they persist.

How then, it may be asked, do democracy and sociocracy differ? How does society differ from the people? If the phrase "the people" really meant the people, the difference would be less. But that shibboleth of democratic states, where it means anything at all that can be described or defined, stands simply for the majority of qualified electors, no matter how small that majority may be. There is a sense in which the action of a majority may be looked upon as the action of society. At least, there is no denying the right of the majority to act for society, for to do this would involve either the denial of the right of government to act at all, or the admission of the right of a minority to act for society. But a majority acting for society is a different thing from society acting for itself, even though, as must always be the case, it acts through an agency chosen by its members. All democratic governments are largely party governments. The electors range themselves on one side or the other of some party line, the winning side considers itself the state as much as Louis the Fourteenth did. The losing party usually then regards the government as something alien to it and hostile, like an invader, and thinks of nothing but to gain strength enough to overthrow it at the next opportunity. While various issues are always brought forward and defended or attacked, it is obvious to the looker-on that the contestants care nothing for these, and merely use them to gain an advantage and win an election.

From the standpoint of society this is child's play. A very slight awakening of the social consciousness will banish it and substitute something more business-like. Once get rid of this puerile gaming spirit and have attention drawn to the real interests of society, and it will be seen that upon nearly all important questions all parties and all citizens are agreed, and that there is no need of this partisan strain upon the public energies. This is clearly shown at every change in the party complexion of the government. The victorious party which has been denouncing the government merely because it was in the hands of its political opponents boasts that it is going to revolutionize the country in the interest of good government, but the moment it comes into power and feels the weight of national responsibility it finds that it has little to do but carry out the laws in the same way that its predecessors had been doing.

There is a vast difference between all this outward show of partisanship and advocacy of so-called principles, and attention to the real interests and necessary business of the nation, which latter is what the government must do. It is a social duty. The pressure which is brought to enforce it is the power of the social will. But in the factitious excitement of partisan struggles where professional politicians and demagogues on the one hand, and the agents of plutocracy on the other, are shouting discordantly in the ears of the people, the real interests of society are, temporarily at least, lost sight of, clouded and obscured, and men lose their grasp on the real issues, forget even their own best interests, which, however selfish, would be a far safer guide, and the general result usually is that these are neglected and nations continue in the hands of mere politicians who are easily managed by the shrewd representatives of wealth.

Sociocracy will change all this. Irrelevant issues will be laid aside. The important objects upon which all but an interested few are agreed will receive their proper degree of attention, and measures will be considered in a non-partisan spirit with the sole purpose of securing these objects. Take as an illustration the postal telegraph question. No one not a stockholder in an existing telegraph company would prefer to pay twenty-five cents for a message if he could send it for ten cents. Where is the room for discussing a question of this nature? What society wants is the cheapest possible system. It wants to know with certainty whether a national postal telegraph system would secure this universally desired object. It is to be expected that the agents of the present telegraph companies would try to show that it would not succeed. This is according to the known laws of psychology as set forth in this work. But why be influenced by the interests of such a small number of persons, however worthy, when all the rest of mankind are interested in the opposite solution? The investigation should be a disinterested and strictly scientific one, and should actually settle the question in one way or the other. If it was found to be a real benefit, the system should be adopted. There are to-day a great number of these strictly social questions before the American people, questions which concern every citizen in the country, aud whose solution would doubtless profoundly affect the state of civilization attainable on this continent. Not only is it impossible to secure this, but it is impossible to secure an investigation of them on their real merits. The same is true of other countries, and in general the prevailing democracies of the world are incompetent to deal with problems of social welfare.

The more extreme and important case referred to a few pages back may make the distinction still more clear. It was shown, and is known to all political economists, that the prices of most of the staple commodities consumed by mankind have no necessary relation to the cost of producing them and placing them in the hands of the consumer. It is always the highest price that the consumer will pay rather than do without. Let us suppose that price to be on an average double what it would cost to produce, transport, exchange, and deliver the goods, allowing in each of these transactions a fair compensation for all services rendered. Is there any member of society who would prefer to pay two dollars for what is thus fairly worth only one? Is there any sane ground for arguing such a question? Certainly not. The individual cannot correct this state of things. No democracy can correct it. But a government that really represented the interests of society would no more tolerate it than an individual would tolerate a continual extortion of money on the part of another without an equivalent.

And so it would be throughout. Society would inquire in a business way without fear, favor, or bias, into everything that concerned its welfare, and if it found obstacles it would remove them, and if it found opportunities it would improve them. In a word, society would do under the same circumstances just what an intelligent individual would do. It would further, in all possible ways, its own interests.

I anticipate the objection that this is an ideal state of things, and that it has never been attained by any people, and to all appearances never can be. No fair-minded critic will, however, add the customary objection that is raised, not wholly without truth, to all socialistic schemes, that they presuppose a change in "human nature." Because in the transformation here foreshadowed the permanence of all the mental attributes is postulated, and I have not only refrained from dwelling upon the moral progress of the world, but have not even enumerated among the social forces the power of sympathy as a factor in civilization. I recognize this factor as one of the derivative ones, destined to perform an important part, but I have preferred to rest the case upon the primary and original egoistic influences, believing that neither meliorism nor sociocracy is dependent upon any sentiment, or upon altruistic props for its support. At least the proofs will be stronger if none of these aids are called in, and if they can be shown to have a legitimate influence, this is only so much added to the weight of evidence.

To the other charge the answer is that ideals are necessary, and also that no ideal is ever fully realized. If it can be shown that society is actually moving toward any ideal the ultimate substantial realization of that ideal is as good as proved. The proofs of such a movement in society to-day are abundant. In many countries the encroachments of egoistic individualism have been checked at a number of important points. In this country alarm has been taken in good earnest at the march of plutocracy under the protection of democracy. Party lines are giving way and there are unmistakable indications that a large proportion of the people are becoming seriously interested in the social progress of the country. For the first time in the history of political parties there has been formed a distinctively industrial party[1] which possesses all the elements of perma-

[1] For the last ten years or more there have been indications in this country that a deep undercurrent of public sentiment was setting in toward the formation of

nence and may soon be a controlling factor in American politics. Though this may not as yet presage a great social revolution, still it is precisely the way in which a reform in the direction indicated should be expected to originate. But whether the present movement prove enduring or ephemeral, the seeds of reform have been sown broadcast throughout the land, and sooner or later they must spring up, grow, and bear their fruit.

For a long time to come social action must be chiefly negative and be confined to the removal of evils that exist, such as have been pointed out in these pages, but a positive stage will ultimately be reached in which society will consider and adopt measures for its own advancement. The question of the respective provinces of social action and individual action cannot be entered into here at length, but it is certain that the former will continue to encroach upon the latter so long as such encroachment is a public benefit. There is one large field in which there is no question on this point, viz., the field covered by what, in modern economic parlance, is called "natural monopoly." The arguments are too familiar to demand restatement here, and the movement is already so well under way that there is little need of further argument. As

such a political party, and while I claim for myself no special gift of prophecy, I was able to foresee this some years before it took any definite form. In the Forum for June, 1887, or about four years before the Cincinnati convention was called, at the close of an article on False Notions of Government, some parts of which I have reproduced in this chapter, occurs the following paragraph which may be said to foreshadow events that followed, and which is as true and salutary now as it was at that date:

"The true solution of the great social problem of this age is to be found in the ultimate establishment of a genuine *people's government*, with ample power to protect society against all forms of injustice, from whatever source, coupled with a warm and dutiful regard for the true interests of each and all, the poor as well as the rich. If this be what is meant by the oft-repeated phrase 'paternal government,' then were this certainly a consummation devoutly to be wished. But in this conception of government there is nothing paternal. It gets rid entirely of the paternal, the patriarchal, the personal element, and becomes nothing more nor less than the effective expression of the public will, the active agency by which society consciously and intelligently governs its own conduct."

to what lies beyond this, however, there is room for much discussion and honest difference of opinion. This is because there has been so little induction. It is the special characteristic of the form of government that I have called sociocracy, resting as it does, directly upon the science of sociology, to investigate the facts bearing on every subject, not for the purpose of depriving any class of citizens of the opportunity to benefit themselves, but purely and solely for the purpose of ascertaining what is for the best interests of society at large.

The socialistic arguments in favor of society taking upon itself the entire industrial operations of the world have never seemed to me conclusive, chiefly because they have consisted so largely of pure theory and a priori deductions. Any one who has become imbued by the pursuit of some special branch of science with the nature of scientific evidence requires the presentation of such evidence before he can accept conclusions in any other department. And this should be the attitude of all in relation to these broader questions of social phenomena. The true economist can scarcely go farther than to say that a given question is an open one, and that he will be ready to accept the logic of facts when these are brought forward. I do not mean that we must not go into the water until we have learned to swim. This, however, suggests the true method of solving such questions. One learns to swim by a series of trials, and society can well afford to try experiments in certain directions and note the results. There are, however, other methods, such as careful estimates of the costs and accurate calculations of the effect based on the uniform laws of social phenomena. Trial is the ultimate test of scientific theory thus formed, and may, in social as in physical science, either establish or overthrow hypotheses. But in social science, no less than in other branches of science, the working hypothesis must always be the chief instrument of successful research.

Until the scientific stage is reached, and as a necessary introduction to it, social problems may properly be clearly stated and such general considerations brought forward as have a direct bearing upon them. I know of no attempts of this nature which I can more warmly recommend than those made by John Stuart Mill in his little work on Liberty,[1] and in his Chapters on Socialism, of which the latter appeared posthumously. They are in marked contrast, by their all-sided wisdom, with the intensely one-sided writings of Herbert Spencer on substantially the same subject ; and yet the two authors are obviously at one on the main points discussed. This candid statement of the true claims of the *laissez faire* school is perfectly legitimate. Equally so are like candid presentations of the opposite side of the question. The more light that can be shed on all sides the better, but in order really to elucidate social problems it must be the dry light of science, as little influenced by feeling as though it were the inhabitants of Jupiter's moons, instead of those of this planet, that were under the field of the intellectual telescope.

[1] Even despotism does not produce its worst effects, so long as Individuality exists under it ; and whatever crushes individuality is despotism, by whatever name it may be called. — JOHN STUART MILL : *On Liberty*, pp. 122–123.

Neither one person, nor any number of persons, is warranted in saying to another human creature of ripe years, that he shall not do with his life for his own benefit what he choses to do with it. — JOHN STUART MILL : *Ibid.*, p. 147.

The strongest of all the arguments against the interference of the public with purely personal conduct, is that when it does interfere, the odds are that it interferes wrongly, and in the wrong place. — JOHN STUART MILL : *Ibid.*, p. 161.

LIST OF AUTHORS AND THEIR WORKS

CITED OR REFERRED TO, WITH CRITICAL AND EXPLANATORY NOTES.[1]

[Figures in full-face type refer to pages of this work.]

It was found undesirable to indicate the sources of the numerous quotations more fully than was consistent with clearness. The present list aims to furnish any additional information that may be desired. The pages referred to in the text are those of the editions mentioned in this list.

ABOUT, EDMOND.

A B C du Travailleur, Deuxième Edition, Paris, 1869. 8°.
Cited on pages **222**, **233**, and **240**.

ADDISON, JOSEPH.

Cato. — The Works of the Right Honorable Joseph Addison, a New Edition with Notes by Richard Hurd, D.D., Lord Bishop of Worcester; in six volumes. Bohn's Standard Library, Addison's Works, Vol. I. London: George Bell & Sons, York Street, 1881. Cato, pp. 162–226.

The celebrated line quoted on page **175** occurs in Cato, Act iv, Scene 1, p. 212.

ALLEN, GRANT.

The Origin of Fruits. Cornhill Magazine, Vol. XXXVIII, August, 1878, pp. 174–188.
Cited on page **248**.

ARGENSON, MARC PIERRE, MARQUIS D'.

See Daire, Dupont de Nemours.

BACON, FRANCIS, LORD.

Novum Organum. The Works of Francis Bacon, Baron of Verulam, Viscount of St. Albans, and Lord High Chancellor of England. Collected and Edited by James Spedding, M.A., of Trinity

[1] The author desires to acknowledge his indebtedness to Mr. David Hutcheson of the Library of Congress for valuable assistance in the preparation of this list, as well as throughout the literary investigations undertaken in connection with the work.

College, Cambridge; Robert Leslie Ellis, M.A., Late Fellow of Trinity College, Cambridge; and Douglas Denon Heath, Barrister-at-Law, Late Fellow of Trinity College, Cambridge. Vol. I, New York: Published by Hurd & Houghton, Cambridge: Riverside Press. 1869.

Cited on pages **190, 196–197.**

BECCARIA, CESARE.

Opere. Milano: Dalla Società tipogr. dei Classici Italiani, 1821.

The Maxim cited on page **282** occurs in the treatise entitled: Dei Delitti e delle Pene. This is published separately at Paris, 1829. See p. 2.

BENTHAM, JEREMY.

The Works of Jeremy Bentham, published under the superintendence of his executor, John Bowring. Edinburgh: William Tait; Simpkin, Marshall & Co., London, 1843.

Cited on page **282.**

BOURDILLON, FRANCIS W.

Light. — Harper's Cyclopedia of British and American Poetry. Edited by Epes Sargent. New York: Harper & Brothers, Franklin Square, 1881, p. 938.

Cited on page **44.**

BROOKS, W. K.

The condition of Women from a Zoölogical Point of View. Popular Science Monthly, New York, Vol. XV, June, 1879, pp. 145–155; July, 1875, pp. 347–356.

Cited on pages **169, 174.**

BÜTTIKOFER, J.

Reisebilder aus Liberia. Resultate geographischer, naturwissenschaftlicher und ethnographischer Untersuchungen während der Jahre 1879–1882 und 1886–1887. Leiden, E. J. Brill 1890. 2 vols. 8°.

Cited on pages **254, 255.**

BYRON, GEORGE GORDON, LORD.

The Poetical Works of Lord Byron. Wm. W. Swayne, Brooklyn and New York.

The line quoted on page **64**, occurs on p. 60 of the above edition and on p. 560 of the London edition, 1851. The motto placed at the head of the Preface (p. v) is from Childe Harold's Pilgrimage, Canto iv, Stanza 185. The other mottos from Byron on pages **163** and **215** are accompanied by adequate references.

CAIRNES, J. E.

Mr. Spencer on Social Evolution. Fortnightly Review, Vol. XXIII (New Series, Vol. XVII), London, January, 1875, pp. 63–82.

Cited on pages **291–292**.

CARLYLE, THOMAS.

Varnhagen von Ense's Memoirs. London and Westminster Review, Vol. XXXII, London, 1839 (December, 1838 to April, 1839), pp. 60–84. — Thomas Carlyle's Collected Works, Library Edition in thirty volumes. Vol. X; Critical and Miscellaneous Essays, Vol. V, pp. 287–322.

The passage cited on page **208** occurs on p. 75 of the former, and on p. 309 of the latter of these volumes.

CARPENTER, WILLIAM B.

Principles of Mental Physiology, with their Applications to the Training and Discipline of the Mind, and the Study of its Morbid Conditions. New York, D. Appleton & Co., 1875.

Cited on pages **12, 15, 171**.

CLARK, JOHN B.

The Philosophy of Wealth. Economic Principles Newly Formulated. Boston, Ginn & Co., 1886.

Cited on pages **117, 199, 240**.

CLARKE, F. W.

An Attempt at a Theory of Odor. See a brief abstract in the Bulletin of the Philosophical Society of Washington, Vol. VIII, Washington, Smithsonian Institution, 1886, p. 27. (Smithsonian Miscellaneous Collections, No. 636. Vol. XXXIII, Article III.)

This very suggestive paper has never been published in full, because, as the author informs me, it is as yet little more than a theory, which, however, he hopes ultimately to establish if true. My knowledge of Prof. Clarke's views is therefore chiefly derived from hearing the paper read, and from subsequent interviews with him in relation to it.

See page **18**.

COKE, SIR EDWARD.

The Reports of Sir Edward Coke, Knt., in thirteen parts. A New Edition, with additional notes and references, and with abstracts of the principal points. . . . By John Henry Thomas . . . and John Farquhar Fraser. . . . In six volumes, London: Joseph Butterworth & Son, and J. Cooke, Dublin, 1826.

Cited on page **276**.

COMTE, AUGUSTE.

Cours de Philosophie Positive, Troisième Edition augmentée d'une Préface par E. Littré. Paris, J. B. Baillière et Fils, 1869. Six volumes, 8°.

Cited on pages **ii, 1, 37, 190, 194, 240.**

CROSS, J. W.

George Eliot's Life as related in her Letters and Journals, arranged and edited by her Husband, J. W. Cross. In three volumes. William Blackwood & Sons, Edinburgh and London, 1884.

Cited on page **281.**

DAIRE, EUGÈNE.

Collection d'Economistes. Nouvelle Edition, Paris, 1844. Tome premier, Œuvres de Turgot. Tome second, Physiocrates (Quesnay, Dupont de Nemours, etc.). Tome troisième, Turgot.

This work is one of the principal sources of information relative to the early French political economists, whose scattered writings are now difficult of access. The aphorisms of the Marquis d'Argenson, de Gournay, and others are to be found here with a full history of their origin. See Dupont de Nemours, Quesnay, Turgot, below.

DARWIN, CHARLES.

Journal of Researches into the Natural History and Geology of the Countries visited during the Voyage of H.M.S. Beagle round the World, under the command of Capt. Fitz Roy, R. N. New Edition. New York: D. Appleton & Co., 1871.

Cited on pages **246–247.**

Autobiography; being Chapter II of The Life and Letters of Charles Darwin, edited by his son Francis Darwin. In two volumes. New York: D. Appleton & Co., 1888. 8°.

Reference on page **280.**

DIOGENES LAERTIUS.

Zeno. — Diogenis Laertii de Clarorum Philosophorum Vitis, Dogmatibus et Apophthegmatibus Libri decem. Ex Italicis Codicibus nunc primum excussis recensuit C. Gabr. Cobet . . . Græce et Latine cum indicibus. Parisiis: Editore Ambrosio Firmin Didot, Instituti Franciæ Typographo. 1850. Zeno, Vol. XII, pp. 159–193.

The passage quoted on page **147** occurs on p. 177 of Vol. XII of this edition. The corresponding Latin is as follows: Primam animantis appetitionem hanc esse dicunt, se ipsum tuendi atque servandi.

DISRAELI, BENJAMIN, EARL OF BEACONSFIELD.

Coningsby, or the New Generation. New Edition. New York George Routledge & Sons.

Cited on page **64**.

DU BARTAS.

Diuine Weekes and Workes. With a Compleate Collection of all the other most delight-full Workes. Translated and written by the famous Philomusus, Iosvah Sylvester. London: printed by Robert Young with Additions, 1641. — The First Weeke: Or Birth of the World. Of the Noble, Learned, and Diuine W. Salustius, Lord of Bartas, 1605.

Cited on page **238**. This couplet occurs on p. 184 of the edition of 1605, and on p. 46 (col. 2) of that of 1641. The original French (Guillaume de Salluste, Seigneur du Bartas) I have not seen.

DU BOIS-REYMOND, EMIL.

Culturgeschichte und Naturwissenschaft. Vortrag gehalten am 24. März 1877 im Verein für wissenschaftliche Vorlesungen zu Köln. Zweiter unveränderter Abdruck. Leipzig: Verlag von Veit & Comp., 1878.

Cited on page **132**.

DUPONT DE NEMOURS, PIERRE SAMUEL.

Abrégé des Principes de l'Economie Politique. 1772.

This work is reproduced in Daire's Collection d'Economistes, Vol. II, Physiocrates, Dupont de Nemours. The citation on page **241** occurs on p. 374 of that volume. In Vol. III of the same work may be found an interesting "Préambule" to Turgot's "Éloge de M. de Gournay," written by Dupont, in which the celebrated saying of the Marquis d'Argenson: "*Pas trop gouverner*," and the historic phrase of de Gournay: "*Laissez faire et laissez passer*," occur.

See further under Quesnay.

ECKERMANN, JOHANN PETER.

Gespräche mit Goethe in den letzten Jahren seines Lebens, 1823–1832. Zweite Ausgabe. Leipzig, 1837. 3 vols. (parts).

The passage quoted on page **63** occurs in a conversation held Jan. 27, 1824.

GEORGE ELIOT.

See Cross, J. W.

The words reproduced on page **281** will be found in the letter which she wrote to James Sully, dated Jan. 19, 1877. Life, etc., Vol. III, p. 267.

GOETHE, JOHANN WOLFGANG VON.
See Eckermann, Johann Peter.

GOLDSMITH, OLIVER.
The Vicar of Wakefield. A Tale supposed to be written by himself. Salisbury: Printed by B. Collins, for F. Newbery, in Pater-Noster-Row, London, 1766. 2 vols. 12mo. — The Works of Oliver Goldsmith. Edited by Peter Cunningham. In four volumes. Vol. I. Boston: Little, Brown & Co., 1854, pp. 292–468.

This last is the edition cited on page **51**. The original edition of 1766 is quoted by the editor, the title-page as given above occupying page 292.

GOURNAY, JEAN CLAUDE MARIE VINCENT, SEIGNEUR DE.
See under Daire, Dupont de Nemours, and Turgot.

GRAY, ASA.
Darwiniana: Essays and Reviews pertaining to Darwinism. New York: D. Appleton & Co., 1877.

See pages **75**, **249**.

HAECKEL, ERNST.
Die heutige Entwickelungslehre im Verhältnisse zur Gesammtwissenschaft. Vortrag in der ersten öffentlichen Sitzung der fünfzigsten Versammlung Deutscher Naturforscher und Aertzte zu München am 18. September 1877. Stuttgart: E. Schweizerbart'sche Verlagshandlung (E. Koch). 1877. 24 S. 8°.

Cited on page **44**.

HAMILTON, SIR WILLIAM.
Lectures on Metaphysics and Logic. Edited by H. L. Mansel and John Veitch. Edinburgh and London, 1859.

Cited on page **20**. The motto used on page **215** is placed opposite the title-page of Vol. I of this edition. Whether the language is entirely his own or was borrowed from earlier authors, I have not been able to learn.

HARTLEY, DAVID.
Observations on Man, his Frame, his Duty, and his Expectations. In two parts: to which are now first added Prayers, and Religious Meditations. To the first part are prefixed, a Sketch of the Life and Character, and a Portrait, of the Author. The Fifth

Edition. Printed by Richard Cruttwell, St. James's-Street, Bath; and sold by Wilkie & Robinson, Pater-Noster-Row, London 1810. 8°.

Cited on pages **20** and **25**. Hartley's first proposition, so prophetic of the present status of psychology, which occurs on p. 7 of Vol. I of this edition, is as follows:

"The white medullary Substance of the Brain, spinal Marrow, and the Nerves proceeding from them, is the immediate Instrument of Sensation and Motion."

HARTMANN, EDUARD VON.

Philosophie des Unbewussten. Zehnte erweiterte Auflage in drei Theilen. — Eduard von Hartmann's Ausgewählte Werke. Zweite wohlfeile Ausgabe. Bände VII, VIII, IX. Leipzig: Verlag von Wilhelm Friedrich, K. R. Hofbuchhändler, 1890.

See pages **64**, **69**, **292**.

HERODOTUS.

Clio. — Harper's Greek and Latin Texts. Herodotus. Recensuit Josephus Williams Blakesley, S.T.B.Coll. SS.Trin. apud Cantabr. quondam Socius. New York: Harper & Brothers, Franklin Square, 1861. Vol. I, pp. 1–107.

Cited on page **312**. The passage is part of a speech made by Solon to Crœsus. In this edition the speech is put in quotation marks as Solon's own language.

HUMBOLDT, ALEXANDER.

Memoiren Alexander von Humboldt's. 2 Bände, Leipzig: Verlag von Ernst Schäfer, 1861.

Cited on pages **63–64**. I copied this passage from Mainländer's Philosophie der Erlösung, p. 209 (see Mainländer, below), where it is simply credited to Humboldt's "Memoiren," without more exact reference, and I have had difficulty in proving its authenticity. I showed it to a number of German scholars none of whom knew of such a work. Most of them doubted its genuineness, and one, in very strong language, declared it a forgery. I finally wrote to Dr. Eduard von Hartmann, as one likely to be informed in such matters. His prompt reply, received on the eve of going to press, contained the desired information as set forth above.

The three paragraphs, as carefully indicated by Hartmann, occur on the three pages, 365, 366, and 367, respectively, of Vol. I, and he further refers me to pp. 306–309 of Vol. I, and to p. 141 of Vol. II, for other passages of similar import.

HUTCHESON, FRANCIS.

An Inquiry into the Original of our Ideas of Beauty and Virtue. In two Treatises. Fifth Edition, corrected.

The second treatise bears the subtitle : Concerning Moral Good and Evil. It is from this that the quotation on page **282** is made.

HUXLEY, THOMAS H.

Administrative Nihilism . An Address to the Members of the Midland Institute, October 9, 1871. In : More Criticisms of Darwin and Administrative Nihilism, by T. H. Huxley. New York : D. Appleton & Co., pp. 57–85.

The passages quoted on page **292** occur on pp. 71 and 72 of this collection of essays.

The Herring : A Lecture delivered at the National Fisheries Exhibition, Norwich, April 21, 1881. Nature, Vol. XXIII, April 28, 1881, p. 682.

Cited on page **246**.

JAMES, EDMUND J.

The Railway Question. The Report of the Committee on Transportation of the American Economic Association. With the Paper read at the Boston Meeting, May 21–25, 1887, on "The Agitation for Federal Regulation of Railways." Publications of the American Economic Association, Vol. II, No. 3, July, 1877.

Cited on pages **265–266**.

KANT, IMMANUEL.

Kritik der reinen Vernunft. Herausgegeben von G. Hartenstein. Leipzig : Leopold Voss. 1868.

Cited on pages **12**, **15**, **71**.

KING, CLARENCE.

Catastrophism and Evolution : An Address delivered at the Sheffield Scientific School at Yale College, New Haven, June 26, 1877. The American Naturalist, Vol. XI, Boston : H. O. Houghton & Co. New York : Hurd & Houghton. The Riverside Press, Cambridge, 1877. August, 1877, pp. 449–470.

Mr. King's use of the phrase "survival of the plastic," mentioned on page **259**, occurs on p. 469 of this volume of the Naturalist.

LA ROCHEFOUCAULD, FRANÇOIS.

Réflexions ou sentences et maximes. Edition publiée par L. Aimé-Martin, Paris, 1822.

Cited on pages **155** and **163**. The maxims are numbered in all editions, but the numbers differ slightly in the different ones.

For example, M. Aimé-Martin states in a foot-note to page 11 that the third motto which I have placed at the head of Chap. XXIV (p. **163**) appears as maxim No. 179 of the fourth edition (which I have not seen), and that La Rochefoucauld afterwards reduced it to the short form that immediately precedes it on page **163**, and placed it at the head of the entire series without number, as an epigram, obviously designed to furnish the key-note or central idea of his philosophy. See further under Pope, below.

Le Conte, Joseph.

Scientific Relation of Sociology to Biology. Popular Science Monthly, Vol. XIV, New York, February, 1879, pp. 325–336, 425–434. Separately paged reprint, pp. 1–21.

Cited on pages **240**, **314**.

Relation of Biology to Sociology. The Berkeleyan, Vol. XXIII. Berkeley, Cal., May, 1887, p. 123. Separately paged reprint, pp. 1–8.

Cited on pages **221**, **292**.

Lucretius.

De Rerum Natura. — Harper's Greek and Latin Texts. T. Lucreti Cari de Rerum Natura Libri sex. Recognovit Hugo A. I. Munro, M. A. New York: Harper & Brothers, Franklin Square, 1861.

Cited on page **51**.

Lyman, D., Jun.

The Moral Sayings of Publius Syrus, a Roman Slave. From the Latin. Cleveland: L. E. Barnard & Co., 1856. 88 pp. 8°.

See page **159** and Publius Syrus, below.

Macaulay, Thomas Babington, Lord.

History of England. — The Works of Lord Macaulay complete. Edited by his Sister Lady Trevelyan. In eight volumes. London: Longmans, Green & Co., 1866.

Cited on page **282**.

Mainländer, Philip.

Die Philosophie der Erlösung. Zweite Auflage, Berlin: Verlag von Theodor Hofmann, 1879.

Cited on page **59**.

Malthus, T. R.

An Essay on the Principle of Population, or a View of its Past and Present Effects on Human Happiness, with an Inquiry into our

Prospects respecting the Future Removal or Mitigation of the Evils which it occasions. Seventh Edition. Reeves & Turner, London, 1872.
Cited on page **242**.

MAUDSLEY, HENRY.
Sex in Mind and in Education. Fortnightly Review, London, Vol. XXI (New Series, Vol. XV), April 1, 1874, pp. 466–483.
Cited on pages **116–117**.

MILL, JOHN STUART.
On Liberty. Boston: Ticknor & Fields, 1863.
Cited on page **331**.

The Subjection of Women. Third Edition. London: Longmans & Co., 1870.
Cited on page **174**.

Chapters on Socialism. Fortnightly Review, Vol. XXXI (New Series, Vol. XXV), 1879, pp. 217–237; 373–382; 513–530. (See p. 226.)
Cited on page **155**.

MONTAIGNE, MICHEL EYQUEM DE.
De la Physionomie. Collection de Moralistes Français. Essais de Montaigne, publiés . . . par Amaury Duval. Tome VI. Paris, 1822, pp. 1–66.
Cited on page **v**.

MORE, SIR THOMAS.
Utopia. Translated into English by Ralph Robinson, 1556. Edited by Edward Arber. English Reprints. London: Murray & Son, No. 14 (bound with Latimer's Sermons, No. 13), 1869.
Cited on pages **155** and **314–315**.

NEWBERRY, J. S.
The Cretaceous Flora of North America. Transactions of the New York Academy of Sciences, Vol. V, February, 1886, pp. 133–137.

The Flora of the Amboy Clays. Bulletin of the Torrey Botanical Club, Vol. XIII, March, 1886, pp. 33–37.
See pages **84–85**.

NICHOLS, HERBERT.
The Origin of Pleasure and Pain. The Philosophical Review, Vol. I. Boston: Ginn & Co., July 1892, pp. 403–432; September, 1892, pp. 518–534.
See pages **8, 21, 138–139**.

PASCAL, BLAISE.

Pensées, Fragments et Lettres, publiés pour la première fois conformément aux manuscrits originaux en grande partie inédits, par M. Prosper Faugère. Paris : Andrieux, Editeur, Rue Sainte-Anne, 11, 1844. Two vols. 8°.

Cited on pages **9, 50, 63, 239, 305.**

PATTEN, SIMON N.

The Principles of Rational Taxation : Published by the Philadelphia Social Science Association. Read at a meeting of the Association, November 21, 1889. 25 pp. 8°.

Cited at length on pages **266** ff.

The Theory of Dynamic Economics. Publications of the University of Pennsylvania. Political Economy and Public Law Series. Vol. III, No. 2. Philadelphia, 1892. 153 pp. 8°.

See page **120.**

PLINY THE YOUNGER.

Epistolæ. — C. Plinii Cæcilii Secundi Epistolæ et Panegyricus. Londini : ex officinâ Jacobi & Richardi Tonson, & Johannis Watts, 1741.

The citation on page **51,** from the fifteenth epistle, second book, occurs on p. 44 of this edition.

PLUTARCH.

Περὶ Τύχης (De Fortuna). — Plvtarchi Chæronensis Omnivm qvæ Exstant Operum. Tomvs secvndvs, continens Moralia, Gulielmo Xylandro interprete. . . . Francofvrti : In Officina Danielis ac Dauidis Aubriorum & Clementis Schleichii, 1620.

Cited on page **195.** The Greek of this edition is printed in ligatures which Dr. Wm. B. Owen of Lafayette College kindly wrote out for me for the passage quoted. The Latin rendering of this passage as placed in the parallel column, is as follows : Atqui nemo terram aqua madefaciens discedit vltro & fortunae opera lateres inde exituros censens.

POPE, ALEXANDER.

Essay on Man. — The Works of Alexander Pope. New Edition. Including several hundred unpublished letters and other new materials. Collected in part by the late Rt. Hon. John Wilson Croker, with introductions and notes. By Whitwell Elwin. Vol. II. Poetry. London : John Murray, Albemarle Street, 1871.

Cited on pages **103** and **132.** The lines on page **103** are not found in the text as published in this and most editions, but are given in a foot-note (note [a] to line 216, p. 392) by the editor, who says that they occur in the "manuscript following line 216." They are preceded by four other lines which help to indicate the growth of the thought in the poet's mind. These are as follows:

"To strangle in its birth each rising crime
Requires but little, — just to think in time.
In ev'ry vice, at first, in some degree
We see some virtue, or we think we see.
Our vices thus," etc.

The editor then adds: "Of the last couplet there is a second version":

"Thus spite of all the Frenchman's witty lies
Most vices are but virtues in disguise."

It deserves to be noticed that Pope's adumbration is of the truth that there are no essentially evil propensities, or *the relativity of evil;* while La Rochefoucauld's adumbration is of the truth that indirection is the essential quality of intellectual action, or *the principle of deception.* These ideas are therefore not opposites or inconsistent with each other, much less "witty lies," but are fundamental truths, though so occult and far-reaching that neither of the writers quoted saw them in their full relations; and Pope's grasp of his conception was so feeble that in revising his manuscripts he seems to have been unable to bring it back to consciousness, and therefore expunged it.

POWELL, J. W.

Mythologic Philosophy. Address of Vice-President, Section B, Natural History, American Association for the Advancement of Science, 28th Meeting, held at Saratoga Springs, N. Y., August, 1879. Proceedings, Vol. XXVIII, Salem, 1880, pp. 251–278.

Cited on page **215**.

PUBLIUS SYRUS.

Collection des Auteurs Latins, avec la Traduction en Français; publiée sous la Direction de M. Nisard, de l'Académie Française, Inspecteur Général de l'Enseignement Supérieur. Vol. IX: Œuvres Complètes d'Horace, de Juvénal, de Perse, de Sulpicia, de Turnus, de Catulle, de Properce, de Gallus et Maximien, de Tibulle, de Phèdre et de Syrus. Paris: Chez Firmin Didot Frères, Fils et Cie, Libraires Imprimeurs de l'Institut de France, rue Jacob, 56. 1869. Publius Syrus, pp. 759–819.

Cited on page **159**. For the English translation see Lyman, D., Jun., above. The maxims are not numbered in Nisard's collection, but Lyman has followed the same order, and his No. 914 occurs on p. 807 (col. 2), and 939 on p. 808 (col. 2). The respective French renderings are as follows:

914. — Qu'un fou se taise, il passera pour un sage.

939. — Le silence tient lieu de sagesse au fou.

QUESNAY, FRANÇOIS.

Maximes Générales du Gouvernement Economique d'un Royaume Agricole. In: Physiocratie, ou Constitution Naturelle du Gouvernement le plus avantageux au Genre Humain. Recueil publié par Du Pont, des Sociétés Royales d'Agriculture de Soissons & d'Orléans, & Correspondant de la Société d'Emulation de Londres. A Leyde, et se trouve à Paris, chez Merlin, rue de la Harpe, 1768. Vol. I, pp. 105–122.

Cited on page **241**.

REID, THOMAS.

Inquiry into the Human Mind, on the Principles of Common Sense. The Works of Thomas Reid, etc., with account of his Life and Writings. By Dugald Stewart. With notes, by the American Editors. In four volumes. Vol. I, Charlestown, printed and published by Samuel Etheridge, Jun'r., 1813, pp. 165–444.

See page **173**.

RICARDO, DAVID.

Principles of Political Economy and Taxation. Edited by E. C. K. Gonner, London, 1891.

Cited on page **242**.

SCHELLING, FRIEDRICH WILHELM JOSEPH VON.

Sämmtliche Werke. In fourteen volumes, 8°. Edited by Karl Friedrich August Schelling. Stuttgart und Augsburg: J. G. Cotta'scher Verlag, 1856–1861.

Cited on page **59**.

SCHOPENHAUER, ARTHUR.

Die Welt als Wille und Vorstellung. Dritte verbesserte und beträchtlich vermehrte Auflage. Leipzig: F. A. Brockhaus. 1859. 2 vols. 8°.

In this work the relations between the feelings, clearly recognized as the dynamic agent, and the intellect, somewhat less clearly recognized as the directive agent, are forcibly set forth, marking, as it seems to me, an epoch in philosophy. I have therefore copied freely from it and placed the leading thoughts of Schopenhauer prominently before the reader in various mottos at the heads of chapters.

Ueber den Willen in der Natur. Eine Erörterung der Bestättigungen, welche die Philosophie des Verfassers, seit ihrem Auftreten, durch die empirischen Wissenschaften erhalten hat. Vierte Auflage, herausgegeben von Julius Frauenstädt. Leipzig: F. A. Brockhaus. 1878.

Cited on page **133**.

SMITH, ADAM.

An Inquiry into the Nature and Causes of the Wealth of Nations. Edited by James E. Thorold Rogers. Oxford, at the Clarendon Press, 1869. 2 vols. 8°.

Cited on page **241**.

SOLON.

See Herodotus.

SOPHOCLES.

Trachiniæ. — Sophoclis quæ exstant Omnia cum Veterum Grammaticorum Scholiis. Superstites Tragœdias VII. Ad optimorum exemplarium fidem recensuit, versione et notis illustravit, deperditarum fragmenta collegit Rich. Franc. Phil. Brunck, regiæ inscriptionum et humaniorum literarum Academiæ Socius. — Accedunt excerpta ex varietate lectionis, quam continet editio Caroli Gottl. Augusti Erfurdt; Demetrii Triclinii scholia metrica; notæ ineditæ Caroli Burneii; et Godfr. Henr. Schæferi annotatio integra. Londini: excudebat A. J. Valpy, A.M. Sumtibus Ricardi Priestley, 1824, Tomus I, pp. 305–381.

Cited on page **312**. This passage opens the Trachiniæ. The Oxford translation is as follows: "There is an ancient saying, renowned among men, that you cannot fully judge of the life of mortals, whether it has been good or bad to an individual before his death." The Tragedies of Sophocles in English Prose. Oxford Translation, London, 1863, p. 203.

SPENCER, HERBERT.

Social Statics: or, The Conditions Essential to Human Happiness specified, and the First of them developed. London: John Chapman, 142 Strand. 1851.

Cited on page **231**.

Social Statics, abridged and revised; together with: The Man *versus* the State. New York: D. Appleton & Co., 1892.

See pages **242**, **245**, **248–249**.

Mr. Martineau on Evolution. Popular Science Monthly, Vol. I, New York, July, 1872, pp. 313–323.

Cited on pages **230–231**.

The Study of Sociology, New York: D. Appleton & Co., 1880.
Cited on pages **116, 175–176.**

The Man *versus* the State: Containing "The New Toryism," "The Coming Slavery," "The Sins of Legislators," and "The Great Political Superstition." Reprinted from The Contemporary Review, with a Postscript. London: Williams and Norgate, 1884.

As bound with Social Statics, abridged and revised (see last title but two, above), it seems to be unchanged except by the addition of a short note. This series of papers constitutes Mr. Spencer's most vigorous attack upon what he regards as the socialistic tendencies of the times, and defence of *laissez faire* or individualism. See page **242.**

First Principles of a New System of Philosophy (A System of Synthetic Philosophy, Vol. I). New York: D. Appleton & Co., 1874.
Cited on page **91.**

The Principles of Psychology, in two volumes (A System of Synthetic Philosophy, Vols. IV, V). New York: D. Appleton & Co., 1873.
Cited on pages **15–16, 36, 50–51, 71.**

The Data of Ethics: Being Part I of The Principles of Ethics, Vol. I (see below). New York: D. Appleton & Co., 1879.
Cited on pages **16, 103, 107.**

Justice: Being Part IV of The Principles of Ethics, or the first part of Vol. II (see below).
See page **242.**

The Principles of Ethics, in two volumes (A System of Synthetic Philosophy, Vols. IX, X). New York: D. Appleton & Co., Vol. I, 1892; Vol. II, 1893.

Cited on pages **162–163, 197, 238, 285.** The last two of these quotations properly belong to the Data of Ethics, but they occur in the lost chapter which did not appear in the edition of 1879, and only first saw the light in the complete volume. The index will refer the reader to many other places where the views of Mr. Spencer are discussed.

SPINOZA, BENEDICT.

Ethica. — Benedicti de Spinoza Opera quotquot reperta sunt. Recognoverunt J. Van Vloten et J. P. N. Land. Volumen prius. Hagæ Comitum, apud Martinum Nijhoff. 1882. Ethica Ordine Geometrico demonstrata, pp. 37–278.

The citations on pages **30, 43, 50,** and **147,** occur respectively on pp. 194, 219, 203, and 204 of the above edition.

STANLEY, HIRAM M.

On Primitive Consciousness. The Philosophical Review, Vol. I, Boston: Ginn & Co., July 1892, pp. 433–442.

Cited on pages **21**, **37**, **138**.

On the Introspective Study of Feeling. Science, Vol. XX, New York, October 7, 1892, pp. 203–205.

Cited on page **47**.

SULLY, JAMES.

Pessimism: A History and a Criticism, London: Henry S. King & Co., 1877.

Cited on page **281**. The word "meliorism" probably first occurs in print in this passage, though taken directly from George Eliot's letter dated Jan. 19, 1877, which Mr. Cross has reproduced in "George Eliot's Life," Vol. III, p. 267, also cited by me on page **281**.

SUMNER, WILLIAM GRAHAM.

What Social Classes Owe to each other. New York: Harper & Brothers, 1883.

See page **100**, note.

TAYLOR, SIR HENRY.

Philip Van Artevelde. A Dramatic Romance. In two parts.—Works of Sir Henry Taylor. London: Henry S. King & Co., 1877. Vol. I, Philip Van Artevelde.

The couplet in the foot-note to page **206** occurs on p. 29 of this volume.

TAYLOR, JEREMY.

Deus justificatus; or a Vindication of the Divine Attributes, in the Question of Original Sin: against the Presbyterian way of understanding it. In a letter to a Person of Quality.—The Whole Works of the Right Rev. Jeremy Taylor, D.D., Lord Bishop of Down, Connor, and Dromore: With a Life of the Author, and a critical examination of his writings, by the Right Rev. Reginald Heber, D.D., Late Lord Bishop of Calcutta. London, 1828. In fifteen volumes. Vol. IX, pp. 309–364.

Cited on page **64**.

TURGOT, ANNE ROBERT JACQUES.

Oeuvres de Mr Turgot, Ministre d'Etat, précédées et accompagnées de Mémoires et de Notes sur sa Vie, son Administration et ses Ouvrages. Paris: De l'Imprimerie de Delance. 1808.

Vol. III (pp. 321–375) contains the "Eloge de M. de Gournay." On page 370 occurs a passage in which it is intimated that the phrase *laissez faire*, used in the economic sense, and universally ascribed to de Gournay, usually coupled with the companion phrase *laissez passer*, may have had an earlier origin in some form, as he seems to affiliate these expressions upon what he refers to as "le mot de M. Gendre à M. Colbert, *laissons-nous faire*." In another article in the same volume (pp. 309–320) entitled : Sur les Economistes, Turgot says (p. 311) of de Gournay : "Il en conclut qu'il ne fallait jamais rançonner ni réglementer le commerce. Il en tira cet axiome : *Laissez faire et laissez passer*."

See page **241**.

VOLTAIRE, FRANÇOIS MARIE AROUET DE.

Le Chapon et la Poularde. Dialogue XIV. — Oeuvres complètes de Voltaire (in seventy volumes). Paris : De l'Imprimerie de la Société Littéraire Typographique, 1784–1789. Tome trente-sixième. Dialogues et Entretiens Philosophiques, pp. 95–101.

Cited on page **159**. The passage occurs on p. 100 of Vol. XXXVI of this edition of Voltaire's works, and is applied by the "Chapon" to men, "ces monstres nos éternels ennemis," whose manifold inconsistencies and hypocricies were under discussion.

The saying that language was given us to conceal our thoughts is commonly ascribed to Talleyrand, but as he was born in 1754 and this dialogue was written in 1766 it must antedate any utterance of the former. Moreover, In *The Bee* of Oct. 20, 1759, Goldsmith wrote : "The true use of speech is not so much to express our wants as to conceal them" ; and in one of the sermons of Robert South (1676) occurs the following sentence : "Speech was given to the ordinary sort of men whereby to communicate their mind ; but to wise men whereby to conceal it."

WARD, LESTER F.

The Local Distribution of Plants and the Theory of Adaptation. Popular Science Monthly, Vol. IX, New York, October, 1876, pp. 676–684.

See page **261**.

The Relation between Insects and Plants, and the Consensus in Animal and Vegetable Life. The American Entomologist, Vol. III (New Series, Vol. I), New York, March, 1880, pp. 63–67; April, 1880, pp. 87–91.

See page **48**.

Politico-Social Functions. Penn Monthly, Vol. XII, Philadelphia, May, 1881, pp. 321–336.

Cited on page **313**.

What Mr. Ward was ready to say. — Herbert Spencer on the Americans and the Americans on Herbert Spencer. Being a Full Report of his Interview, and of the Proceedings at the Farewell Banquet of November 9, 1882. New York: D. Appleton & Co., 1883, pp. 76–79.

Cited on page **314**.

Dynamic Sociology or Applied Social Science, as based upon Statical Sociology and the Less Complex Sciences. New York: D. Appleton & Co., 1883. 2 vols. 8°.

Cited at the heads of nearly all the Chapters and Parts, and constituting the system of philosophy for which the present work aims to supply certain deficiencies and to indicate some of the applications.

Prof. Sumner's 'Social Classes.' Man, Vol. IV, New York, March 1, 1884. A review of Prof. Sumner's book in a rather sarcastic vein, published anonymously.

Cited on pages **100-101**.

Broadening the Way to Success. The Forum, Vol. II, New York, December, 1886, pp. 340–350.

See page **261**.

False Notions of Government. The Forum, Vol. III, New York, June, 1887, pp. 364–372.

Cited on page **329**.

What Shall the Public Schools Teach? The Forum, Vol. V, New York, July, 1888, pp. 574–583.

Cited on page **196**.

Our Better Halves. The Forum, Vol. VI, New York, November, 1888, pp. 266–275.

The principle of *female superiority*, or the law that, biologically considered, the female is the primary sex and the male only secondary or accessory, was first set forth in this paper. It resulted from some quasi-humorous, postprandial remarks at the Six o'clock Club, at Willard's Hotel, Washington, on April 26, 1888. These remarks were briefly reported for the St. Louis Globe, but, inadvertently or otherwise, were credited to Prof. C. V. Riley. I have only seen this item as copied from the *Globe* by the Household Companion (Boston, June, 1888). It is but just to Prof. Riley to say that he admits the error and waives all claim to the idea, and also that he concedes that the principle is sustained by the facts of entomology. This principle is considered in Chap. XIV of the present work, pages **86, 87**.

Genius and Woman's Intuition. The Forum, Vol. IX, New York, June, 1890, pp. 401–408.

The article last mentioned was replied to by Mr. Grant Allen in the same magazine for May, 1889, to which the article now under consideration was a counter-reply. Some portions of it are used with certain alterations in Chap. XXVI, pages **174–175**.

Some Social and Economic Paradoxes. The American Anthropologist, Vol. II, Washington, April, 1889, pp. 119–132.

See page **277**.

The Course of Biologic Evolution. Annual Address of the President of the Biological Society of Washington, delivered January 25, 1890. Proceedings, Vol. V, pp. 23–55. Separately paged reprint, pp. 1–33.

See pages **44**, **48**.

Neo-Darwinism and Neo-Lamarckism. Annual Address of the President of the Biological Society of Washington, delivered January 24, 1891. Proceedings, Vol. VI, Washington, 1891, pp. 11–71.

See page **221**.

The Transmission of Culture. The Forum, Vol. XI, New York, May, 1891, pp. 312–319.

See pages **214–215**, **221**.

Weismann's New Essays. Public Opinion, Vol. XIII, Washington and New York, September 10, 1892, p. 559.

See page **221**.

The Psychologic Basis of Social Economics. Address of the Vice-President of Section I, Economic Science and Statistics, of the American Association for the Advancement of Science, delivered at Rochester, N. Y., August 17, 1892. Proceedings, Vol. XLI, Salem, 1892, pp. 301–321.

See page **254**. A somewhat further condensation was published under the same title in the Annals of the American Academy of Political and Social Science, Vol. III, Philadelphia, January, 1893, pp. 464–482. Publications of the Academy, No. 77.

WEISMANN, AUGUST.

Essays upon Heredity and Kindred Biological Problems. Authorized Translation. Vol. I, edited by Edward B. Poulton, Selmar Schönland, and Arthur E. Shipley. Oxford, at the Clarendon Press, 1889. Vol. II, edited by Edward B. Poulton and Arthur E. Shipley, Oxford, 1892.

The Germ-Plasm, a Theory of Heredity. Translated by W. Newton Parker and Harriet Rönnfeldt, with twenty-four illustrations. New York, Charles Scribner's Sons, 1893.

For the numerous references to Weismann's views see especially pages **26**, **38**, **41**, **86**, **220**, **221**, **245**.

WHATELY, RICHARD.

Elements of Logic, reprinted from the Ninth (Octavo) Edition. Louisville, Ky.: Morton & Griswold, 1854.

Cited on page **171**.

YOUMANS, E. L.

The Centennial Anniversary of the Discovery of Oxygen. Popular Science Monthly, Vol. V, New York, August, 1874, pp. 493–497.

Cited on page **248**.

INDEX.

CPSIA information can be obtained
at www.ICGtesting.com
Printed in the USA
BVHW042202120519
548100BV00009B/307/P

9 781163 293133